RESCUE ME

Caitlin Press Inc.
3375 Ponderosa Way
Qualicum Beach, BC V9K 2J8
www.caitlin-press.com

Text and cover design by Vici Johnstone
Cover and opposite page Shutterstock 157534081
Edited by Christine Savage
Printed in Canada

Caitlin Press Inc. acknowledges financial support from the Government of Canada and the Canada Council for the Arts, and the Province of British Columbia through the British Columbia Arts Council and the Book Publisher's Tax Credit.

Canada Council   Conseil des Arts   BRITISH COLUMBIA   Funded by the   Canada
for the Arts   du Canada   ARTS COUNCIL   Government
                                                                  of Canada

Library and Archives Canada Cataloguing in Publication

Rescue me : behind the scenes of search and rescue / by Cathalynn Cindy Labonté-Smith.
Labonté-Smith, Cathalynn, author.
Canadiana 20220227470 | ISBN 9781773860947 (softcover)
LCSH: Search and rescue operations—Canada—Anecdotes. | LCSH: Search and rescue operations—
   United States—Anecdotes.
LCC TL553.8 .L33 2022 | DDC 363.34/81—dc23

RESCUE ME

Behind the Scenes of Search and Rescue

CATHALYNN LABONTÉ-SMITH

CAITLIN PRESS 2022

To my husband, for his inspiration and his dedication to Sunshine Coast Search and Rescue, and to all the courageous collaborators who generously shared their time and stories to give this book depth and humanity—you have shown me so many new ways to live.

—Cathalynn Labonté-Smith

Disclaimers

The author does not claim to have expertise in areas of search and rescue, criminal investigation, medical training or other technical specialties covered in this book. The author relied on related manuals, publications, public records, interviews of subject matter experts, and other sources for accuracy.

Most of the activities detailed in this book can involve a high degree of risk and should not be attempted by anyone not adequately trained in search and rescue. Attempting these activities, many of which take place in locations that are known to be remote and dangerous, can lead to serious injury or death. Anyone who chooses, despite this strong warning, to undertake any of the potentially life-threatening activities described in this book does so at their own risk.

The opinions expressed in this book are those of the author or interviewees at the time of the writing of this book. The author reserves the right to change her opinion at any time.

SAR members did not provide names of the subjects of the searches, rescues or recoveries described in this book. The author found names in publicly available records, such as federal, state and provincial law enforcement records, print and electronically available newspapers, and social media. If no subject names are provided, then the individuals are referred to only in such terms as "subject," "victim," "missing/lost person," "deceased" or "despondent person." In some older cases, there may have been no way to identify the subjects involved in the incidents.

In researching British Columbia incidents, the government's provincial "Emergency Response Incident Summaries" were extremely helpful.[1]

Contents

Preface

Case "0": Missing Cyclist—Lethbridge, Alberta

My mother, Cecile, says I was a wanderer from the time I could walk. She kept me on a harness and leash so I wouldn't disappear, despite the disapproving looks of strangers at the woman who kept her child on a leash like a dog. Once I outgrew the harness, she still kept a sharp eye on me at all times. Not every child is a natural runaway, as my younger sibling was always within reach of my mother's skirts.

One afternoon, I heard Mom call out to Grandma that she was going to take her bike to the grocery store, as she needed bread. I was pedalling my black tricycle in the opposite direction but turned around and went after her—pumping my legs as quickly as a five-year-old could. I tried to keep up with Mom but quickly lost sight of her. I pedalled out to the main road and thought I spotted her. I followed a woman on a bike, but it turned out she wasn't my mother. In fact, Mom was already home asking Grandma, who had just moved in with us and was unaware of my impulsiveness, where I was.

"I don't know where she is," said my grandma. My panicked mother hopped back on her bike and went in the direction she'd last seen me cycling, then looped around the neighbourhood, estimating how far a little girl could make it on a tricycle.

Meanwhile, I followed Mom's look-alike to a main road of our city, Lethbridge. I passed the grocery store and wondered why Mom hadn't gone in, but I was determined to catch up with her.

Mom knew it was time to call the police when she got back to the house and I still hadn't shown up.

I had covered more than a mile and was about to go under a railway bridge by the Catelli pasta factory when a man called my name. I stopped pedalling.

He said, "Your mom wants you home."

"I'm trying to catch up with her," I said.

"Come with me," he said as he came over, made me dismount, then took my bike. I had no choice but to follow him back to his enormous black and white car. His trunk swallowed up my tiny tricycle. He opened the passenger door for me.

Mom and Grandma were really upset with me when I walked in the door with the police officer, who was surprised at how far I'd gotten in that short period of time. Mom said if I did that again, she would take my trike away.

As an adult, aunt, godmother and former teacher, I reflect upon my escapade and think of the many ways that my story could have had a less than happy ending. As a child, I was in a bubble of innocence, and I'd been focussed on my sole purpose of finding my mother. I was fearless because nothing terrible had ever happened to me.

Now I understand the terror that my mom and grandmother felt in those moments when they didn't know my whereabouts. I had gone with the police officer, a bit unhappy that he'd diverted me from my objective—but the scariest thing is the fact that he could have been anyone.

Writing this book stems not only from the memory of that brief misadventure, but also because of my husband Stephen's experiences in the BC Search and Rescue (BCSAR) organization. Stephen and I enjoy the outdoors, and while we are grateful that we haven't been in a situation where we needed BCSAR, it's comforting to know they are there if we, or our friends or family, ever do. This book is my humble way of giving back to people—from the novice hiker to the most highly trained member of SAR.

The majestic life-saving St. Bernard with the mythical barrel of rum around his neck is associated with saving the lives of skiers and hikers in the mountains and for the most part this myth is true, except for maybe the booze. Shutterstock 1713912484

Introduction

In the pages that follow, search and rescue (SAR) members share cases that are meaningful and memorable to them—how these cases unfolded and how they have affected their lives forever. There are survivor stories that will leave you shaken and in awe of people's will to survive, as well as open missing-person cases that still haunt SAR members and are shared here in hopes that someone will be able to provide information that might bring them home. Mothers of missing children tell heartbreaking stories of searching endlessly and waiting for them to walk through the door, whether it's a day, a week or until the end of their days.

You will read about K9 teams who are key in finding missing persons. Some of these dogs are certified in human remains identification, and others are trained as avalanche dogs. You will also read about horses who have the uncanny ability to find the lost through their sense of hearing and smell.

In any kind of terrain—from deserts to the woods, from mountains to the Arctic or to swamps—there's a SAR team near you. From plane crashes, vehicles dangling over cliffs, ATV rollovers, cars plunged underwater, skiers buried alive in snow, kayakers stranded in floods, canoeists trapped in rapids, or crevasses that can swallow you up in one gulp—there's nowhere that SAR teams won't go to rescue you and your loved ones.

By purchasing *Rescue Me*, you are assisting SAR operations, as some proceeds will go back to SAR units in the greatest need of donations, as a thank-you for their help in the creation of this book.

Early SAR Operations

The first-known civilian SAR operation was in 1656, and it took place at sea. The Dutch merchant ship the *Vergulde Draeck,* laden with chests of silver and other treasures, struck a reef close to the west coast of Australia. Out of a crew of 193, 75 survived and made it to shore. The under steersman and six other crew went back to get help from Batavia, a journey that took forty-one days. Despite several rescue attempts, no confirmed trace of the *Vergulde Draeck* was found, nor were any more survivors. If there were any, they were possibly eaten by cannibals, according to the Government of Western Australia.[2]

Beginning in the 1700s, St. Bernard dogs were used by monks to rescue travellers in the snowy avalanche-prone Alps. St. Bernards, with their keen sense of smell, were able to find people buried in the snow. The dogs covered freezing people with their body to keep them warm. "Over a span of nearly 200 years, about 2,000 people, from lost children to Napoleon's soldiers, were rescued" by St. Bernards.[3] What about the stereotypical image of a barrel of booze around the St. Bernard's neck—is it truth or legend? It all stems from a painting, *Alpine Mastiffs Reanimating a Distressed Traveller,* by Sir Edwin Henry Landseer. In it, one of the St. Bernards has a wooden keg on its collar. While it's controversial whether or not the dogs indeed sported kegs, they did carry packs with essential supplies for lost victims, according to the St. Bernard Club of New South Wales, Australia.

About the Canadian National SAR Program

The National Search and Rescue Program (NSP) oversees all of Canada's SAR organizations and resources, in terms of both response and prevention. NSP is a part of Public Safety and Emergency Preparedness Canada, through the National Search and Rescue Secretariat (NSS). NSS coordinates the National SAR Program, working with federal, provincial and territorial as well as air, ground and marine SAR organizations. Canadian SAR organizations and their responsibilities include:

- Canadian Armed Forces—aviation incidents.
- Canadian Coast Guard—marine incidents.
- Parks Canada—incidents within national parks.
- Provincial and territorial governments—searches for missing

persons, including those who are lost or overdue on land or inland waters.
- Civil Air Search and Rescue Association (CASARA—assists the Royal Canadian Air Force for aeronautical SAR incidents.
- Canadian Coast Guard Auxiliary (CCGA)—assists the Canadian Coast Guard in marine SAR incidents.
- Ground Search and Rescue (GSAR)—often delegated to the police service of jurisdiction.
- Search and Rescue Volunteer Association of Canada (SARVAC)—assists police forces of jurisdictions for GSAR.

There are fifteen thousand specially trained air, ground and marine SAR volunteers who assist the requesting authorities and deliver prevention education with the intention of saving lives.[4]

About SAR in Canada

The roots of the civilian volunteer search and rescue (SAR) organizations across Canada began in the late 1950s and '60s, to safeguard Canadians in the event of a nuclear attack from Russia. As perceived threats from the Cold War diminished by the middle of the 1970s, civil groups began to respond to natural disasters.

The Search and Rescue Volunteer Association of Canada (SARVAC), established in 1996, is a registered Canadian charity supporting Ground SAR (GSAR) volunteers in Canada, and also the general public.

SARVAC represents Canada's thirteen provincial and territorial volunteer GSAR associations, with a board of directors including volunteer representatives from each of the provinces and territories. SARVAC protects the interests of the country's nine thousand GSAR volunteers who provide SAR services on land and shorelines.

About BCSAR

British Columbia has the highest volume of rescues in Canada, due to its vast wilderness and the strength of its outdoor culture. According to the BCSARA website (bcsara.com), there are nineteen hundred search and rescue incidents in BC yearly, with twenty-one hundred people rescued by their three thousand volunteers.

North Shore Rescue (NSR),[5] founded in September 1965, is the busiest SAR in Canada. According to Emergency Management BC's (EMBC) database, there were 1,775 incidents, including air, land and inland water from December 28, 2020, to January 2, 2022. In 2022, there was a sharp uptick in the number of incidents to 2,136 incidents logged from January 3, 2022 to March 31, 2022.

As of April 1, 2022, Emergency Management BC stopped posting weekly incident reports,[6] but still produces annual reports for all types of emergency responses in the province, such as dangerous goods, motor vehicle accidents, environmental incidents, natural disasters, body recoveries, fires and SAR.

NSR (northshorerescue.com) taught urban rescue skills during the Cold War, due to the collective fear that the Russians might drop a nuclear bomb on the Vancouver area, but the organization also assisted in searches for lost hikers and skiers. They later completely focussed on search and rescue, specializing in mountain, canyon and helicopter rescues.

About US SAR

The National Search and Rescue Committee (NSARC) funds SAR in the US, including the US Coast Guard, FEMA Urban SAR, the US Air Force, FAA and the National Park Service. SAR groups go back to the late 1920s. American SAR groups are usually called out by the local sheriff, other law enforcement agencies (such as the FBI), the US Fish and Game Department or national parks rangers. Some SARs receive funding from municipalities and may come under the volunteer fire department category, but most rely upon donations.

Private versus Public SARs

Ending a search is never an easy decision, but if conditions are too dangerous to searchers, there are no further signs of the subject, and the chance that the subject is alive is highly unlikely, then it's done after consultations with experienced SAR managers. A search of a day, four days or even a month may not seem long enough to a desperate family, but sometimes the initial search doesn't turn up any more information than can be found years later. However, sometimes subjects walk out on their own just as the searchers are preparing to leave.

Private SARs may approach families when they are at their most vulnerable during an active investigation, which can interfere with the process, or after the official search is called off. Private SARS who contact families of missing persons claim they don't re- ceive government funds, but many public SAR groups don't receive such funding either.

Private SARs may be registered charitable organizations and have volunteers amongst their membership, but they are run independently. In Canada, that means they don't fall under the NSAR and/or provin- cial SAR organizations, nor are they called out by authorizing agen- cies. The same is true in the US, in that private SAR organizations aren't called out by the sheriff, the US Fish and Game Department or other law enforcement agencies.

Public SARs have structured training and certification, and crim- inal record checks are conducted on the members annually by the local police. Public SAR groups are volunteers who don't solicit donations, don't ask families for compensation, won't put themselves or the pub- lic at risk during a search and won't interfere with evidence that could lead to finding a subject.

This book doesn't include private SAR groups. They have a niche when they're contracted to private companies, such as ski resorts or forestry companies, whereas public SARs never contract out to pri- vate companies. For example, logging companies are required by their jurisdiction's workers' compensation board, such as WorkSafe BC, to treat and evacuate injured workers, which is beyond the scope of pub- lic SARs or ambulances.

Myths about SAR

There are misperceptions that the public and users of public parks have about SAR members. Here are some of the more common myths, as well as an explanation of the reality in each situation.

Myth 1: Police go out on the lookout for rule-breakers, or SAR mem- bers go on patrol looking for people outdoors who need assistance.

Truth: SAR is called out to assist only by requesting agencies. In Can- ada, these agencies include the police, the RCMP and the provin- cial ambulance service. Park rangers patrol provincial parks, and that's why people may have the impression that SAR does the same thing. However, SAR isn't like the ski patrol or police on a beat. In the US, usually the sheriff's office is the requesting authority, although there are exceptions, like the US Fish and Wildlife Service and other law enforcement agencies, like the FBI.

Myth 2: SAR members are paid employees.

Truth: SAR members are volunteers. Some provinces and states don't fund the groups adequately, so they pay out of their own pockets for training and equipment to perform rescues.

Myth 3: SAR work is glamorous.

Truth: SAR involves a lot of walking around at inconvenient times, looking for people who may already be home. A few SAR groups in mountainous regions do most of the dramatic extractions with long-lines from helicopters, because it's extremely expensive in terms of equipment and training. Only a few members within SAR do Human External Transport System (HETS) rescues, where they are hanging from a cable that's swinging from a helicopter.

Myth 4: SAR work is dangerous.

Truth: SAR has become extremely safe, and the safety of the crew is the top priority of every call.

Myth 5: SAR members maintain the trails.

Truth: Clubs, such as trail societies, mountain biking clubs, park rangers and other volunteers maintain trails.

Myths About Missing Persons

When you call 911 to report a missing person, the police, RCMP, ambulance, Armed Forces, Coast Guard, coroner, fire department, Independent Investigations Office (IIO) or sheriff determine when and if they need SAR.

There are several misunderstandings about reporting a missing person, probably brought about from misleading scenes in movies or television. Here are some common myths:

Myth 1: You must wait twenty-four hours to report a missing person.

Truth: The sooner you report someone as missing, the better the odds of finding them, especially if the person left their trip plan with you. Every hour counts when they are overdue, and if you can't reach them, it's time to call 911. After twenty-four hours, the chances of finding someone alive drop dramatically.

Myth 2: You must be related to a missing person to report them missing.

Truth: A friend, neighbour, work colleague, or anyone connected or concerned can contact 911 about a missing person.

Myth 3: A missing-person case is closed if they're not found after a search.

Truth: A missing-person case remains open and active until they are found.

1. New SAR Members

New recruits learn right away that SAR's priorities, in order, are first of all to themselves, secondly to the team, thirdly to bystanders, and finally, to the subject.[7] The subjects are last on the list—because they made the choice to enter the wilderness, whether prepared or unprepared. SAR wants to help those in need, but not at the expense of their own or someone else's life (exceptions are children, the elderly and those with special needs).

If a recruitment ad for SAR were totally honest, it might read something like this:

> Want to get woken up in the middle of the night? Want to search for people in clouds of mosquitoes, swaths of poison oak, swamps up to your armpits or in blinding blizzards? Want to experience heatstroke, frostbite and other major unpleasantries of exposure? Want to lose friends and become a stranger to your friends, family and pets? Want to spend all your spare cash on necessary equipment, training and expenses then get ignored for all your good deeds? Then we're the organization for you.

Truth laid bare, potential SAR members would have a laugh and apply anyway. Every member of a search and rescue group is either recruited for their existing skills or applies to join because their skills set fit the position.

In some SAR groups, new members receive a radio call sign. Some groups use nicknames or the name of their vehicle, like Snowmobile 1. The training is rigorous, and not all of them complete it. There are some elite teams, like the Crag Rats of Colorado, that expect you to come with a high level of mountain skills.

Sunshine Coast, BC
SAR Member in Training, 2020

I choose to focus on the journey of a Member in Training (MIT) from the Sunshine Coast SAR (SCSAR), chiefly because I live in Gibsons on the Sunshine Coast of BC. My husband, Stephen, was accepted to the SCSAR program that year, and it was through Stephen and his cohorts, who had the grit to stay with their training throughout the pandemic, that I became inspired to write this book.

The SAR organization recognizes the supportive role that partners and other family members play in the ability of the SAR member to execute their tasks. There's an impact on the entire household when that call-out comes in the middle of the worst stormy nights, waking up the SAR member, their partner, their kids and/or pets. Hearts race as the radio instructions blast the particulars of the call-out. The SAR member gets dressed in layers while listening to distressing situations that they will soon be walking into. A kiss goodbye and off they go into the dark, often into a storm, to do their best to bring someone home to safety.

Those waiting at home for them never know if the SAR member will be instructed to turn around in a few minutes, or if they will be gone until the next day. Those left at home try to go back to sleep, but their minds race with what scenarios the team might face. Everyone just wants that lost and/or injured soul to be found and rescued.

Steve has been my personal hero for over thirty years, and now through SAR I share his heroism with strangers who are having the worst day of their lives. I know that he's with the rest of his team and they take care of each other.

When Stephen returns from a rescue, we rejoice. When he returns from a recovery, I marvel at how he and his teammates can do what they do. SAR volunteers are provided with training and resources to support them. Many of us don't know how we'd react in a high stress or traumatic situation, and even SAR volunteers are given the choice to attend a call that may be triggering or too traumatic.

Their training revealed to me that anyone with an outdoors background, or at least with a desire to be in the outdoors, can join their ranks, if they commit fully to the lengthy training, have a reasonable fitness level, have a passion for the outdoors, have a deep compassion for others, and fit in with the team. In the case of the 2020 SCSAR cohort, the most challenging part of the training was not the physical demands but learning to navigate with a compass rather than relying on GPS.

Stephen Smith—SCSAR

It was October 2019 when Stephen "Steve" Smith (call sign Sunshine 97), unpacked my survival kit from the trunk of my car, where I stored it for flight training. He raided my kit for supplies for his SAR "ready pack." "This is a really good tarp. Can I have this?" he asked.

"Take anything you need," I said. He swapped my prized items out for his lower-quality ones and snapped up what he didn't already have for his pack. His *Ground Search and Rescue* training manual by Emergency Management BC required that his waterproof ready pack be loaded and ready to go and that he "be self-sufficient for at least twenty-four hours, regardless of conditions."[8]

Sunshine Coast SAR grads of 2020 enjoying avalanche training at Dakota Ridge, December 2020. L to R: Colleen Gould, Ryan Cunce, Stephen Smith, Jeff Staller, Elisha Moussadji, Joachim Pierre, Marc Stokes. Photo credit: Christina J. Tutsch, Instructor, Wonder Outdoor School

Not only should SAR volunteers be prepared to be self-sufficient in all conditions for at least twenty-four hours, but also recreational hikers, snowshoers, cross-country skiers, snowmobilers, snowboarders, ATVers, skijorers, mountain bikers and skiers would all do well to carry survival items as appropriate for the conditions, in addition to a fully charged cellphone or satellite phone and charged external battery.

Steve, who runs, mountain bikes, hikes and blogs on computer-related topics,[9] was approached by members of SCSAR[10] and recruited on the spot for his outdoor experience, fitness, reliability and webmaster skills. He was excited to start his six months of training. Little did we know that in a few months, a world pandemic would overshadow his training, turning a six-month program into a thirteen-month program, with many challenges to his safety and the safety of his eleven cohorts.

Stephen learned invaluable skills, like first aid, overnight survival, search techniques and setting up ropes and knots. His favourite piece of SAR equipment is his headlamp. "We mostly search at night, and it's been my most used piece of equipment," he says.

Pandemic Plans

For every call-out the Members in Training (MITs) had during COVID-19, they wore full personal protection equipment (PPE) in addition to the usual gear. Steve wore SAR-issued waterproof/breathable overalls on top of his technical clothing layers. Over that hot mess, he wore a SAR jacket, face mask, gloves and helmet. Even in the peak of the hot summer, they wore full gear and PPE. If Steve had come into contact with a subject with a suspected or active case of COVID, he planned to stay in our camperized Sprinter van until COVID tests were performed on the subject and himself and found to be negative. Fortunately, he never needed to isolate.

Steve has always enjoyed outdoor life—hiking, mountain biking, long-distance running, snowshoeing, skiing and open-water swimming. "I've seen SAR around now and then and have always been interested in what they do ... now I have the time, interest and availability to get involved," Steve says.

Steve grew up in Horseshoe Bay, West Vancouver, and the surrounding forest was his playground. He joined the Junior Forest Wardens (JFW) in elementary school, where he learned basic first aid, navigation, how to identify species of trees and how to build a fire with one match. He went on campouts and canoe trips with the group.

His family moved to Vancouver Island the summer after he completed Grade 7, and he didn't enjoy the new warden as much, so he dropped out. However, his family continued camping and skiing. Skiing was a more affordable family activity in the seventies than it is today, because of basic rope tows and it being a less luxurious experience.

In his retirement, Steve lives out his forest warden fantasy through SAR. He's available for weekday call-outs, and he's free to go on mutual-aid calls. His drives SAR vehicles, knows the local trails and has never been lost. He keeps fit by running and mountain biking regularly, so he can participate on the longer call-outs. "I'm also a computer professional and HAM radio operator, and I bring these skills to help the group as well. My wife may not like me occasionally having to get up and leave at three in the morning, but she is supportive."

His wife (yours truly) worries when he heads into rough terrain and darkness in terrible weather conditions, especially if water or a helicopter ride is involved. My heart rate goes up when he gets a call, because I'm concerned not only for him and his team, but also for the subject, especially if it's a child, an elderly person or someone with special needs.

Vulnerable people, such as people with special needs or young children, are at higher risk of an unfortunate outcome because they tend to hide from searchers and not respond to searchers calling out to them; for example, when a child goes missing, all resources are called out immediately. All available volunteers respond as quickly as possible, search dog teams often getting to the scene before anyone else, helicopters are readied, and everyone has their adrenaline pumping. Those are the calls SAR members dread the most.[11]

SAR volunteers go to great lengths to search for and save subjects. However, as I mentioned earlier, like any first responders, the subject is officially last on their list of priorities.[12] But after interviewing over sixty SAR members, I'm aware that they forget the rules when it comes to saving a life.

Aside from call-outs that he has actively participated in, Steve says, "There were several call-outs that were resolved before I got there." The full routine still happens with every call-out, whether there's a "stand down" command or not. Team members get into full gear, take their hefty ready packs and drive to the meeting spot, which could be a launch pad for the Zodiac, a helipad, the ferry terminal, a water taxi station, the last known location of the subject or the SAR hall. Every call-out is treated seriously and as an emergency.

The Overnight

The capstone of all MITs' training is the solo overnight camping trip, but the date for this particular group kept getting pushed back because of COVID. Finally, one dry, clear October evening, the overnight was a go. Steve describes this experience as the highlight of his training: "We camped alone overnight, only using what is in our normal search pack. This included a simulated rescue, testing of our survival skills and some good socializing."

They made themselves a shelter from raw materials scavenged in the forest and started a fire without matches. After socially distanced chats, they settled into their shelters to sleep. What made this exercise extraordinary was that one of the MITs was in her third trimester of her first pregnancy; in fact, she was one week overdue. The SAR truck was parked pointed in the direction of the hospital, approximately a five-kilometre drive away, in case she went into labour. Her husband was also on the overnight in his own camp, ready to assist if the baby made an impromptu visit to the camp.

Around three in the morning, the organizers woke the MITs up, screaming that someone was lost. They pulled their groggy selves out of their cozy nests for a full-on simulated search, which ended after about four hours. Hot coffee and breakfast treats arrived around 7:30 a.m. to resurrect the weary MITs.

Steve has gained a lot from BCSAR. He has learned new outdoor skills, gone to a number of areas that he didn't even know existed, flown in helicopters several times and participated in helping a number of people who were injured or lost. He says that despite doing a lot of training, the initial Ground SAR (GSAR) training is just the start. He continues training in rope rescue and SAR management. Steve's only annoyance with SCSAR is that they didn't accept him the first time he applied two years earlier, when he would have skipped all the COVID protocols and delays.

In the cases that follow, Steve recalls the experiences that have had the most impact in his new role as a SAR team member, from an injured mountain biker near his home to travelling to assist another SAR group on a missing person case in a nearby community.

CASE 1: MOUNTAIN BIKER INJURED
SPROCKIDS PARK, GIBSONS, BC

A rescue that stood out to Steve happened one afternoon in May 2020, when a twenty-five-year-old mountain biker was injured on Doug's Detention trail in the popular Sprockids Park.[13] Steve got to the staging area quickly. He says that the injured mountain biker had broken his neck on a crash after going over a jump. They attended to him, packaged him and carried him out on a stretcher to hand over to the BC Ambulance Service, who took him directly to the helipad for a flight to Vancouver General Hospital. "I'm a mountain biker, and it's painful to see an injury that is going to be so life-changing," Stephen said.

Twenty SAR members and two paramedics attended. Steve was one of the stretcher carriers. On the scene, it appeared that the subject was paralyzed from the nipple line down, but in a later briefing, Steve heard that the man was paralyzed from the waist down—a devastating injury, but at least the young man wouldn't be on a breathing machine for the rest of his life, as they had first feared.

CASE 2: MISSING SKATEBOARDER
POWELL RIVER, BC

Until recently, Powell River, on the Upper Sunshine Coast, was a mill town. The mill has now shut down, leaving many people unemployed. To get to this remote and beautiful community from the Lower Mainland is a five-hour journey, if you're lucky and you can sync with both the ferry coming over from Horseshoe Bay in West Vancouver and the small *Malaspina Sky* ferry at Earl's Cove at the other end of the peninsula, but it can take seven or nine hours if you have sailing waits. However, if you are in SAR and are going on a mission, BC Ferries allows your group to have priority boarding to get to the search area, and that was the case when Stephen and I mustered at Earl's Cove for the first ferry at 6:20 a.m. with the rest of the Sunshine Coast SAR members who were able to attend the multi-day search.

On the evening of Friday, August 20, 2021, Vaughn "Vinny" Baumgardt (age thirty-three), a local skateboarder, was last seen around 10:30 p.m. in the 9500 block of Highway 101 in Lang Bay, between the ferry terminal at Saltery Bay and the town of Powell River. Powell River Search and Rescue, after finding no trace of Baumgardt by August 24, called for assistance from SAR teams from the Sunshine Coast, Squamish, Alberni Valley and Westcoast. In total, sixty-six SAR members searched for Baumgardt, as did his family and friends in the community. Baumgardt was described in the RCMP bulletin as five-foot-eight, with blue eyes, dirty blonde hair and a beard. He was last seen wearing jeans and black skater shoes. He wasn't wearing a shirt or a hat.

Stephen took an account from witnesses that they had spotted an altercation between a naked Baumgardt and a motorist. Witnesses also heard motors revving and shouting the next morning at the intersection of Pine Tree Road and Evergreen Road. Unfortunately, the intensive search didn't reveal any clues as to the missing man's disappearance.

An unknown person found Baumgardt's clothes, cellphone and other personal items, folded his clothes and put them neatly on his doorstep. There was a potential sighting of Baumgardt the following week, but RCMP searches on August 27 and 29 turned up empty. The search stalled. One theory is that perhaps he went for a swim and drowned, as he was in the habit of swimming in the ocean.

A Facebook page was launched to make the tight-knit community of Powell River aware of Baumgardt's disappearance and to plead for anyone with information to come forward, and a thousand-dollar reward is offered for information leading to finding him. Divers searched in October, according to the page, but no body was found.

Another theory is that because he was known to walk home from parties along the busy highway, perhaps this time he had been hit by a car and succumbed to his injuries in a ditch. Indeed, search and rescue teams focussed their search along the ditches while looking for the missing man.

Air searches also found no trace of Baumgardt. Search dog teams were brought out, but they found no trace of him either—it was as if he'd disappeared from where he had stood. His mother and father, Sharon and Rob Godkin, continue to await more news.

Suddenly, on March 7, 2022, a new post appeared on the Facebook page: "This past week has seen various rumors circulating. At this time, there are *no* factual confirmations as to the validity of anything. Please stay respectful." What could have happened? What were the rumours? We will have to wait and see if there has been any new information on this case.

2. Avalanches

*Search and rescue is heroic. People don't realize how heroic
they are. —Martin Colwell*

MARTIN COLWELL—LIONS BAY, BC

Martin Colwell, call sign LB 98, lives beside the main trail in Lions
Bay, a small community along the Sea-to-Sky Corridor on the way to
Whistler Blackcomb Ski Resort. He began helping hikers forty years
ago in an unofficial capacity. After a 1981 mudslide destroyed the M
Creek trestle bridge on Highway 99, killing nine people, and another
debris torrent caused the deaths of two boys in the village in February
1983, Martin and a small group of climbers from the community cre-
ated Lions Bay Search and Rescue.[14]

Despite attempts to shore up the cliffs and mountainsides with
nets, concrete and rocks, landslides, rock slides and debris flows are not
uncommon along the Sea-to-Sky Corridor, with its steep cliffs; these
occurrences are caused by natural log jams breaking in the torrential
rain, melting snow and other environmental factors. Britannia Beach
was devastated three times in the twentieth century by landslides and
floods.

A copper mine was built on Britannia Mountain, and "one night
in 1915, a landslide swept into a bunkhouse, killing fifty-six people."
The mine quarters were moved six hundred metres down to Britannia
Beach, but "in 1921, a flood engulfed the town during a winter storm,
killing 37 people and sweeping many houses out to sea. The village was
moved again, this time halfway up the mountain, where it proved to
be a safer location." In 1991, though, Britannia Creek flooded again
during a summer rainstorm, "submerging the flats and burying large
areas under a blanket of thick gravel. Today, rock dikes line the stream
to help prevent future floods."[15]

Martin, a manager for Lions Bay SAR, not only assists in rescues of
hikers, snowshoers, mountain bikers and mountain climbers, but he
also has spent twenty years developing operational software for SAR

The view that you would see if you were fortunate enough to be rescued by an avalanche-certified SAR dog. After ten minutes under the snow you would not make it. Shutterstock 1917530171

teams globally through his company, SAR Technology Inc. His software, Incident Commander Pro, is used to find lost hikers and manage evacuations during natural disasters and firefighting.[16]

Martin feels that SAR needs to embrace new technology. While it sounds impressive that SAR finds 95 percent of subjects within twenty-four hours, Martin says, "Ten percent of SAR subjects are deceased, or missing and presumed deceased. If you look at the 5 percent that aren't found within twenty-four hours, the chance of them being found steadily decreases.

"Better science and technology are where the opportunities are," Martin says. The technology to improve the statistics of successful searches is already there, in the form of drones with better colour- and shape-imaging capabilities, micro planes, long-range planes, drones that fly about twenty-three metres above the ground, GoPros, satellite imagery, mathematical and scientific predictive tools and trail-based tools. Martin also points to existing smart phone applications that can be used by SAR to assist in searches. The main problem, he finds, is getting already maxed-out volunteers onboard to learn new technology.

He loves his old-school SILVA compass. Learning to use a map and compass is a rite of passage for all SAR trainees and, prior to GPS devices being so readily available, everyone used compasses to navigate in the outdoors. In practice, the compass is rarely used now, due to GPS chips in smart phones and tracking beacons, but the compass symbolizes hundreds of years of exploration and discovery. "As such, it has earned a special place for me as a symbol of adventure in the outdoors," says Martin.

CASE 3: FIVE SNOWSHOERS MISSING
MOUNT HARVEY, BC

A search that weighs on Martin was when five hikers climbed too far onto the peak of a cornice, an overhang of snow built up from repeated snowstorms and wind. It is best to avoid cornices, but if you must pass one, it should be approached on the parallel and from a distance. A cornice can be difficult to see, so it's possible to approach one head-on without even knowing it.

On April 8, 2017, a group of six people from a Lower Mainland hiking group attempted the challenging route on Mount Harvey. Five of them snowshoed parallel to a cornice. The sixth snowshoer, who had lagged behind, saw that his compatriots' footprints stopped. He could come to no other conclusion but that his friends had fallen off the cliff. Another hiker along the same route came to the aid of the survivor. The five snowshoers had indeed plunged about five hundred metres to their deaths when the cornice broke off.[17]

Eighty-six members from many SAR groups—including Lions Bay, North Shore Rescue, Coquitlam, Pemberton, Whistler, Surrey and Central Fraser Valley—searched the snow until the five were located and their bodies were recovered. Martin, as the search manager, was in front of a barrage of cameras and reporters that day, as he is any time that there is notable search and rescue involving his group. Cornices can be treacherous in that they are difficult to detect, and this can lead to tragic circumstances, as was the case for these five unfortunate snowshoers.

In *Lost Person Behavior,* Robert Koester says, "Modern snowshoes are simple to use; however, novice snowshoers may get themselves into a situation where they are exhausted, lost, engulfed by an avalanche, or have fallen through the ice on a pond. They are often found at trailheads or on a trail."

After all the years and sometimes tragic outcomes that come with serving in SAR, Martin still finds his involvement with SAR to be extraordinarily satisfying. "The more complicated and complex the puzzle is, the more fun I have in solving the puzzle. I want to work on a search for a ship or yacht that disappears in the middle of the Atlantic Ocean," he says.

Mike Danks—North Shore Rescue, BC

North Shore Rescue's team leader, Mike Danks, joined NSR in 1996 because of his father's influence and love of the outdoors. His father, Allan, is a lifetime member of NSR, and Mike remembers his dad being out on SAR calls at night when he was growing up. His brother, Glenn, is also a firefighter, and he joined NSR as a resource member, working on communications, radio repeaters and other projects.

Mike became a firefighter in 2001 and rose to the rank of assistant chief. After a long career of being a stoic firefighter and SAR member, Mike remembers his life-changing call-out a few days before Christmas in 2014 on Unnecessary Mountain above Lions Bay.

Seven-year-old Erin Moore, her sister and her mother were hiking with a large group. About halfway into the ten-kilometre hike, there was a rock slide on the trail. Erin was struck by boulders and covered by debris. The group unburied her and performed CPR. Nurses who had hiked in by foot, and a helicopter with a doctor and a paramedic onboard, came to Erin's aid. Unfortunately, despite all their efforts, Erin was pronounced deceased at the scene.

"I looked into her eyes," said Mike, who was one of the rescuers trying desperately to save the little girl. Later that evening, as he tucked his own seven-year-old daughter into bed, he looked into her eyes and was deeply shaken.

At that time, Mike had attended every call-out possible over the previous eighteen years. The stress from balancing his job, volunteering at NSR (including training and call-outs at all hours) and parenting three kids all peaked in that one moment of sorrow. That devastating call-out pushed Mike to his breaking point. He dealt with his breakdown by attending a resilient-mind retreat, which was available through the fire department. It reset his life, and he could finally talk about horrific calls like Erin's.

"It was a game changer for me. I could bring it back to my colleagues at the fire department and at NSR—that you don't need to be afraid to talk about the tough calls." His breakthrough moment was when he realized that for the sake of his mental health, he didn't need to go to every call-out.

After twenty-five years in NSR, there are two other rescues that resonate with Mike, and both were snow avalanches. When caught in an avalanche, if you survive being crushed by debris, you only have about ten minutes to be dug out before you will die of suffocation. Because of the urgency, avalanche rescues are given Code Alpha—the highest priority.

On March 4, 2017, a skier was caught in an avalanche on Tony Baker Gully in Cypress Bowl. He was wearing an avalanche beacon. His skiing partner located the beacon and used an avalanche probe to find him. Four experienced backcountry skiers were on the ridge, and they skied down to help dig the subject out with their shovels.

Mike and two other NSR members were lowered by helicopter to continue digging out the subject, remove him by longline via the helicopter, then load him into a waiting ambulance. He made a full recovery, thanks to Mike and NSR.

Mike found out later that the man lived a block away from him. "He was so kind. He collected shells from all the countries he visited and made decorative pieces for us from the shells. He invited us for Christmas dinner."

Case 4: Snowshoers Trapped on Runner Peak
Mount Seymour, BC

In February 2019, Brock Fisher and Remigiusz "Remi" Michalowski, both experienced mountaineers, were on their way to see Runner Peak on Mount Seymour when opaque fog rolled in. They thought they were firmly on the summit of the saddle and took off the rope that linked them together. Remi was ahead of Brock when they took a few steps and then froze, realizing that they were off track and on bad snow.

"I heard a loud crack—*bang!*—that shook my body and deafened me. I was picked up off my feet. I kept my eyes open, tracked the ground and saw a tree," Brock said. He pushed his body to the left, reached out and grasped the tree as he was dangling over the cliff. He clambered up, straddled the tree and tied himself to it. He took off

Doug Reid (yellow helmet) and Mike Danks (black helmet) extracting Brock Fisher (centre) from the avalanche that nearly took his life. Photo Credit: Grant Baldwin

his snowshoes and built a platform using nearby trees. He pressed the SOS button on his two-way satellite messenger device (SPOT) and called Remi every two minutes. Remi didn't answer. He called 911 on his cellphone. Next, he called Remi's girlfriend and mother to tell them what had happened. Then he called his wife and brother-in-law to tell them to come to the mountain.

The RCMP and SAR called him with an update, but the news wasn't good. The visibility was so bad that they said they might not be able to get him out until morning. Fifty-four NSR members, including Mike, came to assist, but the thick fog and high avalanche risk made it impossible to reach the scene. They waited at a staging position below, as well as above in case Mike and his teammate, Doug Reid, became buried in an avalanche themselves.

Three helicopters were dispatched. Mike and Doug did a hover exit, put Brock in a harness and did a longline extraction with the help of a helicopter. As they flew away, Brock saw the cliff that Remi had fallen sixty to ninety metres from, and he started to process what had just happened. When Brock got to the lodge, he saw Remi's mother and sister. He told them as gently as possible about Remi's accident, without completely crushing all of their hope.

The avalanche risk was extremely high, so the team waited for the weather to clear before returning to search for Remi's body. The next morning, Mike received a call from Mount Seymour that Remi's family were frantic and had arrived with shovels to go up the mountain to look for him themselves. Media swarmed the area.

"My heart sank. That was the hardest drive of my life. I dreaded talking to the family," said Mike. He contacted Police Victim Services to meet with him and the family.

The mother was devastated, in shock, and incredulous that they weren't out looking for her son. "You're soft," she said to Mike.

"That had a high impact on me," said Mike.

He took the mother to the station and held her hands. He showed her photographs of the avalanche site. She wanted the army to come in. However, the Canadian Armed Forces are limited in their services to lost aircraft and watercraft, and to situations when life and limb are at risk beyond what SAR could do. More lives couldn't be risked in the recovery of her son's body.

"Your son is not alive. He has zero chance of survival," Mike explained. The next day, after the Whistler Blackcomb avalanche control team had stabilized the area, SAR members, including avalanche dogs with their handlers from Canadian Avalanche Rescue Dog Association (CARDA), searched the area. Remi's body was recovered forty-eight hours after the avalanche. He had suffered major trauma when he was swept over the cliff band.

Brock put mountaineering and climbing aside after losing his best climbing partner. Instead, he now enjoys mountain biking with his wife. "I put her through a nightmare," Brock, a graphic designer, said. He continued, "I get nervous when my friends go to the backcountry in local Pacific coastal mountains. Conditions are too unreliable. Ask yourself how stable conditions were for the past five days before going out. Further north, conditions are more stable," Brock advised.

He's unbelievably grateful for all that Mike and his team did to save him but hates that he became a case number for SAR. He feels that there's a stigma attached to being rescued—that the public lumps expert outdoorspeople in with the inexperienced and unprepared.

Mike would like people to be supportive of each other. He'd like to see the end of shaming on social media when people enjoying the outdoors make missteps. "Everyone is fragile right now with the pandemic. Listen to your friends and your workmates. We're not robots." He also wants the public to know that SAR drops everything to search for you when you need them. Bringing a subject home safely is the adrenaline high they need to balance out the haunting calls. Calling 911 as soon as someone knows they need help increases their odds of survival. We are as delicate as shells underfoot when it comes to the vagaries of nature.

3. Caves

Unlike the other BCSAR groups, BC Cave Rescue (BCCR) has no outside funding other than the Emergency Management BC (EMBC) operational allowances and reimbursements. Three applications for gaming grants have been turned down on technicalities, and BCCR is ineligible for regular funding through the BC Search and Rescue Association (BCSARA). It does not fit the template for community-based Ground SAR (GSAR) groups, as it is organized through the BC Speleological Federation (BCSF), which represents the interests of organized caving groups in the province. From the beginning, except for private donations, BCCR has raised their own funds, paid for their own equipment and shelled out for their own training.

The most the cave rescuers get in swag in exchange for their hard work and volunteerism is a T-shirt, making it challenging to attract new volunteers. The T-shirt motto makes all the hard work and expense worth it, however: "Interfering with natural selection since 1984."

There are only about a thousand cavers in organizations throughout Canada. Fortunately, enthusiastic cavers see cave rescue training as a way both to improve their personal technical skills and safety, and to contribute to a service that anyone venturing into a cave, including their companions and even themselves, may someday need.

Their main source of fundraising is from the basic caving and cave rescue courses that they hold a couple of times a year for a modest fee of $150. They also receive private donations. Phil Whitfield, whose story appears below, says it's a point of pride amongst their membership that they are self-funded and that it says a lot about the caring nature of the caving community.

There haven't been many cave-related rescues, and thankfully few fatalities, but when their expertise is needed, there's a handful of committed, highly trained experts spread between BC and Alberta that can mobilize quickly to the mouth of any cave. Most caves are located in provincial parks and are remote, and it requires a massive effort to coordinate a rescue.

A cave Search and Rescue member properly harnessed to a rope system descends into a challenging environment for a search with no light and no communications equipment. Shutterstock 1867616776

The two mammoth underground BCSAR rescue operations covered in this chapter happened not because of human error, but because of the fragile properties of limestone on the interior of the caves that became worn away from friction of ropes and cams—cleats placed into cave walls that ropes are secured to—rather than because of any error of the experienced cavers themselves; in other words, they were freak accidents.

Phil Whitfield—Kamloops, BC

Born and raised in Victoria, Phil Whitfield got hooked on caving at the age of seventeen, and he started his caving career at Horne Lake Caves in 1964. Six years later, he helped revitalize Canada's first caving organization, the Vancouver Island Cave Exploration Group, and became active with the US National Speleological Society, presiding over its Northwest Caving Association for twelve years.

After moving to Nelson in 1975, he became involved in winter SAR through his career with BC Parks, which began in 1971. Between 1982 and 1984, he organized BC Cave Rescue, primarily for the safety of the provincial caving community.

Transferred to Kamloops in 1984, Phil joined Kamloops SAR (KSAR) and was invited to become involved with its rope rescue team. He attended a week-long Provincial Emergency Program (PEP) rope rescue instructors' seminar in Penticton in 1985–86, initiating a thirty-four-year run as a SAR rope rescue instructor. Serving as president of KSAR for several years, he also represented the Emergency Management BC Central Region groups, including Barriere SAR, Central Okanagan SAR, Kamloops SAR, Keremeos SAR, Logan Lake SAR, Nicola Valley SAR, Oliver–Osoyoos SAR, Penticton & District SAR, Princeton Ground SAR, Shuswap SAR, Vernon SAR, and Wells Gray SAR, on the Provincial SAR Advisory Committee in the early 1990s. Phil was the regional planning manager for the southern interior region of BC Parks from 1984 to 1995. He moved to a regional management position with the Land Use Coordination Office from 1996 until he retired in 2002. Phil also retired from KSAR in 2004, but he continued to be active in caving organizations, cave rescue instruction and rope rescue instruction.

In 2011 BCCR and the Alberta Cave Rescue Organization (ACRO), who have worked closely together since 2001, formed the

Alberta/BC Rescue Cave Service (ABCCRS) to share resources, training and to assist each other with search and rescue incidents.

After over thirty years, Phil stepped back as the BC provincial coordinator for ABCCRS in 2013, in part to put more time into improving the SAR rope rescue program. From 2015 to 2018, he was on the team that updated the rope program and produced the new *SAR Rope Rescue Manual,* published by Province of BC, EMBC with a grant from Canada Council's SAR New Initiative Fund (SAR NIF).[18]

Disillusioned with the transition process into the new rope rescue curriculum, he retired as an instructor in 2019. However, when his successor as BCCR coordinator moved to Atlantic Canada in 2020, Phil came out of his short-lived retirement from SAR.

Phil shared the following highlights of the cave rescues he has been involved in during his over five decades of caving experience, in his role of rescue coordinator.

CASE 5: CAVER INJURED
ARCTOMYS CAVE, BC

From October 17 to 21, 1991, Phil managed the most extensive and expensive cave rescue and recovery in Canadian history at Arctomys Cave, Mount Robson Provincial Park. At the time, Arctomys, at 536 metres deep, was the deepest known cave in Canada; however, Bisaro Anima Cave, 683 metres, near Fernie, BC, has since surpassed that record. The deepest cave in the world is found in Russia—the Veryovkina Cave, at 2,212 metres.

According to Phil's report on the Arctomys accident, three men from Jasper, Alberta—Rick Blak, Ron Lacelle and Hugo Mulyk—and Chris Zimmerman of Valemount, BC, took a helicopter twenty kilometres from the Yellowhead Highway and up almost two thousand metres to the entrance of the Arctomys Cave. Rick and Ron each had ten years of caving experience, so they split into two teams; each of the experienced cavers paired up with a less experienced man.

Rick and Chris went into the cave first, at around two in the afternoon, then Ron and Hugo followed three hours later. At around eleven that night, they met up at an area called the Straw Gallery. Half an hour later, Rick used a handline—a free rope tied to an anchor, in this case rock outcropping—to avoid water on a 3-metre drop just below the Elbow at 405 metres deep.[19] Suddenly, a four-hundred-kilogram outcropping of rock that anchored the handline broke loose. The boulder slid, crushing Rick's pelvis and knocking him unconscious.

Ron and Hugo broached the rock slide in front of them, reaching the accident site within fifteen minutes to find Rick conscious and in agony. He was unable to use his right leg, and his speech was slurred. The three men tried to rescue Rick themselves, and they began to carry him toward the Elbow; however, after less than an hour, they realized they needed help. Chris, a Mount Robson park ranger (as were Rick and Hugo), had industrial first aid training, so he stayed with his colleague. Chris had no space blankets, garbage bags or extra clothes to keep Rick or himself warm.

Ron and Hugo reached the mouth of the cave at 5:30 a.m. on October 18, after climbing back in almost virtual darkness because of trouble with their headlamps. Their base camp was under fresh snow. Their VHF radio calls to BC Parks failed to hit a repeater and were unanswered. After considering their options, they set off for the highway at eight that morning. Eight and a half long hours later, they reached a telephone booth and called the RCMP and BC Parks for help.

BC Parks called Phil at 5:15 p.m. on Friday, October 18, within forty-five minutes of receiving Ron and Hugo's call from a telephone booth on the highway that they hiked to after getting out of the cave. A massive rescue, involving over a hundred first responders and volunteers, was launched.

Into the early morning of Saturday, October 19, SAR and Parks Canada personnel arrived at Mount Robson and cavers converged from Prince George, Vancouver Island and Alberta. The cave rescue equipment cache and three cavers from Vancouver Island were flown to Kamloops airport, where Phil, a Kamloops resident, met them at 2:30 a.m. They then drove in Phil's truck to the rescue base at Mount Robson Park, arriving at 7:25 a.m. Having good luck with the weather, nine other Vancouver Island cavers were able to be flown directly to Valemount and by the end of the day, thirty-nine underground and five surface support personnel had been airlifted to a camp at the cave entrance. A Bell 204 helicopter was on standby and radio communications from the cave to the base camp were set up with a portable repeater.

The plan to extract Rick was to move the ninety-kilogram stretcher up 405 metres through a passage of about one-kilometre from the Elbow to the entrance, which required considerable rigging.

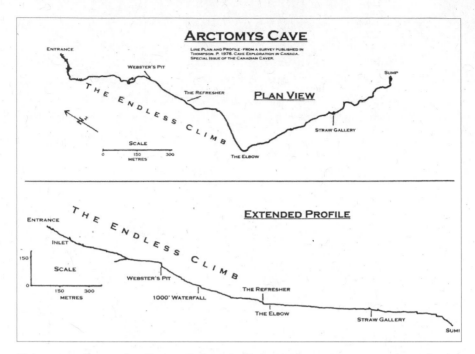

This map shows the Straw Gallery, where the cavers met up deep in the cave prior to the accident, and the Cascades, downstream from the Elbow, where the accident occurred as Rick tried to traverse the water on the three-metre climb. You can see how steep and long the rescue was back to the mouth of the cave. Arctomys Cave Map. Source: Phil Whitfield

The stretcher would be moved using head and tail belays—ropes and attachments that allow the stretcher to be lowered vertically or horizontally in a controlled manner by including both a self-braking function and backup rope to protect against human error or the failure of components of the system[20]—up to five metres above the floor of the cave. This required rotating a huge team of members underground so they could take turns to prevent burnout.

Chris and Rick had discussed that it was better for Chris to head out of the cave. They wanted to save the rescuers from potentially having to recover two bodies from the narrow passageways and depth of the cave.[21] With great reluctance, Chris left Rick's side and started his climb out of the cave. His light failed before he reached the entrance, but he was found and led out by the members of the first rescue team at around 9:30 a.m., hypothermic and shaken after having spent forty-three hours underground.

Chris, now seventy-seven years old, says, "During the long hours waiting for help, Rick was incredibly strong and brave. We could not tell time, since neither one of us had a watch. Finally, Rick said, 'I can't last much longer; I think you have to go for help too.' I am grateful for the rescuers saving my life since I had run out of light and was very weak and disoriented when they found me."

Phil was airlifted to the base camp to coordinate the underground operation around 2:30 p.m., October 19, and an hour later, the initial response team reported that they had found Rick deceased. It took until 12:30 p.m. on Monday, October 21, two and a half grueling days of toil, for the rescuers to bring the stretcher with Rick's body to the opening of the cave.

The Arctomys fatality was the third to occur underground in Canadian history. The rescue/recovery involved 109 personnel, two aircraft and helicopter transport. The total estimated cost of the rescue was $100,000 (equivalent to approximately $250,000 in 2020).

Phil's analysis found that the unpredictable anchor failure that caused the original accident was "virtually unavoidable" and that the caving party "responded appropriately but could have carried hypothermia gear and could have had their lighting better prepared, though neither precaution would likely have affected the final outcome of the accident."[22]

As a result of the accident, BCCR acquired a personal locator beacon for use by remote caving expeditions and set up protocol for having such expeditions arrange to have a standby team prepared to respond immediately if alerted. Despite its tragic outcome, the operation was a model of successful inter-agency cooperation and demonstrated the capabilities of organized cavers as an effective team of technical rescue specialists responding at a provincial scale.

CASE 6: CAVER INJURED
FANG CAVE, BC

Unlike the drawn-out rescue and delays that occurred due to complicated logistics at Mount Robson, Phil found that the rescue at Fang Cave was quite the opposite, and everything went expeditiously to the benefit of the subject, John Huybers.

Exactly eighteen years after the Arctomys rescue, on October 17, 2009, John and three companions went to the Evanoff Provincial Park to explore the Fang Cave. John, forty-six at the time, was a professional forester and a highly accomplished mountaineer, rock and ice climber and backcountry hiker.

On the return trip that afternoon, John was ten metres down a tight shaft called the Corkscrew when a five-hundred-kilogram rock slab toppled from the wall and pinned him to the ground in a pool of water, puncturing a lung and breaking nine of his ribs, both collarbones, his right shoulder and a finger. His group hurried to his aid and somehow managed to ease the slab off of him.

Another group happened to be in the cave, even though it usually only saw a dozen or so visitors a year. One of the group members had just finished a cave rescue course. As luck would have it, the group with the injured caver had a satellite phone, and they were able to reach Prince George SAR. In a couple of hours, a helicopter came to the rescue, landing in a meadow near the entrance.

The rescuers formed a chain to pass John's stretcher along the cave's steep slope for 610 vertical metres. He was rescued from the cave at midnight. When they reached the mouth of the cave, there were fifty to sixty SAR members, including four military SAR technicians who had parachuted in from the Squadron 442 airplane.[23]

Phil says the main reason for the successful outcome for the subject was that the group had a satellite phone and could call for help right away. But there were other important factors that contributed to saving this severely injured subject, such as:

- The location being near Prince George, which has an extremely experienced cave rescue team.
- The helicopter team's arrival just before dark before they were grounded for the night.
- The 442 Squadron's addition of four SAR tech parachutists to the rescue team, and their helicopter being available to evacuate the subject in the dark.
- The presence of the second caving group, which included someone trained in cave rescue.
- Fast, efficient and safe cave-rescue stretcher-handling techniques from the cave entrance down to where the subject could be transported to hospital.

- Four SAR techs with skills to reverse the failing condition of the patient.
- The subject's own physical and mental stamina.
- The outstanding cooperation of all the authorities and twenty-five SAR members involved.[24]

Phil started out by offering rope rescue and cave rescue skills to the caving community, and he added his talents for planning, organizing and managing. He jokes: "[I] must have been a decent role model, as our daughter is now a full-time paramedic with BC Ambulance after having ridden a few stretchers in rope rescue practices as a teenager."

After five decades of service, he still enjoys contributing to his caving community and the greater public. What keeps him in the SAR game? "Comradeship and friendships, enjoyment of learning technical skills and applying my own abilities to promote cooperative efforts and continuously improve systems."

Phil encourages anyone interested in SAR that it is "a good hobby if one enjoys helping others, working with a great bunch of dedicated people and becoming more aware of risk factors in our environments and in human behaviour."

CHRISTIAN STENNER—ALBERTA

Christian Stenner is the Alberta provincial coordinator of the Alberta Cave Rescue Organization (ACRO). Amongst the membership are some of the top cavers in the country, if not the world, who are trained and ready for rescues anywhere on the planet. Christian, whose day job is in corporate security, says that cave SAR is just like above-ground SAR, except that "there are no lights, no GPS, no radio or cellphones; you have to crawl on your hands and knees everywhere [and] bring in all your equipment; and there's no transportation."

He has eighteen years of experience in caving, including exploration in the Rockies, Mount Meager (an active volcano in BC), Glacier National Park, Central America, Mexico and the Pacific Northwest of the US. Christian prepares and trains cavers for companion rescues. If it's at all possible to assist an injured caver to make it to the surface, it's much faster to get them the help they need. Christian says that otherwise, the amount of time it takes to get help is significantly longer: "If you are five hours of travel from the entrance of a cave, it will take five hours for someone to get out to call 911, plus the time [it takes] for agencies to organize a response, plus five hours for responders to reach the subject once they get to the cave. There is no hope of maintaining the 'golden hour' to get to a hospital," he says.

The general rule of extraction of a subject from a cave is that for every hour it takes to get into the cave, it takes a day to get them out of the cave on a stretcher. If the subject is five hours from the mouth of the cave, it will take five days to get them out of the cave by "caterpillaring" them along. Caterpillaring means that the stretcher bearers hold onto the stretcher, then continuously slide it up to the next position. The front stretcher bearers move to the back of the line and wait for their turn to hold onto the back of the stretcher again; in this way, everyone has a chance to rest briefly.

A stretcher is a critical component of any rescue with a non-ambulatory casualty, but the PETZL NEST stretcher, Christian's favourite piece of SAR equipment, is designed specifically for cave rescue, so it's a game changer in comparison to using regular SAR stretchers. "It's light and compact with simple and effective straps for securing the casualty that even a caver can understand," Christian says. "It can be configured for traverses, [and it] raises and lowers horizontally or vertically." Having equipment designed for the specific rescue environment is important, and the NEST is one example of cave-specific equipment.

Christian says a cave rescue can take a hundred or more people from many agencies. He referred to a cave rescue in Germany in June 2014, at the Riesending or "Big Thing" cave, when it took more than seven hundred people to rescue Johann Westhauser. An experienced caver, Johann was almost six kilometres inside and one kilometre deep from the entrance in the nineteen-kilometre-long cave when a falling rock struck him on the head. Despite wearing a helmet, he suffered a brain injury too severe for him to walk out.

One of the cavers in the party of three went for help, leaving the other caver to stay with Johann. It took four days for the doctor to reach Johann. The interior of the cave is windy and has deep ravines that are challenging, even for experienced climbers and cavers. It took twelve days for rescuers working in shifts of sixty men to carry Johann's stretcher to the surface. Johann suffered a brain bleed and spent two weeks recovering in hospital. He went back to caving and climbing two years later.

The rescue cost nearly a million Euros and involved 728 people from five countries due to the depth and technical difficulty. The cave's entrance was later gated and access restricted due to this incident.[25]

Case 7: Caver Stuck
Rat's Nest Cave—Canmore, Alberta

In 2016 Christian was involved in a challenging rescue of a man on a guided tour of Rat's Nest Cave in Grotto Mountain, near Canmore. The man had gotten stuck between pinch points in an area called the Laundry Chute. The guide tried for several hours to free the man before going back to the surface to call for help on his cellphone.

Fifty people from six agencies arrived just before eleven that night, many hours after the man had become trapped. A chisel was successfully used to chip away and remove the rock until the angle of rock caused the tool to skip across the rock rather than chip into it. Other ideas, like Vaseline and medications, were floated. Medications and verbal coaching were then used to relax the patient's tense muscles and relieve his anxiety so that he could move past the pinch point. A careful balance in the medication was essential to ensure he was still ambulatory, as it would've complicated the rescue further if he had required a stretcher.

Since communication devices don't work underground, runners relayed messages from underground to the cave entrance and vice versa, adding to the time needed for the rescue. After trying many tactics to remove enough rock to free the patient and considering but ultimately rejecting the use of micro-explosives, they thought that a pneumatic chisel that ran on compressed air could work. The equipment was hiked up to the mountain and down into the cave.

The subject was kept as comfortable as possible and fed hot food and coffee from an iconic Canadian fast-food chain throughout that long night. After the rescuers had spent about sixteen hours using the pneumatic drill, he was finally freed in the early morning of the following day.

The man moved past the restriction without pain and was able to move back through the cave to the entrance on foot, with assistance. Fortunately, he had only been five or ten minutes away from the cave entrance. Seventy rescuers were involved by the end of the operation, including shifts of rescuers operating the drill, a medical team, cave rescue specialists, message runners and the command centre.

CASE 8: CAVER INJURED
BISARO ANIMA CAVE, BC

In November 2019, Christian and a team of twelve cavers and divers went to Canada's deepest cave, Bisaro Anima, near Fernie. With the divers onboard, the team wanted to add to the explored depth of 674 metres by scuba diving into the crystal-clear pool at the bottom of the cave. They planned to spend a week underground to accomplish their mission, which they had spent two years planning.

Christian said that being inside the cave was like "living in a refrigerator." It was cold, filthy and wet. Bisaro Anima had spacious rooms, but there were also some tight places. There were four camps in the cave. The group split up between the camps, because none of them were large enough for more than three or four cavers at a time.

Everything went smoothly the first day, but on the second day, at four hundred metres deep into the cave, lead diver Kathleen Graham slipped and fell. Her ankle was badly broken.

Kathleen crawled all the way out of the cave. She was able to bear some weight on the injured foot and ascend over twenty pitches. Pitches are steep sections requiring rope to repel down and climb up. It took three excruciating days for her to climb out of the cave.[26]

If she had waited in the cave, it would have taken two weeks to rescue her due to the depth of the cave, tight restrictions that a stretcher couldn't fit through and many vertical sections requiring complex rope systems. Rescue teams would've mustered to the area and needed more than a hundred cave rescuers for such a deep cave. As blindingly painful as it was for Kathleen to self-rescue, it was the best option at the time.

She spent two more days on the surface, instead of calling for a helicopter evacuation, so that she could wait while the remainder of the team finished their expedition and exited the cave. It was a full week from the time of her accident until she finally got an operation and her ankle was pinned back together.

Cave rescues are particularly difficult. Christian says his specialty team members are the best cavers and are really good at what they do, but the last thing they want to do is have to attend call-outs in caves, given the limitations imposed on them by the cave environment.

4. Deserts

The wilderness is not Disneyland. It's a real place. New Mexico is harsh terrain, not a theme park or a resort.
—Zöe Halena

ZöE HALENA
SOCORRO, NEW MEXICO

Zöe Halena was a freshman when she joined student Socorro Search and Rescue (SSAR) in 2013. A student at the New Mexico Institute of Mining and Technology (NMIMT), Zöe is now pursuing her Ph.D. For work, she researches geobiology in caves.

SSAR is a member team of the New Mexico Search and Rescue Council (NMSARC). (Student SARs don't exist in Canada due to onerous regulations that discourage SARs from starting them.) While she was growing up in Wisconsin and Northern Michigan, Zöe's parents encouraged her love of the outdoors from an early age.

Most of SSAR's call-outs are for tourists. However, in 2017, Zöe was called out on the search overnight for a missing despondent subject, and she found the body. The deceased turned out to be a student from her own university who died by suicide. She heard her classmates talk about the deceased—who was someone she knew of but who wasn't a classmate of hers—for weeks and months, but she was bound by the confidentiality agreement of her SAR not to disclose anything.

Zöe became a team leader in 2014. "It's different being a volunteer when you're young. You have a big sense of responsibility [that] others don't have. It can be isolating. My peers have small problems in comparison to SAR activities. Spending time outdoors, you can't relax, because you have knowledge of what can go wrong," Zöe says.

Zöe says she relies on her SAR equipment in the field. "I purchased a ZOLEO satellite communicator in the past year, and I have found that very useful." The ZOLEO is similar to the Garmin inReach in that it uses the Motorola Iridium satellite network to provide communication in areas without cell coverage, like much of the wilderness areas in New Mexico, and it has a Bluetooth connection to cellphones so the user can text. "When I run missions, it's critical for me to both be at incident base and able to communicate with my teams in the field, but also to be able to stay in touch with the 'rest of the world' that we need to coordinate with during a SAR mission," Zöe says.

Case 9: Hiker Missing
La Luz Trail, New Mexico

In September 2020, Zöe was called out to her largest incident, in terms of the number of searchers involved—a mutual aid mission that took searchers to the peak of the La Luz Trail, which is one of the most challenging of the Sandia Crest trails at an elevation of 3,255 metres (an elevation gain of 975 metres, similar to the gruelling Grouse Grind located north of Vancouver, BC).

Gibran Hernandez-Avila (age forty) went for a hike on the popular Sandia Crest Trail, which traverses the Sandia Mountains, within an hour's drive on the Albuquerque International Sunport airport. In the winter, this range has the desert at its feet and can have snow at its peaks, but the missing person alert went out for him on a warm September day.

From September 15 to 20, the temperature rose to twenty-nine degrees Celsius and dropped to no lower than twelve degrees Celsius at night, according to the Kirtland Airforce Base weather station an hour away from the Sandia mountains.[27] Gibran's most pressing need wasn't shelter nor food. He would need water, as without it he would succumb to dehydration within three days.

Zöe was on the search for over forty-eight hours, with breaks for eating and sleeping, which is the maximum time most searchers stay on a search before taking a leave due to the physical, mental and emotional toll of the search. It is rare that searchers stay on a task overnight due to the physical strain and exhaustion caused by harsh conditions, like heat, cold, steep terrain, high altitude, strong wind, and storms encountered in wilderness searches. Remember that SAR and other first responders carry packs of about thirty pounds or more of gear and water on their backs, adding to their fatigue. Searchers usually work from first light until three or four o'clock in the afternoon. Approximately one hundred searchers from twenty teams attended the search for Gibran, including Albuquerque police, New Mexico State Police, NMSARC and K9 teams.[28]

Gibran had posted videos online of his progress that he took with his cellphone, providing vital information for the searchers. When Gibran stopped posting, he was reported missing by his friends and girlfriend. He had been missing for about a week when a searcher using a drone spotted something blue. A SAR rope rescue member rappelled down to the object, which turned out to be Gibran's backpack. Some of his other belongings, including his cellphone, were found in the area. The cellphone data showed that Gibran had made it to the top of La Luz Trail and kept on going, but he must have slipped and fallen from a cliff, perhaps during the night when visibility was at its worst.[29]

Zöe says that the discovery of the backpack, the rappelling and the use of a drone led to the discovery of Gibran's body, and all of that

Search and Rescue dogs can be subject to heat exhaustion and have to be kept cool, hydrated and rested. All Canada Photos KPHFH3

happened on the final day of the mission. "We were able to find those items and the body because after three days of initial searching in a different location, the cellphone forensics narrowed down his possible location to this area," Zöe says.

Zöe's confidence as an incident commander is growing. "Every SAR mission, you learn something new," she says. She feels that debriefing needs more emphasis, and she reaches out to members after incidents. She would like to see more critical-incident resources available to members.

"SAR has shaped how I've come into adulthood, to make something more of myself. I'm peers with a wide range of people. It's been eye-opening. I want to do SAR for the rest of my life," Zöe says. The following are some of the guidelines that she has learned:

- Individuals will be found where no one thought they would be.
- Expect the unexpected.
- Don't get trapped into one way of thinking.
- There are factors beyond subjects' control.

Phyllis Wright—Mesilla Valley, New Mexico

No one understands the amount of water and electrolytes they need.
—Phyllis Wright

Phyllis Wright of Las Cruces, New Mexico, joined the Mesilla Valley Search and Rescue (MVSAR)[30] in 2002. MVSAR has thirty-five members and attends twenty-five to thirty call-outs every year. They are located about sixty-four kilometres north of the Mexican border and on the back side of the Organ Mountains.

The MVSAR is a paramilitary SAR that has a drone team supplied with a drone that has thermal imaging capabilities (FLIR) to assist in searches. Phyllis says that the authorities her group works with have drones with audio capabilities, and some can drop food and water to subjects.

MVSAR members are reimbursed for the gas burned to get to and from calls, and for their health insurance, although they receive no worker's compensation if they are injured on duty. The group runs on donations from the subjects' families and the general public.

Phyllis' group has been called out to assist the US Border Patrol, the El Paso Army Base, the National Forest, and the Desert Peaks National Park rangers. Searches can involve a helicopter provided by the state police.

CASE 10: FREE CLIMBER INJURED
MESILLA VALLEY, NEW MEXICO

In 2010, Phyllis attended a call-out for a free climber who was a Grade 12 student. The young man fell twelve metres, then rolled through a field of cacti. "He was so broken," said Phyllis. He was unrecognizable through his injuries; he was concussed, both legs, arms, shoulders, clavicles and all of his ribs were broken, and his entire body was covered in cactus spines. To get an IV line into him, the paramedics had to drill into his leg bone because so much of his skin was covered in cactus needles that they couldn't get access to a vein in his hands or arms.

Despite his serious injuries, the teenager kept up a positive attitude and made it to his graduation in a wheelchair. Undaunted he fully recovered and joined the MVSAR, then later became a teacher.

Phyllis says with temperatures reaching up to forty-three degrees Celsius in the New Mexico desert in the daytime and no accessible water, it puts people at serious risk of dehydration if they get stranded or lost. The majority of call-outs are for hikers or the occasional ATV or UTV rider who runs out of gas.

Phyllis says their call-outs mostly involve tourists who are unprepared, especially in the summer. "They attempt a long hike in the late morning and are unprepared for the rapid drop in temperature at night," she says. Temperatures can drop by as much as twenty degrees Celsius or more from the heatstroke-inducing daytime temperatures to freezing nighttime temperatures that can cause life-threatening hypothermia.

Phyllis wants to get to more subjects and get to them faster. She finds that recoveries of deceased subjects are the hardest part of being in SAR, even though they offer much needed closure for the family.

5. Dives

We are the shepherds who look after the flock.
—Corey Cooper

COREY COOPER—AUBURN, WASHINGTON

As a diver, Corey Cooper says that all of his missions are recoveries. "I'd have to be in my gear, watching someone drown, for it to be a rescue," he says. Corey joined Explorer SAR (ESAR) in Skagit County in 1998 when he was only sixteen years old. ESAR is a youth SAR program run by youth with an adult SAR advisor. Corey became a team leader, then a field leader, meaning that he's able to organize an entire mission.

Corey feels that his experiences and skills learned in ESAR set him up for success. He became a firefighter when he graduated from high school. At age twenty-one, he joined the reserve police force as well. After struggling for seven years to make a living, he was going to join the military in 2009. His fate was changed one day when he was out on his motorcycle. A car flew over four lanes of traffic and T-boned his motorbike.

The car hit him so violently that it sheared off his right leg below the knee. His leg was barely hanging on. He took off his belt and made a tourniquet out of it, then asked a good Samaritan to put pressure on it for him. Corey had to learn to walk all over again with a prosthetic leg.

For the last four years, he's worked as a corrections officer for the State of Washington, including a fourteen-month assignment in a violent sex offenders' facility. Currently, he works in a re-entry program for inmates, which is a more supervised program than a halfway house.

Corey joined the Kitsap Underwater SAR in 2012, and he is now vice-president. He has grown the team to nineteen divers and five support team members. They are called out approximately five times per year on recovery missions, and they train monthly. The team receives no funding. Each diver spends about fifteen thousand dollars or more for their diving gear, including tanks, regulators and dry suits, and this

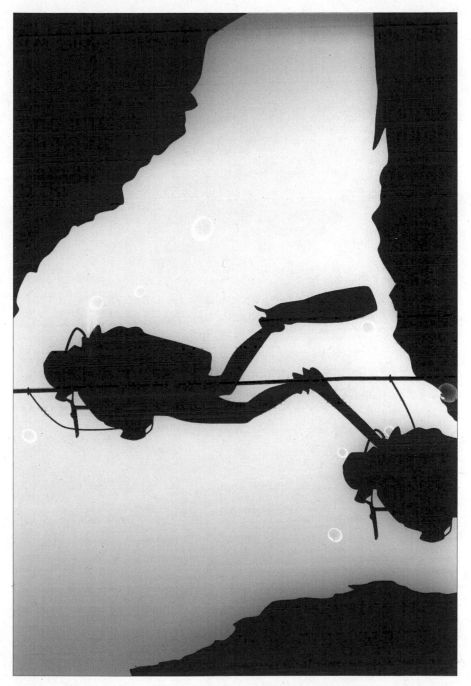

Search and Rescue divers' missions are almost always recoveries not rescues. Shutterstock 20991

does not include the cost of training and travel. With over seven hundred dives logged, Corey's equipment needs replacement.

For diving, he uses a special prosthetic leg that he keeps in his dry suit. He also has a dedicated prosthetic leg for swimming, and a new prosthetic blade-type running leg, in addition to his everyday leg.

During his first three years of diving, Corey dove in a wetsuit. He was cold all the time, especially on SAR missions. "You get out of the water and you're on the police boat, waiting to get back in and do another dive, so you stay suited up." He invested in a dry suit, which he said was well worth the cost: "A dry suit is so much easier to get in and out of, plus you stay dry and warm."

Case 11: Missing Women
Green River, Washington

While this story doesn't involve diving, it is a high-profile case that has stayed with Corey. Growing up in Skagit County in the '80s, Corey remembers hearing his parents talking about a serial killer who murdered mostly teenaged sex workers and runaways on the strip of what is now the Sea-Tac airport area. The murderer was called the Green River Killer because he dumped the bodies of his victims in and around the Green River.

One of the suspects was Gary Leon Ridgway, a truck painter who lived near the river. Police arrested him in 1980 for soliciting a prostitute but let him go after he passed a polygraph test. Finally, in 2001, DNA tests had developed enough to tie Ridgway's DNA samples to the victims.

In exchange for a sentence of life in prison instead of the death penalty, Ridgway revealed the locations of the bodies of his victims. He claimed to have murdered eighty women, but he couldn't remember where he'd put them all. Ridgway was convicted for killing forty-eight, and a forty-ninth victim was later found, making him the most notorious serial killer in the US.

Corey was nineteen at the time of Ridgway's arrest. His ESAR group was called out to clear the property next to Ridgway's for evidence, then Ridgway's house, and then a golf course. Next, the team went to a wooded area on the banks of the Green River, five minutes away from Ridgway's house.

The police detective told them to find fruit trees. "We found crab-apple trees and cut through the brush to clear the area. A team member found a working drain and dug around. He found a mud-encrusted human bone that was about a foot long and porous," Corey says.

They radioed the detective, who put a call-out statewide for other SAR members to come and join the search. They spent the weekend digging out the mud, carefully noting where each bucket came from, and putting the mud through screens, "like archaeologists," said Corey. They found many human bones—important evidence for the trial and for the grieving families of the missing women.

Gary Ridgway, now seventy-three, is serving his life sentence at the Washington State Penitentiary in Walla Walla, Washington, a minimum- to maximum-security prison.[31]

CASE 12: MALE TRAPPED IN CAR
HOOD CANAL BRIDGE, WASHINGTON

The Hood Canal Bridge is a floating bridge in western Washington that crosses the Hood Canal of Puget Sound; it connects the Olympic and Kitsap Peninsulas. On the night of May 16, 2016, Bruce Hilton Cowing (age fifty-nine), a Department of Transport employee, drove his truck off the bridge. Crashing through a railing, Bruce's truck plunged 105 metres (344 feet) deep into the water and ended up about 46 metres (150 feet) from shore.

No one had witnessed the truck entering the water. It wasn't until the next morning, when Bruce's wife called to find out where her husband was, that the search began. It took a week for a marine salvage company to locate the truck using a submersible and another three days to secure it before Corey and his dive team were called in by the sheriff's department.

Salvage divers put chains around the truck to secure it. With great difficulty, Corey pulled the upside-down, deceased man out of the truck. He wrapped one of his arms around a chain to give himself some stability in the strong current, then let air out of his buoyancy compensator vest to stay under the water.

Media helicopters circled overhead, so he wanted to bag the body before surfacing. Crabs and octopi had been at the remains for the past ten days. Corey got the bag on the feet, then the arms; however, the head kept banging against his diving mask. He managed to get the deceased into the bag and zipped up. He put Bruce's body into the waiting basket. The crane operator pulled the basket up to where a boat was waiting to take the remains in the bag to shore.

Corey was in danger every second of the twenty-six minutes it took to carry out the recovery. The truck could've broken away from the chains and taken him with it. Thankfully, the chains held, he made it back to the surface, and the body was recovered. The family had closure in this case, but often people are never found before a search is called off.

"Our mission time is limited before the search is over," says Corey. He says, "Even the [SAR] dogs are sad and put their heads down if people aren't found."

Corey's frustration is that "people don't know we exist." In the media, his team isn't mentioned by name, even when they play a critical role, such as in the Hood Canal Bridge recovery. In another case, ESAR offered their services to a family unofficially after the Seattle police diver had searched for a week at University Bridge without success. Four of their divers found the subject in a day.[32] Being mentioned in the media might help to bring in the much-needed donations to their group.

His advice to the general public is to always be prepared. For example, even for a day hike, bring a pack with food, water, a whistle and a signalling mirror. If you get lost in the dark, it's important not to move, as you could make your situation worse (for example, you could fall off a cliff). If you're going to be in or on the water, wear a life jacket.

Corey recalls a friend of his from the fire department who went paddle boarding with a buddy who hadn't brought a PFD, so the firefighter lent him his. Unfortunately, the firefighter fell off his paddleboard, there was no leash on it, and he drowned. Corey wasn't able to go to the scene at the time, as he was on another rescue.

Corey's future goals include growing the team; getting more people trained in learning side-scan sonar, which can locate bodies underwater; and fixing the administrative backlog. In terms of growing the team, he brought in his wife to help with shore support.

To cope with the stress of his work and SAR recoveries, Corey does recreational diving and metal detecting, and he's just moved to a farm that he and his wife plan to turn into their own personal petting zoo.

6. Ground

CHRISTIE FALK—ABBOTSFORD, BC

Christie Falk grew up practising martial arts, and she taught fitness and kickboxing. She works at a hospital in the shipping and receiving department. Her background isn't typical of other SAR members in this book. While she has always loved the outdoors, her family and friends didn't "play" that way, so she didn't have many opportunities as a youngster to pursue outdoor adventures, such as backpacking, hiking or going on extended backcountry trips. However, since joining Central Fraser Valley SAR (CFVSAR) seven years ago, she's more than made up for her lack of early activities in the woods.

Christie has completed most of the training possible within her SAR group. She is an "organized avalanche rescue" team member, a ground search team leader and a SAR manager, and she is trained in rope rescue and helicopter-hover exit. "I love the diversity. It's super interesting," she says.

So why is she now taking a six-month leave of absence from CFVSAR? Christie has a huge goal ahead of her. "Being in SAR gave me the confidence that I could be successful," says Christie. Being outside, engaging with the community, helping people in need and performing emergency management gave her belief in herself that she can become an RCMP officer.

CASE 13: DOG WALKER MISSING
COQUITLAM, BC

Dog walker Annette Poitras took her border collie, Chloe, and two clients' dogs, Roxy the boxer and a pug/beagle cross (puggle), Bubba, for a walk on a rainy, cold afternoon on Monday, November 20, 2017. She parked her van at the parking lot at the Westwood Plateau in Coquitlam, on the corner of Parkway Boulevard and Plateau Boulevard, but she failed to tell her husband, daughter or friends where she was going for what was supposed to be a quick walk. Her husband, Marcel, reported her missing when she didn't return home.

Coquitlam SAR was called in to assist the Coquitlam RCMP at eight o'clock that evening. Annette, in her fifties, was fit, familiar with the area and dressed appropriately for a decent afternoon—but certainly not for overnight or for what was to befall her over the next couple of days. She didn't have her pack of survival essentials, which she usually carried with her, on that walk. Coquitlam SAR was hopeful that the dogs would keep her warm, so overall, her chances of surviving until they found her were good, despite the rotten weather conditions.[33]

They called out her name as they did their sweep, but there was no answer from Annette and no barking from the dogs. By the next morning, November 21, there was still no sign of her or the dogs, and the search team was exhausted by the cold wet conditions, and dense forest. Soon, other SAR teams arrived from Coquitlam, Maple Ridge, Surrey, North Shore Rescue, Lions Bay, Central Fraser Valley, Chilliwack, Mission, Kent Harrison, Squamish, Arrowsmith, Comox Valley, Metchosin, Peninsula Emergency Measures Organization from Saanich, Campbell River, Sunshine Coast, Nicola Valley, Castlegar, Penticton and Kamloops. In total, 155 SAR members participated in the search. Helicopters were also used to look for Annette. At the end

Rope teams are an essential part of BC rescue operations due to the coastal terrain and number of caves in the region. Shutterstock 1141260602

of the second day of her disappearance, the searchers still had no sign of their subject. There was now a great concern for Annette's condition, as they wondered if she would still be conscious and able to respond to their calls.

"Annette's story reached all over the globe through the media; I believe it was because of her being a dog walker and the dogs being with her," says Christie, who entered the search on the third day. She grew more anxious as the hours ticked away. "We went in knowing there was a high probability that she could be non-responsive at this point, with it being November and the nights being so cold and wet," she recalls. "We did a sweep in the area between the road and the river and called out to her. As we started our second pass, I heard dogs barking and a voice. It was hard to hear over the rushing of the river. I looked at my teammates in surprise and excitement. Could she be alive? Was this really happening? My heart skipped a beat."

The team leader confirmed this was Annette and the dogs by announcing, "We found her." Annette and her dogs were on the opposite side of the river. They got over to her in the pouring rain. The dogs were protective of Annette, but eventually the rescuers were able

Cellphones provide important clues in the digital age for finding missing persons. Shutterstock 6199136327

to win their trust and get to Annette. A longline helicopter team was called in to bring out Annette, the dogs and some of the SAR team members.

"Being the only female on the team, I helped her put on warm, dry clothes and chatted with her. She was so concerned about the dogs and wanted them to be taken out first. I reassured her that they were going to be taken care of, but she was going to be taken out first," says Christie.

Once Annette was packaged up, she and two SAR members were longlined out of the forest. Annette was brought to a waiting ambulance and taken to hospital. Next, the dogs were rescued by a longline, then some of the SAR crew. However, Christie was one of the SAR members who had to find their way back out on foot.

It turns out that it was Bubba, the puggle, who had led to the misadventure by running off the path. Annette went off the trail into the woods to look for her charge, but she got lost, fell, hit her head and became unconscious. In the fall, she'd also injured her back and lost her mobility. She sheltered under a log with the two dogs, and eventually, Bubba returned to them and cuddled with Annette.[34] Dogs have an amazing ability to air scent and track humans. As hard as it may be, perhaps it might keep everyone safer if we waited for our canines to find their way back to us, rather than put ourselves in harm's way to find them?

Christie feels that what contributed to Annette's survival was multifold. "The dogs helped keep her warm, but it was her survival mindset. She thought, 'These dogs need me. I will survive.' She had passion and care for the dogs, and they saved her life. By herself, she would have been a lot less likely to have survived."

Christie wants the public to have a healthy respect for the outdoors. "The outdoors has so much to offer. Embrace it," she says. But she cautions to be wise and learn how to survive outside, just like being street smart. "Just like being in the city, [where] you know to lock your car and not walk down dark alleys at night, you need to learn the threats that exist in the woods," she says.

Annette Poitras's Story

When I spoke with her in January 2021, it had been three years since Annette's "ordeal," as she calls it. She still has nightmares and flash-backs from the three days when she was lost in the deep woods with the three dogs. She still gets spooked when helicopters fly overhead.

"But it's getting better," she says. Chloe, her border collie, is doing well, Roxy, the young boxer, is recovering from her second surgery for a torn ligament. "Roxy clings to me and looks up at me now when we walk in the rain. I believe dogs remember," she says. Bubba, a senior dog now, is no longer her client. He isn't as mobile as he used to be on that day when he took off into the woods.

"I was freaking out," she says. Unconcerned for her own safety, Annette had gone off the trail to look for Bubba, which led to her falling, then getting disoriented and lost. She recalls being concerned about what her client must have been thinking about Bubba—that maybe she'd kidnapped him. She also worried about her responsibilities that she was missing, while she was hunkered down by a log.

Bubba came back to them the morning of the second day and dug a shelter under the ferns. Annette tried to do the same but was too weak. She protected Roxy from the rain with one of her two raincoats, because the boxer was shivering in the cold and wet. Chloe stared at her and guarded her the whole time.

"Roxy had it the worst. She shivered and had sores and blisters," she says. Annette's own teeth had violently chattered the whole time.

On the third day and feeling close to death, Annette says, "I laid there and thought, have I done everything I wanted to do with my life? I thought that I had done a lot of things. I was at peace. Everything was in slow motion. I wasn't afraid to die. I was okay," she says. Roxy began to bark, and Annette shushed her. It was then that she heard a whistle.

"I am here," she had called out.

"Where did they come from? My angels," she says. "I cried with joy," she says, when she realized she'd been found. The first SAR member to reach her coaxed the dogs away from her with pieces of granola bar.

When she realized that she was going to be hooked to a helicopter by a line and flown out, Annette was "freaked right out. I said, 'No way! Can't you carry me out?' I was so scared. I really didn't want to see

Annette Poitras, a dog walker, survived for three days in the woods of co-quitlam, BC, along with three dogs. Here, she is packaged to be longlined to a helicopter and brought to safety. Photo: Jon Lavoie

or hear anything." The SAR members put goggles on her and tucked her in.

She was in the hospital for five days recovering from severe dehydration and hypothermia. Her body had gone into a state of rhabdomyolysis (rhabdo), an extremely painful condition where her muscle tissue was breaking down. When she had fallen from the slippery log, it had knocked the wind out of her and rendered her unconscious. She'd been without water for three days, the maximum that you can survive without water. On the second day, it had snowed in the morning, but luckily, a "pineapple express" had moved in and the temperature went up, which likely contributed to her survival.

"I thought I could make it another day, but when they found me, they told me that I wouldn't [have]," she says.

Annette took a lot of time off from her dog-walking business after her ordeal. When she started back, she had friends accompany her on her dog walks. She hasn't gone back to the trail where she came so close to losing her life.

Her story went viral on social media, and as a result, she's raised a lot of money for Coquitlam SAR, both from donations that came in immediately after her rescue and from the continued sales of the book co-written by Ann K. Bruinn and Marcel Poitras, Annette's husband: *Three-Dogs Nights: The Search and Rescue of Annette Poitras*. Annette has had several marriage proposals from men from all over the world, much to the couple's amusement.

Annette no longer leaves for a dog walk without her pack of essential supplies, just in case she has to spend a night in the woods. Her kit includes a headlamp and a whistle, which "carries ten times as far as yelling," she informs me. Because you can't rely on a phone (her lost cellphone was never found), she has a SPOT device with her. The SPOT is a centrally monitored GPS tracking device. She now makes a trip plan and makes sure she tells someone where she's going and when she'll be back every time she goes into the woods.

If a dog were to run off the trail, Annette will now wait at the same spot for up to two hours for the dog to return, then go back to her van. She has become a safety advocate on the trails. She has turned around other hikers for wearing improper footwear, like flip flops, or for having inadequate clothing for the conditions. She has also turned back hikers who are going up too late in the day with no packs and no water and told them what they need to carry.

Annette continues to walk dogs by herself, much to Marcel's dismay. However, she's familiar with the trails and feels safe with all the dogs around her. She's had one other mishap since 2017. She fell off a monster of a log and broke two ribs in 2020. She was able to walk out on her own but waited a week to go to the hospital due to the pandemic. Obviously, she has a high tolerance for pain.

She now says that she takes life day by day. "I don't plan things." She experiences survivor's guilt when people lose their loved ones. "I want the world to know about SAR. Before my ordeal, I didn't know anything about SAR. I didn't know they were volunteers. What hurts me is when people don't thank SAR when they're rescued," she says.

MICHAEL ST. JOHN
MARIN COUNTY, CALIFORNIA

Michael "Mike" St. John is the leader of the SAR unit at the Marin County sheriff's office, which is located just across from the Golden Gate Bridge in San Francisco, California. In an interview, Michael said he joined Marin SAR (MSAR) in 1979, the year it was established, and he assumed the role of unit leader in 1988, at which time he was a firefighter. The one-hundred-member-strong group conducts fifty to sixty call-outs for the sheriff's office yearly. In 2020 they went on fifty-nine missions, some that lasted two to three days, for a total of eighty-nine days in the field, with fourteen rescues.

Marin SAR aids in the administrative work to find missing persons, which includes tasks like tracking bank cards and cellphone data as well as coordinating and conducting interviews with families of missing persons. They focus on gathering evidence for law enforcement, missing-person investigations and abductions.

The sheriff's office gives them some funding every year, maintains their vehicles and gives them garage space, but Marin SAR raises an incredible eighty thousand dollars per year in donations to meet their needs.

The Marin SAR program brings onboard youth members from the age of fourteen to eighteen from local high schools. The youth SAR group has found eighteen subjects. One young man, Luca, made six finds on his own. Nearly all the young members have gone on to college, and 15 to 20 percent of them have returned to join SAR as adults. Mike says that youth members "see better, hear better and hold no bias." They will search areas that adult members rule out.

Mike is proud of their state-of-the-art, paperless command centre. They use software like SARTopo and CalTopo, a Cloud-based app, to track their searchers. They've had access to mobile Wi-Fi on large searches. They find e-bikes to be huge time savers on the trails.

CASE 14: MISSING COUPLE
INVERNESS, CALIFORNIA

On Valentine's Day in 2020, Carol Kiparsky (seventy-seven at the time) and Ian Irwin (then seventy-two) of Palo Alto, went for a romantic sunset hike from their vacation home on Via De La Vista in Marin County, but it turned into an endless nightmare when they got lost in the dark and had to survive on their own for nine days. A massive search, involving approximately four hundred people, was launched to find them.

MSAR was called out to help search the Tomales Bay State Park area.[35] Mike says they used all their resources, including drones, four e-bikes and a borrowed parabolic microphone, which amplifies sound by five times, making it more likely to hear a subject calling for help.

With the couple still missing after eight days, the rescuers were resigned to the fact that this was likely now a recovery mission. However, on February 22, searchers heard them calling for help off the trail in dense bush. Ian had an injured ankle, a cut on his forehead, facial injuries, and they were both cold, tired and hungry, having survived only on fiddle head tops, and other edible plants, and sips of muddy puddle water, but they were alive. The couple were taken out by helicopter to the hospital, where they were both treated for hypothermia, and Ian was treated for his head and facial injuries, as well as nerve damage to his feet.

The couple recovered and even returned to hike where they got lost, but now they bring a cellphone with them.[36]

In addition to mutual aid cases like the search for Carol and Ian, MSAR has assisted in major disasters, like the tragic California fires. The largest fire—the Camp Fire in Butte County, named after Camp Creek Road, where the fire initially ignited due to electrical transmission wires[37]—started on November 8, 2018. Eighty-five people were killed, and fifteen people were injured, including firefighters. Camp Fire consumed over 386 square kilometres (240 square miles), destroying

18,804 structures in seventeen days. When it ended on November 25, 2018, it was the deadliest and most destructive wildfire ever recorded in California history.[38]

Mike says that parks are overwhelmed with visitors, and SAR volunteers struggle for better support so they can handle the extra call-outs. After forty-two years in SAR, he looks forward to spending time away. He plans a trip to the Grand Canyon for three weeks, where he will teach a course in search management.

Bryan Courtois—Bristol, Maine

Bryan Courtois has been a part of SAR since 1996. In 2012 he became president of Pinetree Search and Rescue (PTSAR) and education director for the Maine Association for Search and Rescue (MASAR). He holds a drone pilot's licence and assists as a flanker with Maine SAR dogs (MESARD). He's a tool and die maker, with a relevant background for SAR as a registered Maine guide, wilderness first responder and avid all-season outdoorsman.

He enjoys hunting, hiking, backpacking and skijoring. Bryan says, "Skijoring is dog sledding lite." Bryan uses one or two sled dogs to pull him along on cross-country skis, instead of a sled and a pack of dogs.

Bryan hikes and camps year-round. He's hiked and backpacked all of the Appalachian Trail in Maine and New Hampshire in three- to twelve-day-long sections, including in the winter. He earned the rank of Eagle Scout and served twenty-five years as a leader with the Boy Scouts of America. He has taught beginner hiking and backpacking, lost-person scenarios for people studying to take the Maine Guide exam, Appalachian Mountain Club (AMC) trip leaders, and Boy Scout and Girl Scout leaders.

Bryan has done several multi-day dog sled trips, including ten days with the Baffin Island Inuit in May of 2000, seal hunting, fishing and looking for polar bears. "In 2004 I spent ten days with the Cree of Oujé-Bougoumou, Quebec, dog sledding, fishing, hunting, and learning traditional crafts," he says. In 2014 he also took a trip to Kuujjuaq, Quebec, where he hunted ptarmigan, fished and saw musk ox.

Bryan said that his most valuable equipment is a pair of neoprene gloves, because they're "best for searching in cold and wet conditions. Gore-Tex does not keep me dry at those conditions. If it is not wet, fleece or other gloves work." He remembers one of the worst search conditions he has ever been in, and he didn't have neoprene gloves at that time. The temperature was minus-one Celsius (thirty degrees Fahrenheit). They were searching for an area of young dense spruce. It had snowed during the previous day and night. "We had to search a solid wall of snow. Touching anything sent a cascade of wet snow down wherever we touched. Within minutes everyone was soaked. We persevered and finished our grid. Now I always carry a pair," Bryan says.

Bryan Courtois enjoying a skijoring outing with a Maine SAR dog, Griz, a malamute who was eight years old in this picture. Photo: Janet Courtois

PTSAR has a large team with fifty-nine members, including fourteen MASAR-certified search team members and two MASAR search team leaders.[39]

Every member pays annual dues of twenty dollars, even though they pay for all SAR expenses out of pocket. They receive no compensation for the hours they put in searching, rescuing and recovering missing people, nor do they receive federal, state or municipal funding.

The team is usually called out once a month. They cover a high-density population in their urban area, but they also work in diverse terrain in the woods, like the northern end of the Appalachian Trail (AT).

According to the Appalachian Trail Conservancy, the AT is 3,531 kilometres (2,194.3 miles) long and covers scenic woods in the Appalachian Mountains across fourteen states. The trail, which was completed in 1937, is jointly managed by the National Park Service, US Forest Service, the Appalachian Trail Conservancy, numerous state agencies and thousands of volunteers.[40]

The Appalachian Trail Conservancy estimates that three million visitors hike a portion of the AT a year, but only about a quarter of them complete the entire trail each season. Since the AT opened, more than twenty thousand hikers have finished the entire trail, including thru-hikes and multi-year section hikes. Someone who completes the trail in one or multiple years is called a "two-thousand-miler."[41]

Case 15: Missing Hiker
Appalachian Trail

Bryan was part of the mammoth search for missing hiker Geraldine "Gerry" Largay (age sixty-six), trail name "Inchworm," in July 2013. Gerry, a retired military nurse, was determined to be a two-thousand-miler and even took a course on how to do the six-month hike. She was an experienced hiker with a female trail partner to accompany her in the day. Most nights Gerry came down from the trail to spend the night in a hotel with her husband, George (trail name "Sherpa"), due to a back problem that limited how much she could carry in her backpack.

She and her girlfriend were doing a "flip-flop hike" starting at Harpers Ferry to Mount Katahdin in Maine, then driving back to Harpers Ferry and hiking south to Springer Mountain in Georgia. The women made slow but steady progress after starting out on April 23, until Gerry's hiking friend was called away for family reasons at the end of June, leaving Gerry alone on the more challenging Maine part of the trail. She was in the White Mountains, and it was too far to hike down every evening to meet up with her husband, so she stayed in lean-tos and huts along the trail.

According to Bryan, the West Virginia part of the trail is busy, but the Maine leg of the trail is less frequented, and the surrounding brush is extremely thick. On July 22, 2013, with 1,609 kilometres (1,000 miles) hiked, halfway through her journey, Gerry stepped off the trail to answer the call of nature. She couldn't find her way back to the trail. She had a tiny compass, but it was too small to be functional.

Gerry became impossibly lost in the thick woods. She climbed upward hoping to find a cell signal and sent texts to George, none of which he received. She had a tent, a sleeping bag and a few essentials, and she set up a camp under a tree. When he stopped receiving texts from her, George alerted the authorities that his wife was missing and a search was launched.

Bryan says it was the state's largest and most expensive search, with hundreds of searchers and K9 teams in the field for the first three weeks that she was missing. Helicopters with thermal imaging cameras swept the area. Game wardens talked to hikers and asked them to keep a look out for "Inchworm."

"We held out hope for quite a while. She had supplies, although not a lot. She didn't know how to use a compass or maps," says Bryan. No clues of Gerry's whereabouts were found, and months went by. George became a person of interest to the police briefly but was cleared. However, social media was quite accusatory of Gerry's husband.[42]

On October 14, 2015, more than two years after Gerry's disappearance, a forester was performing an inventory of trees on land used by the US Navy's remote SERE survival school in Redington Township, Maine. On a hill about 146 metres (160 yards) inside the navy property, along the border of the AT, he discovered an abandoned campsite. He saw a collapsed black tent and a backpack, and inside the tent was human remains in a sleeping bag.

When the authorities arrived, it was confirmed that it was Gerry's skeleton in her sleeping bag next to her ID. She had tried to get the attention of the helicopters overhead, from the looks of the scorched trees surrounding her campsite and a shiny emergency blanket hanging from branches, but the thicket was too dense for them to spot her.[43]

Her diary, in which she wrote about her last days, was found among her personal items sealed in a waterproof bag. There were entries made every day until August 18, 2013. There were instructions for what searchers should do: "When you find my body ..."

There was creek water nearby, and Gerry had a bottle of water next to her body, so it was unlikely that she died of dehydration. She was obviously unfamiliar with the wild plants in the area that could've sustained her a little longer, like wild berries, greens and roots. She survived anywhere from nineteen to twenty-six days before she died of starvation.

A nearly complete transcript of the content of her journal can be found in *When You Find My Body: The Disappearance of Geraldine Largay on the Appalachian Trail* by D. Dauphinee. A detailed account of the twenty-six-month search is also found in the book. The family made a memorial cross on the trail close to where Gerry was found.

As a takeaway from Gerry's tragedy, Bryan says, "If you get lost, stay where you are," preferably on the trail or near the trail in an open space where you can be found.

CHRIS MUSHUMANSKI—VANDERHOOF, BC

You can say I drank the SAR Kool-Aid.
—Chris Mushumanski

By day, Chris Mushumanski is a teacher and counsellor for a distance-learning public school. But outside of teaching hours, he dons a waterproof jacket and has been an active member with Nechako Valley SAR (NVSAR) since 1997. In 2013 he joined the BC Search and Rescue Association (BCSARA) board as secretary and became a Critical Incident Stress Management (CISM) peer.

Chris came to SAR through a friend, who had similar outdoor backgrounds and wanted to help others and reinforce that safety net in their community. The first weekend he joined was a long training session on a Saturday in September 1997. As they started training, an RCMP vehicle pulled up and asked them to head over to Prince George to help PGSAR search for two missing teenagers. The search drew a lot of public attention.

They drove an hour and a half, and just as they started searching for the missing teenagers, they were found in good shape. The training was postponed, but then the next morning at four o'clock, another call came in for a missing eighty-year-old mining prospector north of Fort St. James.

They drove three hours up logging roads and arrived in the middle of nowhere. They shot a gun into the air to draw the prospector's attention. Over the hill came a reply shot. They helped the prospector find his way out of the bush with the sound of their gunshots. Happy ending number two in two days. As they returned to the SAR hall, Chris's friend asked him what he thought about SAR. He said, "This is easy; we drive to PG and after a few minutes of searching, the kids were found. Drive to Fort St. James and shoot a gun, and there's our man. I can do this!" As Chris now says, "Little did I know ..."

With his breadth of outdoor experience, strong organization and communication skills and counselling training, Chris is an effective search manager. He communicates and listens well, and he can see multiple steps down the road, so he knows what needs to be done next. His unique set of skills is invaluable when he's managing searches and working with the CISM program.

"Many times, during SAR calls, the family or friends of the subject are having the worst day of their lives. I believe SAR brings a sense of calm, purpose, action and hope for them. I try my best to remember [to] embody all these skills and philosophies each time," Chris says.

The busy father, husband and teacher has a supportive family when it comes to his SAR commitments. He's missed out on major holidays, birthdays, anniversaries and a few concerts and plays that his daughters were in due to SAR calls. He says, "That can be very hard on my family, but they are supportive and forgiving. I couldn't do this without them."

As a teacher, Chris can get away for calls in the summer more easily. "In 2015 my family was back east on an extended trip. In July I was away on ten different SAR and CISM tasks, for a total of twenty-one days. It was awesome and guilt-free!" he says.

Chris devotes an extraordinary amount of time to SAR. Nechako Valley SAR is a small group that responds to about twelve to fifteen calls a year. He says, "Our busiest year had twenty-four calls—nothing crazy by NSR standards, but we did have four calls in twenty-four hours. With all the SAR hats I wear, I shudder to [admit] that I usually regularly put in over a thousand hours a year."

CASE 16: GIRL MISSING
VANDERHOOF, BC

An incident that weighs on Chris is the search for Madison "Maddy" Scott in 2011 at Hogsback Lake, southeast of Vanderhoof. Her tent was still at the campsite where she had been camping with friends, but Maddy was missing. Her truck, a white 1990 Ford F150, was found with all her belongings inside the cab, except her keys and cellphone.

Maddy was last seen in the very early hours of Saturday, May 28. SAR was requested on Sunday, shortly after she was reported missing. The initial search was quite large, with around a hundred people looking for Maddy. They covered a large area thoroughly and safely and documented it all for the RCMP file.

It was incredibly hard for Chris to update Maddy's parents throughout the day, and even worse to give them the final briefing that night, as there were no clues found in the area searched. The RCMP suspended the SAR efforts until any new information or other areas to search were identified.

"Over the years, we have put in twenty-five-plus days and easily over fifteen-hundred person hours on this file. Sadly, Madison has not been located, but it certainly has not been due to a lack of effort, including her tireless family and friends," Chris says.

Since Maddy was last seen by friends who were leaving the overnight party and campout, she's never been seen again. Sergeant Matt MacLeod of the RCMP's North District Major Crime Unit believes that foul play occurred sometime between 4:00 and 8:30 a.m. on May 28 after everyone else had left the campground.[44]

In the YouTube video *The Vanishing of Madison Scott*,[45] her mother, Dawn, describes her daughter as someone who is "independent, witty, loves her family and friends and just loves life."

Maddy has ginger hair, weighs 170 pounds, is five-foot-four, and has green eyes. The RCMP continue to investigate her disappearance and urge anyone with information to come forward.

Chris says the search for Maddy Scott was the beginning of a transformation of his group. Thanks to extensive grant writing and countless hours spent in broadening their skills and response capabilities, nine years later they got a SAR hall and garage, a mobile base to operate from, rescue tools and vehicles they needed, and a highly trained membership.

Case 17: Four Females Missing
Prince George Area, BC

Chris was involved in an evidence search on the troubling Cody Legebokoff investigation. Cody was nineteen years old at the time of his arrest for the murder of four females, making him one of Canada's youngest serial killers. One of the victims included a former student of Chris's, fifteen-year-old Loren Leslie, who went missing on November 27, 2010.

Chris says, "I taught Cody as well—small-town dynamics, when you teach and volunteer for many years. It was extremely hard to first hear about the news of Loren's death, followed a few days later with Cody being charged, and being asked to help with the evidence search."

On November 27, 2010, an officer saw Cody speeding in his pickup truck after entering the highway from a logging access road and pulled him over. Blood was found on Cody's clothing and tools, which was enough evidence to arrest him and launch an investigation into the other three missing women in the area.[46]

It was an incredibly hard few weeks that followed after December in 2010, which extended to a few years as they helped the RCMP and Prince George SAR look for evidence related to the murders of three other missing women, Natasha Montgomery (twenty-three), Jill Stuchenko (thirty-five) and Cynthia Maas (thirty-five). As demanding as the searches were, it was extremely meaningful to Chris to help bring justice to the families.

In her victim impact report to the court, Natasha Montgomery's mother, Louanne, described her daughter as "a beautiful person, inside and out. She always had a huge smile. When she was in the room, everyone knew she was there. She had a huge, bubbly personality; she was friendly to everyone and always found a way to make you feel good … She liked to draw, scrapbooking, played the clarinet and trumpet, she liked to sing and do many types of crafts."

The mother of two from Quesnel played softball and enjoyed many outdoor activities. She was in Prince George when she went missing. Her body hasn't been found; however, her blood was found in Legebokoff's apartment and on the murder weapon.[47]

Jill Stuchenko was a warm, loving mother of five children, aged two to fourteen. She was a talented singer who dreamed of being famous one day.[48]

Cynthia (Cindy) Maas was born with a disability, making her vulnerable to someone like Cody. "She was an innocent. She had dreams and aspirations for her life," said her sister Judy.

Donna Leslie, Loren's mother, addressed the court, saying, "I am shattered, heartbroken and will never be the same." Her father, Doug Leslie, described Loren as a "fun-loving, innocent little girl … all I have left is a deep sadness that never ends, that never leaves me."[49]

In September of 2014, Legebokoff, was sentenced to life in prison, with no eligibility for parole for twenty-five years, on four counts of first-degree murder, occurring between 2009 and 2010.

CRITICAL INCIDENT STRESS MANAGEMENT (CISM)

Chris finds his work with the CISM program within SAR, which helps volunteers deal with critical-incident stress, a profoundly meaningful way to give back and to be there when a group, a SAR member or their family member needs support. In the US, psychological first aid can sometimes be offered to SAR members through sheriffs' offices.

The CISM program is available after the tough calls, like body recoveries, rescues where a high level of trauma occurred or lifesaving first aid was provided, high-profile searches or rescues, near misses, the tragic times when SAR members have died in training or on task, prolonged calls like helping with evacuation notice delivery, and even successful searches, such as when a child is found. Chris says that all of these instances have the potential to profoundly impact the group and its members.

Chris says he's gained a family of SAR members across the province, as well as experiences not found in any other organization, world-class training and the opportunity to make a real, measurable difference. "There is no one else out there equipped, trained and available like the GSAR community. Those are the same reasons I continue to this day," he says. He feels that the SAR community is one of most dedicated professional groups he's ever had the pleasure to work with. "They *love* doing search and rescue, and they are outstanding at it," he says.

Jim McAllister—Sidney, BC

A knock on the door led Jim "SAR Jim" McAllister to a full career and a life's passion. He didn't look to join SAR. Instead, SAR came looking for him one early September evening in 1977 in Golden, BC. Jim opened the door to reveal an RCMP officer, who asked, "Are you Jim McAllister?" Having recently moved to Golden, Jim wondered what he might have done wrong.

The officer said, "I understand you are a scuba diver. There has been a drowning in a remote lake, and our dive team can't make it. Would you be willing to search for the body? If you are willing, we will have you registered as a search and rescue volunteer to afford some protection." After checking with his wife, who was eight months pregnant with their first child, Jim indicated he would help, and carried out the task as requested.

After that incident, Jim attended the Golden and District SAR meetings. One of the first calls he went on was a rope rescue of a young couple who had missed a curve and driven off a cliff in the Kicking Horse canyon; their van was hung up on rocks about seventy-six metres down. There was another steep slope of forty-six metres down to the railway tracks and river. Jim watched the rope rescue team set up a load and belay (safety rope) system—"load" meaning what "is being lowered or raised by rope in a rope rescue system and which may include stretcher, subject and attendant(s) where the rope is bearing some or all of their weight."[50] Their only equipment was fifty-five metres of high-stretch climbing rope with steel brake bars.

Despite several complications, the couple was rescued and no one was injured. This led Jim to think that there must be a better way to get the equipment to where it was needed. "Several of us 'newbies' formed a society, raised funds [and] purchased a used ambulance, six-hundred-foot rescue ropes and proper equipment. After completing rope rescue training, my scuba diving experience drew me into swiftwater rescue, then SAR management," says Jim.

"SAR Jim," as those in the community call him, currently serves as treasurer on the executive of BCSARA. He's been a member since the late 1970s, and he has spearheaded many changes within the organization, from the days of pagers to today's use of GPS, cellphones and night-vision goggles.

Jim moved to Cranbrook in 1990 and joined SAR there. He became the regional representative on the Provincial SAR Advisory Committee in 1995–96 while co-writing the *Strategic Plan for SAR in BC*. From there, he says, "In 2002, during the cuts to government services, I got the position as the SAR specialist at the Provincial Emergency Program in Victoria." He then became the manager of programs and retired as the director of Emergency Management Services and Programs in 2008. He was co-chair of the Ground SAR Council of Canada, formed Avalanche Canada, and managed the development of AdventureSmart and other safety programs.

Of his long SAR career, Jim says, "SAR has had an extremely positive impact on my life. I can go anywhere in the province and see people I have met along the way." Jim estimates that as a SAR volunteer, he was on 350 calls in the Kootenays and oversaw many more. His volunteer hours exceed five hundred a year.

Jim enjoys sailing in his retirement, an activity he finds overlaps with his SAR work in interesting ways. His favourite SAR equipment was a Prusik knot—a length of seven- to nine-millimetre cord with the ends tied together with a double fisherman's knot, then wrapped around a larger rope with a Prusik knot and clipped into an anchor or harness. This slides along the rope until under pressure and then locks. Used in rope rescue as a non-mechanical friction stop and also as a climbing aid, the Prusik has a lot of uses outside SAR as well. "As a sailor, I use it on anchor lines, to relieve pressure when a line gets jammed, and even to climb the mast," says Jim.

CASE 18: SHEILAH SWEATMAN—CRESTON, BC

Jim McCallister became acquainted with Sheilah Sweatman when they were both bloggers on a website for the *Callout: Search and Rescue* TV series started prior to when he retired from EMBC in 2008.

Sheilah was a SAR member with many special skills and a wonderful personality. Her parents, Teddi and Wynn Sweatman, say that she was also an accomplished artist and a certified carpenter. Their daughter, "Sheesh," was a "powerhouse within the Nelson SAR community and everywhere she went. She loved the work she did with SAR."

Sheilah lived in the Selkirk Mountains near Nelson, BC. She enjoyed snowboarding, mountain biking, rafting, hiking and was training for her first triathlon. She worked at a vet clinic and was training her puppy, Freya, to be a search dog.

Sheilah was on a swiftwater call-out on Goat River, near Creston, BC, where a car had gone off the road and become submerged on June 29, 2011.[51] The body of a woman was in the car and Sheilah's instructions were to hook a cable to the car. At the coroner's inquest a video was showed that Sheilah was thrown from a raft near the car when the car began moving downstream.

When she came off the raft, her leg became tangled up in the cable. For five minutes she managed to keep her head above, then she was dragged under by the cable attached to the car. Her SAR team members tried to reach her by rowing a boat to her, swimming and throwing her ropes, but their efforts failed to save her.[52]

Her loss drove a lot of changes in operations, policy and procedures in the SAR system, so that members wouldn't be placed in that precarious situation on a body recovery again. Central Okanagan SAR named a rescue boat *Sweatman* in her honour. Nelson SAR landscaped a garden around Sheilah's Monument. Also, the Sheilah Sweatman Gymnasium at Queenston School in her hometown of Winnipeg, Manitoba, was named in her memory.

Though Jim is retired from his role with SAR, he has taken it upon himself to spend countless hours preserving the memory of Sheilah Sweatman. The Search and Rescue Volunteer Memorial monument, that Jim was instrumental in organizing, was unveiled on the grounds of the legislative assembly in Victoria on March 2, 2017.[53] Sheilah's death was a major catalyst to have the memorial erected to recognize the air, marine and ground SAR volunteers who have died during training or responses. Jim wrote a book about the project, *A Monument to Remember: The British Columbia Search and Rescue Volunteer Memorial Project*; proceeds from his book go toward maintaining the memorial.[54]

Jim was involved in the formation of the SAR Volunteer Safety Program prior to and after her death. "As a Director with EMBC I announced the formation of the program in 2007, after retiring I came back as a contractor to work on its development and release in 2009, as a Director at large for BCSARA I assisted with the Swiftwater Task-force that was formed shortly after Sheilah's death on June 29, 2011, which resulted in changes to the safety program and responded to the enquiry recommendations, and led the formation of the BCSARA/EMBC Joint SAR Volunteer Safety Committee in 2012 partly in response to Sheilah's death."

BC SAR's swiftwater safety guidelines, as well as their operational guidelines, can be found online in the *SAR Safety Program Operating Guidelines*.[55]

Case 19: Hitchhiker Missing
Prince George, BC

The searches that stay with Jim are the ones when the subject isn't found. "The summer of 2002, I was in Prince George twice for the search for Nicole Hoar, who went missing along the Highway of Tears and has never been found."

The Highway of Tears is a 725-kilometre stretch of Highway 16 in BC's north between Prince George and Prince Rupert, where forty women and girls, the majority of whom are First Nations, have gone missing or been found deceased since 1969.[56] In 2005, the RCMP launched Project E-PANA to investigate thirteen homicides in the area of Highway 16 and adjacent Highways 97 and 5; in 2007, the RCMP acknowledged that eighteen women had been murdered or disappeared from the Highway of Tears.[57]

Jim was the Search and Rescue Specialist for EMBC during the extensive initial search for Nicole Hoar. "My attending the search was to assist the EMBC Regional Manager by providing expertise and to assist if other resources were required," he said. "There was over 1,500 kilometres of roadways searched by vehicle, plane and helicopter, and by walking roadsides looking for clues, while the RCMP conducted their investigation, during the weeklong search. [At that time] there were no presumptions made in relation to other missing women along the highway from a search perspective."

The case is still open and RCMP still search for Nicole Hoar, who was twenty-five years old at the time of her disappearance in June 2002. She was from Red Deer, Alberta, but she was working in the Prince George area as a tree planter at the time. She was hitchhiking to see her sister in Smithers, west of Prince George. She was last seen at a gas station, but she was never seen again, despite over fourteen hundred tips being called in.

If you have any information at all about Nicole Hoar or any of the other missing women, please contact the RCMP, regardless of how insignificant you might feel that information might be.

CASE 20: BOY MISSING
SALMON RIVER, BC

Another missing-person incident that troubles Jim is when Debbie and David Malthus of Dawson Creek, BC, took their foster son, Joseph Andrews, on vacation at a campground by the Salmon River, north of Prince George. Joseph went missing on August 4, 2002, while tubing on the river. At first it was thought that the boy, who was wearing a shirt, shorts, yellow baseball cap and an orange PFD, had had an accident while floating on the yellow tube, which had a long yellow rope attached to it.

The search lasted for eight days, and it involved up to 120 searchers, including forest fire crews, RCMP dog teams, aircraft and trackers. RCMP search planes and helicopters searched the Salmon River and used a "sewer camera" to check under the log jams. Not finding him in the water, they moved their search to the woods, but there was still nothing of Joseph to be found.[58]

Jim says he coined the term "the next tree syndrome" when he was driving volunteers to the airport to go home. "So many of them said, 'But if I had looked around the next tree, he might have been there.'"

Since then no trace of Joseph has surfaced, not even the yellow inner tube, yellow rope, or his clothing, not in the water or in the surrounding woods. No tips, clues or sightings came in from the public. Police interviewed each of the hundreds of campers staying at the campground that weekend, as well as anyone living in Salmon Valley, but there were no leads. Police, searchers and a helicopter searched the area again in December 2002, once the trees shed their leaves, but there were no clues as to the boy's disappearance. Joseph would have been twenty-nine years old now, if he had survived his trip down the river.[59]

"SAR Jim" continued volunteering with BCSAR for over forty years because of the "sense of community within BCSAR and elsewhere in the country and the world." He remained on the BCSARA board to see that "the volunteers receive sustainable funding and recognition as first responders on the same level as paid professionals."

Jim has now retired from the BCSARA board, having achieved his objectives of sustainable funding, the memorial and the safety program. He's now "taking time to write some of the many stories that should be recorded to show the contribution of the volunteers."

Sue Duxbury—Sunshine Coast, BC

"I'm Sunshine 07, also known as 007," jokes Sue Duxbury. Sue grew up in Penmaenmawr, North Wales, in a family where volunteerism was a way of life. Her dad was on call for the coast guard, called the Royal National Lifeboat Institution. "He was also on call for the local fire department. My dad always joked that if the siren and the maroons went off at the same time, he'd be torn in half," says Sue. She moved to the Sunshine Coast in 1978 and has been there ever since.

Case 21: Female Hitchhiker Missing
Sechelt, BC

Sue joined SCSAR in 1993, but her desire to make a difference started much earlier. On August 7, 1980, she and her future mother-in-law were icing her three-tier wedding cake, and her neighbour, seventeen-year-old Mary Ellen "Marnie" Jamieson, was helping. The tiers sank, as the columns between the tiers weren't properly supported, which was both a disastrous and laughable situation.

Pretty, blue-eyed, blonde Marnie left with both women in a happy mood about the upcoming wedding. Marnie was casual about hitchhiking home on Sunshine Coast Highway 101. Hitchhiking was a common way of getting around the Sunshine Coast back then and is still in practice today, particularly between the ferry terminals at each end of the peninsula, where bus service is infrequent and taxis are rare and costly.

But the wedding celebrations would have a pall cast over them when Marnie was reported missing the following day. Her body was found four days later on the side of a logging road in Sechelt. The cause of her death was asphyxiation.

Clifford Olson, the notorious serial killer of at least eleven children between the ages of nine and eighteen, was a suspect in Marnie's murder, as he did travel to the Sunshine Coast to visit family frequently. He also left his victims on back roads, like he did with Marnie. Strangling and stabbing were Olson's hallmarks; however, his most common method was blows to the head with a hammer. In the end, Olson was never charged with the teenager's death, but Sue's gut feeling is that he murdered her friend.[60]

DNA testing and crime technology weren't nearly as sophisticated then as they are now. However, Olson's victims were all found in the Vancouver area, including Surrey, White Rock, Richmond, Burnaby, Chilliwack and Whistler. It's not inconceivable that he may have taken the ferry and committed Marnie's murder, but he has taken that and any other locations of his unfound murders to his grave. He died at Ste.-Anne-des-Plaines prison in Quebec on September 11, 2011, at the age of seventy-one.

SCSAR was started by Bill Lawson, an auxiliary RCMP member. He recognized that the auxiliary was not really prepared or trained for searches, and they needed a SAR group.

In those early years, says Sue, "I learned a lot on the fly. We had boots and a compass and rain gear. Call-outs were done using a telephone tree." Maps were studied, and tasks were planned on someone's tailgate. The club met once a month for training exercises. She was one of two women amongst male loggers, surveyors, mill workers and backcountry skiers. She describes the growth of the group as reactive.

SCSAR never had a rope team until they needed one, at which time, Richard "Richy" Till and Bob Charters trained them. Sue says that it was a steep learning curve. "Similarly, we never had any swift-water training until after we'd been wading in creeks to pull people out," she says.

At first, there was no specific training program. They covered basic first aid, map and compass navigation, and radio operation, but it was a lot less organized. "We also used our kids as subjects for training. I'd pay them in Clif Bars. Now we aren't allowed to use under-nine-teens, although we still use our grown kids and spouses," says Sue.

CASE 22: CLIMBER INJURED
GRAY CREEK, BC

Sue recalls her "firsts" most vividly. For example, "Your first recovery call usually sticks." In the late 1990s in Sechelt, a group of teens were rock climbing at a waterfall on Gray Creek when one of them had difficulties with the rope and couldn't make it up the cliff. He told the others to cut his line, as he was over the water and thought he could swim to land and work his way back up. They cut his line, but the water pulled him under, and he drowned.

At the time, there was no swiftwater training or SAR teams dedicated to swiftwater rescues. Sue and her team waded across feeder creeks to reach the site. It was treacherous to carry the subject out, with slippery rocks and dense vegetation. Members are no longer allowed to enter the water without swiftwater training.

CASE 23: ELDER MISSING—PORPOISE BAY, BC

You remember your first recovery, and your first successful find.
Rhody was my first never-solved to this day.
—Sue Duxbury

Sue's first unsolved missing-person case was an elderly lady. "Rhody Lake went missing in November 2005. We never found anything. No clue, no clothing, nothing."

On a brisk late-April day in 2022, at a coffee shop in Sechelt, BC, Jennifer Lake Tipper, daughter of Rhody Lake, had a reunion with Alec Tebbutt, president of Sunshine Coast Search and Rescue, who had been the search manager on her mother's case back in 2005. Jennifer recounted the timeline on the day her eighty-year-old mother disappeared. A successful magazine editor, Rhody—"not the kind of person you expect would disappear," according to Jennifer—went for a walk at Porpoise Bay at 8:30 a.m. on Sunday, November 27, 2005, according to a neighbour who had seen her. Jennifer says that her mother went for a second walk at 12:30 p.m. on that snowy day according to witnesses in the neighbourhood.

At about two that afternoon, Jennifer's brother saw their mother leave for another walk up the road, which has no shoulder and where cars frequently speed. Rhody was spotted at the top of Sandy Hook Road. "It was unusual for my mom to walk that many times in a day," Jennifer said. It was also out of character for her to walk the approximately four kilometres to Porpoise Bay, double the length of the walk she would usually take. Jennifer speculated that perhaps her mom had gotten a ride from someone. She describes her mother as trusting and said that she would be unafraid of hopping into any car that came along.

The ninety-third Grey Cup was held that afternoon at BC Place stadium in Vancouver. The Edmonton Eskimos won in a 38–35 rare overtime victory over the Montreal Alouettes. Likely, everyone was inside their homes, entranced by the thrilling game on their televisions, when Rhody left for that third walk of the day. She was wearing brown corduroy pants, a wool sweater, a blue and yellow vest, a bright rust hat, gloves, a backpack and hiking boots, and she carried a walking stick festooned with bear bells.

Rhody was an avid, seasoned hiker, both on her own and in groups. "She knew what to do," says Jennifer, who felt that if it got dark that afternoon and her mother got lost in the woods, she would have known to find somewhere to shelter for the night.

Rhody's son left the house at about the same time that afternoon and didn't return until 11:30 p.m. that night, after watching the game with friends. The next morning, he was alarmed to find that his mother wasn't at home; her bed was made and didn't appear to have been slept in. He called around to her friends to see if she had walked over to have tea with them, but none of them had heard from her. Rhody didn't have a cellphone; in fact, she refused to have one.

At about nine that morning, he called Jennifer, who lives in Burnaby, about their mother's disappearance. Jennifer left home at noon, having waited in hopes that her mother would turn up, then headed for the Horseshoe Bay ferry. She arrived at her mother's home in Sechelt at 4:30 p.m.

"The police stopped me and told me there was a missing person. Search and Rescue was there. The Salvation Army was there," says Jennifer. Alec explains that the Salvation Army truck provided food for the search team and the family. Jennifer's other brother drove to join them as soon as he could.

Local psychics showed up at the house to assist with the search, and they offered various readings that were followed up on, such as the possibility that Rhody had been attacked by a bear, fallen into the shallow estuary, fallen into a gulley or been kidnapped and taken away in a car. A neighbour had seen a cougar in a tree, but no evidence of Rhody's body was found.

There was a sighting of Rhody with a man with a dog at the entrance to Porpoise Bay Provincial Park; however, the man was never identified, nor has he come forward.

The search went on for six days and included SAR teams from the Lower Mainland and Vancouver Island, as well as an RCMP search-dog team. They searched the shorelines from the air, and searchers were longlined into the surrounding forest to conduct searches over the vast terrain. However, dive teams weren't engaged. After the thorough search and no evidence being found, the search was called off.

Alec recalls a former SAR member reporting the scent of rotting flesh in the area not soon after Rhody disappeared, so they bushwhacked through dense blackberries and salal, but nothing was found. Two years after her mother's disappearance, Jennifer hired a private investigator, who brought in their own search dog and re-interviewed witnesses, but they were unable to turn up any clues as to Rhody's whereabouts. Another search was conducted five years later, and again after ten years.

The Sunshine Coast RCMP believe that her disappearance was non-criminal in nature. Corporal Don Newman wrote in an affidavit: "The possibility that she fell into the Sechelt Inlet or that an animal moved her remains is substantial.[61] Alec agrees that the most likely scenario was that Rhody was attacked by an animal, although he admits that in a previous search where a wild animal was involved, the subject's bones were found scattered, whereas there have been no physical clues found in Rhody's case.

Jennifer feels that her mother may have had an accident, such as a fall where she hit her head, or that foul play was involved, like someone hit her with their car accidentally and put her lifeless body in their trunk.

After ten years, Jennifer applied for a death certificate through the court, which was granted. The family was then able to settle the estate, and also held a memorial.

"It's tormenting," Jennifer says of her mother's disappearance. "SAR was amazing and helpful. I have total gratitude. I knew it was equally hard for them to end the search. SAR was our rock. They brought us back to reality. They brought sanity to the situation," she says. "I wish we'd had social media back then," she adds.

"We have solved missing-person cases with social media. We've had hundreds and sometimes thousands of responses on Facebook. There's a lot more eyes," says Alec. Jennifer would like her mother to be remembered as a writer, an artist and an outgoing, outspoken advocate for health issues, who was fairly active, despite having had a mini-stroke and some falls in the year prior to her disappearance.

"You remember your first recovery, and your first successful find," Sue says. "Rhody was my first never-solved."

Case 24: Two Teenagers Missing
Sechelt, BC

There's an impressive conveyor belt that runs from a dock in Sechelt all the way to a gravel pit on the hill about three kilometres away. In the mid-1990s, Sue Duxbury says local teen males found ways to get into the gravel pit for a ride on the conveyor belt. Two teenage males died that way when the pile of gravel they were on unexpectedly dropped into an underground horizontal conveyor. The fatal accident was paramount in Sue's mind when two more teenagers went missing in Sechelt and were suspected of joy-riding the conveyor belt into the gravel pit.

Members were dispersed throughout the gravel pit site, but equipment was still running. Sue, a new SAR manager at the time, called the night manager of the site to get the machinery shut down, and he got his crew to help with the search. Within fifteen minutes, the teen girls were found hiding in a maintenance shack. Sue was elated that they were found safe but also dismayed that people were still getting into the site to take joy rides on the conveyor belt.

The RCMP arrived and gave the girls a talking-to before they were released into the custody of their parents. The schools in the area then educated their students about the dangers of the conveyor belt by inviting every Grade 6 class for a visit. The gravel pit operators shored up the fences in hopes that no one else would get in.

Case 25: Boy Missing
Petgill Lake, BC

Sue says another mutual-aid call of the highest priority was a search for a child who had gotten lost in the woods around Petgill Lake. The SCSAR group took the first ferry from Langdale terminal over to Horseshoe Bay and then drove north to access the Petgill Lake trailhead, which is in the Squamish area. The hike started across from the Murrin Provincial Park parking lot, across the highway from the Petgill Lake trailhead and is a six-hour round trip up to Petgill Lake and back, with an elevation gain of 640 metres.[62]

The boy, who was about twelve years old, had become separated from his dad while they were fishing. The dad headed back to the car and waited before calling SAR. The boy wasn't found the first day. Sue says they covered a considerable area around the lake both on foot and by helicopter for about a ten-kilometre radius.

The second day, the boy showed up on the highway in Britannia Beach, three kilometres away from where their car was parked. In a show of incredible resilience, he had covered twenty-four kilometres along the power line parallel to the highway before hiking down to the highway. Sue recently completed the Organized Avalanche Response Team Leader program on Brohm Ridge near Squamish. "We actually witnessed an avalanche come down in an adjacent valley to where we were working. It was both awesome and terrifying," she says.

In the future, Sue's goals are to "up my medical training so I can give pain meds." Within SAR, she sees more use of drones in the field and emergency locator transmitters (ELTs) on dementia patients. Other innovative tools she would like to see are more rugged mountain e-bikes to allow SAR members to cover greater distances on a search, and a modular bridge, designed by Richard Till, that can be easily mobilized for gaps over water during evacuations. In 2022, the Sunshine Coast SAR team received two mountain e-bikes and they are waiting for a third bike to arrive.

ANDY EVANS—SECHELT, BC

Andy Evans, call sign Sunshine 56, joined Powell River SAR in the fall of 2008. He juggled his job as the manager of the town's mall with his MIT training, which he completed on March 20, 2009. Andy joined the team "under the influence of several of my closest hiking partners that were excited to get some young blood involved in the group."

Andy quickly moved into the role of VP of the newly formed society and was instrumental in helping set it up and securing their new building. He trained the new MITs. He also obtained his HAM radio licence in April 2010 (VA7SAZ) and became an organized avalanche response team member in January 2010.

In the summer of 2014, Andy moved to Sechelt and joined SCSAR. Just as though he were a brand-new SAR member, he had to do six months of probation, which took him until the spring of 2015. Since then, he's completed SARMed 1, utility terrain vehicle (UTV) training and snowmobile training. Andy has recruited and trained over twenty new members for the group, and he will be key in intake sessions to come. He was one of two of the trainers for the graduating class of MITs in 2020 for SCSAR.

Andy, who is currently a landscaper, joined BCSAR because he loves the outdoors and wants to share his knowledge and skills with others, but primarily he "joined to help people in need, whether they're in medical need, lost or in distress."

He brought his advanced skills in the outdoors and a keen interest in snow-related rescue to BCSAR. More recently, he's focussed on his medical skills. He's found that he excels with trauma in the field. "I am usually on one of the first teams to respond to medical calls."

Andy feels that SAR has made him a more compassionate person. Sometimes on calls they deal with people in distress and medical trauma. "SAR taught me to look at each situation individually and focus on the needs of our subject. Not every call is easy; some do not end the way we want them to and are very sad. Luckily, we have a great team of people available to us to help us through these situations," says Andy.

Secretive Society of Mushroom Pickers—BC

The wild mushroom trade in BC is a multimillion-dollar business fuelled by restauranteurs' demands. A mushroom picker can make thousands of dollars per day, depending upon the type of mushrooms and their level of picking experience.

Foraging with minimal equipment—just a small mushroom knife, brush, basket and a guidebook, with your nose to the ground like a truffle pig—is a fun outing. The woods can yield lots of edible fungus, like lobster, cauliflower, chanterelle, tree fungus, puffball and other mushroom delicacies to make creamy soups or sauces with. But you can easily get lost and/or injured with your head down, and a strong urge to pick in places that might be just beyond your reach or out of your hiking skill level can lead to a fall or to getting lost.

According the Government of BC's online guide to mushroom picking, the gathering of wild mushrooms is an important part of First Nations' foodstuffs and income. Other pickers must not trespass on First Nations land. Individuals and commercial picking operations are allowed to harvest mushrooms on Crown land, as long as they comply with "applicable legislation related to the use of Crown land and respect the rights of private property owners, First Nations and other stakeholders."

During every mushroom season, BCSAR has many call-outs for mushroom pickers getting lost. Most of the time they are found, although they may have to spend a night outdoors before they're found, and that's risky during the late October season. Every year at least one lost mushroom picker goes missing for an extended period and is found deceased.

Mike Ritcey of Kamloops SAR (KSAR) explains the reason pickers get lost: "With your head down, picking mushrooms, you're not paying attention to which way you came in or which way you have to go to get out." He advises mushroom pickers to "bring a GPS or compass; know the area and bring a map; find out where the roads in and out are; bring the essentials; and let people know their plans and route."[63]

This last piece of advice goes against the culture of secrecy amongst the pickers. They don't want anyone to know where their picking grounds are, as they hope to best their competitors. However, having a trip plan and informing someone they trust if they're overdue from a mushroom picking trip can be a matter of life and death for gatherers.

Majority of subjects (83%) go out alone. Most subjects eventually wander out to a road or trail or they may even return home. Subjects in the wilderness tend to be found along canyons, creeks or drainages. Medical and trauma scenes are possible. Subjects have poor long-term survivability because of limited clothing and equipment.[64]

Case 26: Mother and Child Missing—Powell River, BC

One of the challenges of being a SAR member for Andy is when subjects are in psychological distress. "Some are successful in their desire to go forward with their plans.[65] This is very hard on every member of the team." The other difficult challenge for Andy are calls that involve children, as in the following missing-persons case.

"I'm a dad first and a SAR volunteer second. When we get a call that involves a child, it is always difficult for every member of the team," says Andy. On this call, Heather Thompson and her daughter, who was only twenty months old, went out to pick mushrooms the morning of October 24, 2012. When they didn't return by evening, Heather's boyfriend reported them missing. Her van and her belongings were found in the Duck Lake area.[66]

Andy recalls, "We immediately started searching the area for the mom and child. It was completely dark, so we were hopeful that we would find them soon. We searched until 2:00 a.m. with no luck. It was a hard decision for us to call off the search for the night."

The team returned at first light. They had called for mutual aid overnight. SAR teams from Vancouver Island and the Lower Sunshine Coast were on their way. Powell River is a small community of about thirteen thousand people, and word gets around quickly. PRSAR had over two hundred people converge on their stage area. The RCMP had a helicopter in the air, and civilians searched trails and drove along the roads. Andy searched while riding an MTV on the trails.

However, they still hadn't been found by the middle of the day, and PRSAR was getting worried about the subjects spending another night out in the woods. "How could we not find them, with this many people in the field? All of a sudden, it came over the air: 'We've got them! The helicopter spotted mom and child!'" Andy recounts.

They immediately dispatched teams to the area. The mom and her child were in good condition, along with their family dog. This was an extremely emotional search for Andy, as his daughter was young at the time. As a parent, he had related closely to this search.

This was the best of all possible outcomes. The pair were cold after being out in minus one weather overnight, but they were going to be okay.

Andy has been on over 150 calls. He says, "Whether we are out on a call, reading up on a new procedure or policy, spending time on our weekend updating our medical, or going to an avalanche course, our time is just completely immeasurable." He says that he has "gained invaluable knowledge and leadership skills from being involved on the team." He adds, "I continue to volunteer because in all honesty, I really just like to help people, as well as I love to share my knowledge with others."

STEVE TORY—TUMBLER RIDGE, BC

Steve Tory, an IT consultant, joined Tumbler Ridge SAR (TRSAR) in 2014. He was already a volunteer firefighter and thought it would be interesting. Several of his firefighter friends were in SAR, so he knew what he was in for. He was also inspired by his childhood Scout leader, who had been in SAR.

TRSAR gets about twelve calls per year. Steve says they are fortunate in that the population in the north, for the most part, is still afraid of wilderness, and people know better than to count on getting cellphone signals. Their group can call in surrounding BCSAR groups, like Prince George SAR, for assistance if needed, and they can also rely on the help of STARS (Shock Trauma Air Rescue Service) in Grande Prairie, Alberta, for night flight evacuations. STARS is an Alberta and Saskatchewan organization that is mostly funded by industry. Steve says STARS flies to the Tumbler Ridge area about once a year to assist and is an amazing asset.

Steve estimates he puts in about five hundred volunteer hours every year in SAR. He says his group specializes in Ground SAR and avalanche operations, and he has a rope-rescue team in development. In the long-term, they would like to add swiftwater rescue because the nearest swiftwater team is a two-hour drive away.

Case 27: Two Hikers Lost in Boulder Gardens
Tumbler Ridge, BC

On October 6, 2019, two hikers, a mother and daughter, went for a day hike on the Boulder Gardens trail, a two-hour, four-kilometre-long, moderately difficult trail that's steep and rocky in places. The women missed the initial trailhead, and after hiking for a while, they ran into two grizzly bears. Fortunately, the grizzlies must have had their bellies full of berries and didn't pursue the women as they moved off the trail and into the wilderness of Babcock Mountain. This departure from the trail left them without their bearings and they became hopelessly lost.

After gaining some elevation, they found cell service and called for help. They were sheltering in a culvert under an abandoned mining road. A TRSAR member and professional archaeologist, Craig Waters, was confident he knew where they were by their description of the area. The SAR team, including a pregnant member, were able to drive straight to the lost women on ATVs. The subjects were quite surprised to be rescued by an expectant mother, who stayed on the mountain with another member while the hikers were ferried to safety. Steve explains that it was a low-risk rescue and the pregnant member was in no danger as it was her first trimester.

After the rescue, the members received thank-you cards and fresh socks from the rescued subjects. One of the subjects was a teacher, and her class made a poster to thank the members for saving their teacher. Steve calls these two the greatest rescue subjects of all time, because of how appreciative grateful they were to the SAR members.

Case 28: Two Hikers Lost
Bootski Lake, BC

On the opposite end of the spectrum from the previous rescue, two well-prepared subjects were hiking Bootski Lake, a strenuous ten-kilometre alpine hike. Steve says he's seen chunks of ice the size of cars floating in the lake as late as July. The elevation is only about six hundred metres, but the lake is sheltered. It's called Bootski because people can ski just on their boots to the lake, without the help of skis.

On October 8, 2017, Marianne McCullough and Nicole Amirault were hiking Bootski Lake with a dog when fog disoriented them. They did everything right in terms of being prepared for the bush, except for bringing a navigational or communication device. They didn't have a cellphone, GPS or compass.

They built a lean-to with a platform and covered it with a tarp, so they were protected from the snowstorm in the night. The dog caught a grouse for their supper. Steve says their shelter was excellent, even better than any shelter he's built.

In the morning, a search was launched with thirty-nine search personnel, including seventeen Tumbler Ridge SAR members, four South Peace SAR members, thirteen from North Peace SAR, and air searchers.[67] Marianne and Nicole built a fire to make smoke signals. After seven hours of searching, and on the second pass of the spotter plane, their smoke signals were detected from the air.

The helicopter landed near the subjects' camp, and they were walked out and flown to safety. Without them being so prepared, Steve says the outcome could have been much worse.

More than half of the time, Steve has rescued people out of their predicaments, gotten them in the cab of the rescue truck with a hot drink and a snack, and then they've asked him about his job with TRSAR. "It's almost like I'm their Uber driver," Steve says. He informs them that he was in bed sleeping before the phone rang to come and rescue them in the middle of the night and that he is a volunteer. When he informs them that the team comes out in the worst of conditions to help others in need, they tend to be blown away.

Steve enjoys the training and sense of community that SAR gives him. He can travel anywhere in the province and always be welcomed into a SAR member's home like family. He spoke of a course on tracking held in Princeton for fifty SAR members a few years ago and how amazing it was to develop those skills. He would like to see TRSAR improve its helicopter capabilities in the future, as well as build a swiftwater team to keep up with the recreational river boating in the area. Satellite communicators are Steve's indispensable pieces of equipment. "They are a valuable source of comms on rescue operations. Everyone in the backcountry ought to have one," he says.

The other passion Steve has is volunteering with the Tumbler Ridge Geopark. On September 23, 2014, it became the second UN-ESCO Global Geopark in North America. Apparently, 75 percent of the world's Tyrannosaurid tracks were discovered in the area since the original trackway discoveries in the 1990s. Where was TRSAR when those dinosaurs needed rescuing?

7. Ice

"Binty" Massey—Whistler, BC

"My brother couldn't say my name when he was little, and my mom picked up on it, so that's what everyone calls me," says Vincent "Binty" Massey of Whistler SAR (WSAR). He is extraordinary in all that he undertakes, which includes pottery,[68] building houses and saving lives.

This grandfather of four joined WSAR in 1988 and has performed about a hundred direct rescues. He's certified for avalanche, snowmobile, helicopter longline (HETS), rope and swiftwater rescues.

Binty has seen many changes over the past three decades. He attributes the phenomenal growth in the passion for backcountry activities to generational and social media influences. Children grow up enjoying the backcountry with their parents and grandparents, and it instills a passion for the outdoors in the younger generation and becomes part of their lifestyle. He takes his own grandkids skiing.

The other growth factor in rescues, in Binty's opinion, is that Whistler and Blackcomb have ski lifts that take people to the backcountry and out-of-bounds areas within minutes. Ticket vendors and chairlifts don't know the intentions of the people they carry to the top.

Going into the backcountry means you're prepared and have the knowledge and experience needed to go off-trail into areas that are within your ability and skill level. Going out-of-bounds means you're recklessly entering dangerous territory that is clearly marked as such, and often, those who do so are unprepared and under-skilled. You can safely enjoy the backcountry with preparation and appropriate training and by avoiding treacherous out-of-bounds areas.

Binty says that the SAR work for their thirty-two members, ten of whom are new to the longest serving, Brad Sills, who joined in 1976, never stops, whether it's for lost hikers and injured mountain bikers in the summer, or backcountry snowboarders, skiers, snowshoers, snowmobilers and snow bikers in the winter.

Ice rescues put rescuers in great peril when there is no helicopter available, and even if there is a helicopter available it is extremely dangerous. Shutterstock 1904218387

"We're constantly doing hot loads onto the helicopter," he says. Hot loading a helicopter means that the engine doesn't shut down when loading.

In addition to making beautiful pottery, when Binty isn't on SAR calls, he guides ice cave tours. His wife, Cheryl, also an artist and basket weaver, is incredibly supportive of his involvement with SAR.

CASE 29: ICE SAILOR FALLEN THROUGH ICE
GREEN LAKE, BC

On March 5, 2005, Binty drove by Green Lake and saw bystanders watching a man who had fallen through thin ice while ice sailing and was flailing and struggling to save himself. Binty spotted his neighbour, mountain rescuer Paul Skelton, in the crowd and asked him what they were going to do about it. They raced over to Blackcomb Helicopters to see if they could find a pilot. Steven Flynn, a helicopter pilot, had just driven past the scene too and knew the man would need a rescue team if he were to survive. He rushed to the heliport, where Paul and Binty were waiting.[69]

The man had been in the freezing water for forty minutes by the time they arrived. "He stopped moving and was resting his arms on the ice," says Binty. Steven hovered so close to the surface that one of the helicopter's skids touched the ice. Paul and Binty leaned over on the pilot's side and hauled the 250-pound, soaking-wet victim to safety, while the pilot kept the helicopter from tipping into the lake. To watch a short film about Binty and this particular rescue, see: youtube/6pMNMQcjoJ4.

For their act of bravery, Binty and the other two men received the Governor General's Medal of Bravery in 2008. The medal is intended for everyday heroes who risk their lives with no regard for their own survival, whether the person they saved was a loved one or a stranger.

CASE 30: MISSING SNOWSHOER
CYPRESS PROVINCIAL PARK, VANCOUVER, BC

Binty says that social media spurs people on to take pictures of how "gnarly" it is out in the wild. He says that the drive for more and more extreme Instagram and YouTube posts can lead to carelessness. People end up posting their last picture just before they disappear forever, slipping and falling to their deaths off a precipice or waterfall.

However, cellphones are valuable rescue tools, as SAR can ping a cellphone to find a subject's location even if they can't call out. Pinging a cellphone means that an authority, like the RCMP, calls the service provider to get the cellphone's GPS coordinates. The authority then passes along the coordinates to the SAR manager, who gives the location to the search team.

Nikki Donnelly (age twenty-one) of Ontario became lost on the afternoon of Thursday, January 14, 2021, while snowshoeing on the Howe Sound Crest Trail up to St. Mark's Summit in Cypress Provincial Park. The summit is not recommended as a place to go in the winter, but it is still heavily used.

Nikki ventured solo into unfamiliar backcountry in a high-risk area. The conditions were slippery and treacherous. Both inexperienced and experienced snowshoers alike use this well-travelled area for day use, and she wasn't prepared to spend the night outdoors. Social media shows that she made it to the peak and took a panoramic video of the view with her phone.

Nikki called her boyfriend in Ontario to let him know she had made it to the peak. She called him again several hours later to tell him she was lost. The message was then relayed to local authorities on the North Shore of Vancouver, unfortunately delaying the onset of the search.

North Shore Rescue (NSR) sent in ground SAR and a helicopter with night-vision technology, as it was already dark by the time the message got through and a search ensued. At about two in the morning, a storm moved in, and the search was paused.[70]

SAR pinged her cellphone around 4:30 a.m. and determined the area where they would be able to find her. Her cellphone went dead after that time. In the morning, the search resumed, and Nikki was found in a drainage area mid-morning. SAR members recovered her body from the steep area that she fell into with a longline attached to a helicopter. She was later pronounced deceased by the medical authorities.

In her panicked state, it is unfortunate that she called her boyfriend instead of 911. While it might be easy to blame someone like Nikki for making choices that led to a devastating outcome, the most important lesson of Nikki's story is to always reach out for help in life-threatening situations before it's too late, regardless of potential embarrassment or punishment brought on by breaking the rules or making a mistake.

CASE 31: SNOWBOARDER MISSING
BLACKCOMB MOUNTAIN, WHISTLER, BC

Julie Abrahamsen, a twenty-year-old woman visiting from Norway, went snowboarding in the backcountry at Whistler Blackcomb in January 2015. Her father, Knut, called her cellphone from Norway that evening. Uncharacteristically, Julie didn't pick up her phone. Her roommates didn't think anything of her absence overnight, thinking that perhaps she had stayed with a friend or gone to Vancouver.

Her father's concern grew when Julie didn't answer her phone the second night. Her roommates noticed that her snowboarding gear was missing, and they became worried. On the third day, Julie was reported missing.

Binty and another WSAR member went up in a rescue helicopter to look for Julie. They spotted tracks that appeared wandering at Wedge Mountain along Wedge Creek. Binty says you can tell the tracks of a lost person, because they circle around and seem aimless, instead of in a straight purposeful direction.

The helicopter pilot let the two rescuers off. They followed what they were sure were Julie's tracks and saw that they ended at a creek. They were terrified that she'd been swept away by the water. They kept walking along the creek—relieved to see that her tracks reappeared and went into the woods.

It was getting dark, and they knew that they would be spending the night in the pouring rain, because the helicopter wouldn't be able to fly back in the night to pick them up. They called Julie's name as they walked through the forest. They didn't expect to hear an answer because they felt that she would most likely be deceased due to the harsh and wet conditions. She likely would've passed away from hypothermia within the first twenty-four hours of going missing in the woods.

"Hello," they heard in the trees. It was Julie. She was wearing a thick Norwegian knit sweater and other appropriate clothing but was soaked to the bone. "Why are you looking for me?" she asked Binty and his fellow searcher.

They explained that it was because she wouldn't get out on her own. Julie was heading for a canyon, and there was no way, once she turned around, that she would survive another three days in the wild.

They gave her warm, dry clothes and made a shelter for the night. The next morning, they had to wait a few hours for suitable weather to bring a helicopter back. They also had to trek with her for almost a kilometre to find a good place for the helicopter to land. Binty attributes the young woman's survival to her toughness. Julie said that in Norway, you can go down from any of the mountains and reach a road, and that was what she was attempting to do.

Her father, Knut, flew out to thank the rescue crew, and he donated a large sum of money to the WSAR for rescuing his daughter. Binty had them over to his home for dinner. The next day, he took Knut and Julie skiing and showed them where she had taken the wrong turn.

Binty says the story didn't end there. Years later, he heard from Knut. Julie, the independent and tough young woman, was in Costa Rica when she got lost again, this time while hiking. Julie was lost for a week, and Knut flew out to Costa Rica to help with the search before she was found.

Binty stepped down from the considerable physical, time and emotional demands of his volunteer position at WSAR. He moved to the Sunshine Coast in July 2022 to retire.

James Vieno—Timmins, Ontario

James Vieno, vice-president of the Timmins Porcupine Search and Rescue, (TPSAR), is a technical advisor for mining hardware. He's worked for a heavy equipment dealer that works with the largest gold mine in Canada, as well as for iron and diamond mines. He has a forestry degree and mapping skills, both valuable assets to bring to TPSAR.

James's boss was the president of TPSAR and brought him into the organization in 1997. James says he joined because the team shares the same core values as he has, and he enjoys the community involvement and serving the community. He says his SAR team recruits the best of the best members. James also teaches "Train the Trainer" sessions for SAR trainers and does Hug-a-Tree presentations—an AdventureSmart program for children to help them survive if they get lost in the woods. He puts in almost five hundred volunteer hours annually. James's favourite piece of SAR gear is his pair of Irish Setter boots. "I have walked many, many, many kilometres in them, and I have never had sore feet."

The group has seventy-two members and goes on call-outs two to three times a year. James attributes the low number of calls to people using their cellphones for navigation and to call for help. TPSAR isn't funded by their home province of Ontario. They hold a boot drive on Mother's Day to raise funds to cover insurance costs, and they also work with a local bingo hall for donations.

CASE 32: ICE FISHERS OVERDUE
TIMMINS, ONTARIO

James remembers that it was Superbowl weekend, February 5, 2006, when a grandfather and his grandson were two days overdue from an ice fishing trip. James and his team followed the path that the pair had taken for five kilometres in snowshoes to an outfitters cabin. They passed eight-by-four-foot blocks of ice floating in the water.

"One searcher fell through the ice," says James. He passed him a walking stick and pulled him out of the freezing water, and he changed into warm dry clothes. They wore red headlights to keep their night vision as they walked another two kilometres. They spotted a flash from a small fire around four in the morning. James says that when you're out on a call, your senses are heightened.

They followed the flash and found the grandfather and grandson stranded on the ice. The engine on one snowmobile was blown, and the second snowmobile was stuck in the slushy ice and snow. The grandson was so cold he could barely talk. His feet were bare and frozen, because his boots had melted in the fire when he got his feet too close to the flames. The grandfather was hypothermic.

The rescuers connected command, packed up the subjects and put glow sticks down for the air ambulance. The helicopter hovered above unstable ice. James carried out the grandfather on piggyback. The grandfather insisted on taking the trout he had caught with him.

CASE 33: RIDER INJURED, HIGH FALLS TRAIL
MUSKOKA, ONTARIO

In May of 2008 at High Falls Trail in Muskoka, Ontario, three riders had their horses walk across the icy river. High Falls is a popular hiking area with a trail that leads to a waterfall. One of the riders was on a Clydesdale draft horse. The man was six-foot-six and weighed at least three hundred pounds. The Clydesdale slipped on the ice and fell on top of the rider, who sustained many broken bones.

TPSAR was called out in the middle of the night to rescue the man. The other riders made camp while they waited. An ambulance was brought in to wait while SAR went in to get the injured man. James took a quad to track the horses, and he took along a paramedic.

They found the injured man down a 90- to 122-metre incline. One of the riders had lost her pack and asked James if he had any food on him. James had a granola bar with him, which he planned on eating, but he couldn't say no to her. The woman took the granola bar and promptly fed it to her horse, making James regret handing over his only snack.

With much effort, they carried the injured man and drove him out on the ATV to the waiting ambulance. He made a full recovery and later donated to the SAR group.

For James, SAR is a family activity, as his wife, Julie, a former secretary, is now a member, and both their son and daughter are in SAR. "I was a wreck the first time my son went out on a call," James says.

James reminds people to call 911 in an emergency. While it's natural to want to call your spouse or your parents, your chances of being found quickly are much higher if you call 911 first.

John Mitchell—Dawson City, Yukon

It doesn't matter who does it; the goal is to get Granny off the mountain.

—John "Mitch" Mitchell

John "Mitch" Mitchell joined Yukon Search and Rescue (YSAR) in the early '90s. YSAR has 120 members from Beaver Creek, Carcross, Carmacks, Dawson City, Faro, Haines Junction and Whitehorse. When Mitch joined Dawson City SAR, the members had to wear too many hats administratively. Overwhelmed with work, the key players left, leaving behind a boat, a truck, backpacks and compasses.

Mitch stepped in as leader to rebuild the team because the RCMP and the community needed SAR help. He brought his experience as a Canadian ranger in a northern reserve unit of the Canadian Armed Forces. He has bush skills cultivated from forty-five years of living, working and playing in Yukon. Mitch, who is semi-retired, does some project management in housing construction for the local First Nations.

He says the thirty-member YSAR group has about six call-outs per year and are able to reach an incident scene up to 160 kilometres from their location in Dawson City within ninety minutes. "In the winter, daylight hours are critical. We have a 9:00 a.m. to 4:00 p.m. window, which limits our aerial searches."

Mitch and his SAR/ranger team break and mark the trail for the Yukon Quest Sled Dog Race when it goes through Dawson City, and they also provide a backup rescue capability for mushers and volunteers out on the trail. Mitch gives the trail report to the racers. YSAR is highly visible in the community.

We can do a lot in Yukon with yellow rope and duct tape.

—John "Mitch" Mitchell

Mitch's favourite piece of SAR equipment is his parka because every pocket is packed full of what will allow him to have a relatively comfortable overnight bush camp. The sleeve pocket has his fire-starter, a small folding knife, bug dope (in the summer), a small first-aid kit and a survival blanket.

"My favourite edged tool is a kukri with a fire-starting flint added to it. The kukri is a large [curved] knife used by the Gurkhas of Nepal that can serve either as an axe or as a knife. It's very ergonomically efficient and the most versatile tool I've ever owned," Mitch says.

CASE 34: MISSING CROSS-COUNTRY SKIER
DAWSON CITY, YUKON

The evening of November 30, 2015, a Dawson City woman went cross-country skiing on the Midnight Dome trails above Dawson, and she took a shortcut that led to a steep hill. She slid down about forty-six metres. "The last forty feet [twelve metres] was a vertical drop onto the edge of the Klondike River. She sustained many broken bones, from her feet to her pelvis, to her arm, to her collarbones," Mitch says.

She somehow crawled about two hundred metres over the ice, in hopes of reaching the highway, but eventually ended up on glare ice (smooth, glassy ice) and was unable to move any further. Luckily, she had told someone when and where she was going, making it easier to find her. [71]

Mitch and his team tracked her to the slope in the dark of night. Mitch coordinated the group into two teams, with one team on snowmobiles going around the Klondike River to reach her from that side and another team working their way in on foot across difficult terrain from the same side to the river's edge.

The snowmobile team couldn't get to her. They backtracked to the top of the slope and set up ropes to rappel down from the original route she took. The ground searchers on foot reached her first, and within minutes the rappel team got down too. Six rescuers gingerly picked their way over the thin ice on the river and pockets of open ponds to get to her.

The team moved her off the wafer-thin ice and got a fire going on shore to warm her up, then performed first aid. They scouted the route through the dark to a recovery area and used a toboggan to sled her out to the ambulance.

For their incredible bravery, without regard for their own safety, the YSAR team received the Commissioner's Award for Bravery. But this was not Mitch's first award for bravery—he received the Governor General's Medal of Bravery on June 27, 2001, and a personal Commissioner's Award for Bravery on January 9, 2000 for saving the life of a young boy.

On April 10, 1998, Mitch was at work when he heard noises, then looked out his window and saw a six-year-old boy being viciously attacked by two Rottweilers. Mitch fended off the dogs with only a bucket and a small wood stove. Using the bucket as a shield and the wood stove to beat the dogs back, he got the boy to his feet and fought the dogs off as he got the boy to the safety of his truck. He drove the badly injured boy to the nursing station. The boy was evacuated to Vancouver, where he underwent many surgeries. As a teen, the boy joined the Junior Canadian Rangers group that Mitch leads.[72]

For his volunteer work with the Junior Canadian Rangers program, and for being a positive role model and a mentor for Yukon youth, Mitch was awarded the Community Safety Award by Justice Minister Mike Nixon in 2012. Mitch was also the first Canadian ranger to receive the Military Medal of Merit for leading his team on a mission to save another rescue group that got lost in zero visibility, sub-zero conditions.[73]

Case 35: Stranded Canoeists
Dawson City, Yukon

In 2015 there was a rapid and unexpected rise in the water levels on the Ogilvie River due to heavy rain. The Dempster Highway washed out in five locations, and in one spot the water level reached up to the windows of parked trucks.

The high waters prevented the normal practice of lining or towing stranded vessels upstream to a recovery point and a couple of canoeists became stranded on a small island of floating timber.

Mitch was on the rescue helicopter that found the couple after they called for help. There was nowhere for the helicopter to land, so all he could do was drop an axe and a saw down so that they could clear a landing area.

The stranded man wasn't a lumberjack, but he worked extremely hard to make a hole in the woods. The woman contributed what she could, as exhausted as she was. They managed to create "a very small chopper pad with a latticework of trees," says Mitch. The helicopter made a vertical descent and perched by the tip of one skid on a stump, and the couple were able to enter the helicopter as it hovered in front of them.

Mitch once visited a SAR group on Vancouver Island. "They had more equipment just in storage than we have in all of Yukon," he says. His team provides their own Ski-Doos and other equipment. Drones for use in searches on the Klondike River would be invaluable for his crew, as would a landing craft with a ramp. Without the presence of the Canadian Coast Guard or Royal Canadian Marine SAR, YSAR are forced to rely on their personal boats in dire emergencies.

8. K9s

A number of us who volunteer for SAR had things go wrong but were able to walk away. That's why we help. Even the best-made plans can be ravaged by nature. Plan well and have a good communication system set up that has multiple redundancies.
—*Michelle Liebe Hofstee*

For every scent receptor in a human's nose, a dog has fifty. A dog's sense of smell is ten thousand to a hundred thousand times better than ours, making us comparatively "nose blind." While so much of our world is processed through our vision, a dog's world is a scent map.

Dogs can even tell time through scent. As any dog owner can tell you, dogs know when it's mealtime, walk time and bedtime. Scientists believe this is because different times of day smell differently to them. Dogs smell in stereo—the left side and the right side of the nose aren't connected.

The iconic rescue dog, the St. Bernard, isn't as ideal a SAR dog as you might think. St. Bernards are slower to cover an area than other breeds of working dogs. Handlers need to be able to pick up their dogs to get them in and out of helicopters and vehicles, if they're injured, or in other circumstances. St. Bernards weigh between up to 120 kilograms, so they are ruled out just by their sheer bulk. Most search dogs are a manageable 23 to 32 kilograms.

Search dogs are valuable members of the SAR teams. Each of them can do as much searching as up to fifteen human searchers in the same amount of time. The canines are much beloved pets to their handlers, as well as working dogs.

Myths About Search Dogs

Myth 1: Dogs can't smell in the rain or in water.

Truth: Search dogs can air scent in the rain and can smell underwater and even under mud.

Myth 2: Dogs can't pick up scent in cold or snow.

Truth: It makes it more difficult, but they can, or we wouldn't have avalanche dogs.

Myth 3: Dogs can't search at night.

Truth: Dogs have good night vision, but they mostly rely on their superior sense of smell.

Myth 4: When not on duty, SAR dogs are kept caged.

Truth: SAR dogs are treated as pets and have the run of the house when they aren't training or on call-outs.

Myth 5: Anyone can turn their dog into a SAR dog.

Truth: To become a dog handler with your own dog on a SAR team is highly unlikely. For most SAR groups, you would have to be accepted into a SAR group, train and be in GSAR for at least two years. Your dog would have to meet all the obedience, temperament, physical and drive requirements. Then you would need to train for likely a year before being validated by an RCMP dog validator. Your dog would need to be six months to two years old when they started training; otherwise they are too old. You would have already been in GSAR for two years by this time, so it would be too late.

Myth 6: SAR dogs are the same as police dogs.

Truth: SAR dogs aren't involved with searches for and apprehension of criminals or sniffing for illegal substances. However, SAR dogs may be tasked by police or RCMP to search for evidence related to a criminal investigation, such as clothing, bones or even a deceased person. SAR dogs are friendly, non-aggressive and good around children. However, police dogs are used on searches for lost subjects as well as for searches for criminals.

MIKE RITCEY—KAMLOOPS, BC

Mike Ritcey, call sign Kilo 99, has had working dogs his entire life. He describes his current and third SAR dog, Ranger, a three-year-old yellow Lab, as "a young, high drive, lovable male dog. He is very high energy and has an excellent work ethic. He wants to please." Mike adds, "He brings hope to anyone that sees him get out of the truck. His energy and confidence are infectious."

Ranger came from Saskatchewan. "I asked for a high-drive dog and was not disappointed. You need a dog with a strong hunt or ball

Search and Rescue dogs tend to come from specialized breeders. The pup's parents are usually working dogs themselves. The dogs come to the handler's home at eight weeks old and start their training right away. They begin with playing with small items of clothing that have been worn, like socks and mitts. Shutterstock 1882401460

drive—one with a no-quit switch." Ranger has a long career ahead of him. SAR dogs can work until they are eight years old and sometimes until they are ten, versus police dogs that retire after seven or eight years.

Ranger and Mike showcase their partnership in a documentary called *Sit. Stay. Search.*[74] in which you can watch the pair and other teams go through training exercises. Mike says that Ranger works at "110 percent." Every time Ranger is on the job, he makes Mike look good.

Mike firmly believes that dogs are a person's best hope for being found. Some of the reasons dogs are so efficient at searching are that they are willing to work in the rain, they can go anywhere and they are reliable. Dogs have such a keen sense of smell that they can find subjects inside of car trunks, which are supposed to be airtight, or even under water, he says.

Drones, on the other hand, can't fly in poor-visibility weather and are limited as to where they can fly. Mike says, "I've had subjects tell me they've seen drones right in front of them, waved at them and the drones didn't see them. They've seen them pass over them several times, and the drones didn't pick them up."

Mike joined Kamloops SAR (KSAR) in 1976, when there were no dog teams. He was a paramedic for thirty years, as well as a big-game hunting guide. As a guide he trained dogs to track cougar, bear and deer, so when it came time to train dogs to search for humans, it wasn't a drastic switch for him.

Mike explains that dogs track not only by scent, but also by ground disturbance, "bleeding" and what we leave behind. Bleeding is like when you cut the grass and can smell the bruising of the blades. When humans disturb the ground, it's totally different than when a bear does.

On the dog intelligence scale, German shepherds are third, golden retrievers are fourth, Labrador retrievers seventh and Austrian Malinois twenty-second. These are some of the most common SAR dog breeds used in BC. "Bloodhounds don't have the obedience or recall required, but they are great for tracking animals."

KSAR has approximately fifty call-outs a year, giving Mike up to fifty potential opportunities to reunite a missing soul with their loved ones. "Bringing someone back to their parents or loved ones is indescribable—pretty emotional," he says.

He has an understanding family and no personal life because he puts in over six hundred hours a year into call-outs and training. He's had to abandon family celebrations, even his wedding anniversary, to go on call-outs.

CASE 36: TWO HIKERS MISSING
CATHEDRAL LAKES, BC

What Mike struggles with on searches that go on for many days and subjects remain missing is when to stop, even though that's not SAR's call to make. The final decision on starting and stopping a search lies with the authorizing requesting agency. This is what parents, friends and families of missing subjects often don't understand. SAR managers have input, as they are the subject matter experts, but the final say rests on the shoulders of the requesting agency.

Mike refers to a search for two overdue hikers in Cathedral Provincial Park in late June 2015, which makes him question if every unresolved search has gone on long enough—because sometimes even people who are unprepared survive when they theoretically shouldn't. Mike has seen people beat the statistics in extreme conditions and come home.

When Lynne Carmody and Rick Moynan of North Bay, Ontario, didn't return from their planned day hike from Cathedral Lakes Lodge, a search ensued. Forty SAR members from many groups and three helicopters looked for them for six days. The couple were middle-aged and had no supplies with them, as they were only headed out for the day. At some point, they wandered off the trail and got lost.[75]

"Lots of tough country up there. By day five, I was starting to think they must have fallen off a cliff," says Mike. The search focussed on the ridges and the meadows, as they thought the couple would seek the high points or the open areas to make themselves most visible.

The heat soared up to forty degrees during the search. Mike says that some of the SAR dogs got sick from the heat. There were no sightings or clues as to the couple's whereabouts. On the last day of the search, a helicopter took the family of the lost hikers up on a peak to say their goodbyes.

As the search teams were packing up on June 28, 2015, the couple came stumbling out of the trees, to everyone's surprise and great relief.

Lynne later wrote a letter, which was published in a local newspaper, expressing their gratitude to the searchers and explaining what had happened. After they left the trail, ending up lost in thick woods, they made a shelter for the night. They heard the helicopters the next day, so they climbed higher and stayed there for five days. After realizing the helicopters weren't going to find them, based on where they were searching, they walked back to the lodge, using the position of the sun to help them navigate. It took them eight and half hours to make it back.[76]

CASE 37: MISSING MALE
SUN PEAKS, BC

On February 17, 2018, Ryan Shtuka, who had recently moved from Beaumont, Alberta, to Sun Peaks, left a house party on Burfield Drive at around two in the morning. He was reported missing hours later. Twenty-three KSAR members responded, including Mike and Ranger, and local volunteers also came out to search for him. After the extensive search was conducted for twenty-four hours straight without locating Ryan, SAR was stood down and the RCMP took over the investigation.[77]

No trace of Ryan has ever been found.[78] However, Mike remains undaunted, and he and Ranger have been to the search area almost once a month, since the original search, looking for evidence of Ryan's disappearance. Ranger has brought him gloves, hats, scarves and all manner of clothing every time they've searched the area, but none of the items have matched what Ryan was wearing at the time he went missing.

After repeated searches, Mike believes that Ryan "never got lost." The distance between where the house party was held and where Ryan lived was simply too close for him to have gotten lost along the way. The snow off the path was 1.2 metres deep—much too deep to walk in. Mike believes that if he'd strayed off the ploughed road, Ryan would not have gotten far at all. There was no water in the creek at the time, and cadaver dogs were used, but still no trace of Ryan was found.

Mike can only conclude that Ryan isn't in the area; however, he plans to go back with Ranger to the area again to search for "a bone, hat, belt, jacket, shoe, anything."

Mike says that SAR dogs can find individuals by their unique scent. You can give a dog something that a subject has worn or touched, and they will search for that person when they're given a command they are trained for, such as "Show me." If the search area is frequented by a lot of people, it can be helpful to give the dog something that will help them home in on the cone of scent that an individual gives off, in order to prevent the dog from becoming confused when other people cross the path.

Mike doesn't plan to retire from KSAR. He has Ranger to keep partnering with, and he is also excited about the new 12,000 square foot dog-training facility that he is already training in.

"We will be putting on Human Remains Detection training open to everyone, as well as drug detection [training]," he says. "Other groups will rent out space for training, for example, first aid classes and ambulance training. St. John's was looking at it to train their service dogs … the centre has great potential."

MICHELLE LIEBE HOFSTEE

Michelle Liebe Hofstee, call sign Kilo 92, wanted to be like her mom, who volunteered in church groups, but she found SAR to be truer to her passions and gifts. She's been a whitewater rafter and kayaker since 1991, and she thought those skills would be an asset to SAR. As a mother of two young girls, what she likes about SAR is that it's a practical outlet for her paddling skills, offers a flexible schedule, and she has their strong support that family comes first.

Michelle joined Kamloops SAR in 2012, and she added Merritt SAR (MSAR) in 2020. She's worn many hats: team leader, manager of Ground SAR and swiftwater rescue team leader, as well as an ice rescue, rope rescue, K9 and avalanche team member. Now a teacher in Ashcroft, BC, Michelle treasures her time with SAR, as well as her Osprey SAR pack: "It was given to me by Lauren Russell Wilson when her husband, Neil, passed away. It reminds me of the people who support us and that the reason I joined SAR was to help people," she says.

BCSAR has presented Michelle with many opportunities. She and Gertie, her German shepherd, were cast as a SAR team in a full-length movie, *Beyond the Woods* (2019), a dark detective/thriller set in the woods in the winter and filmed in the Kamloops area in minus-twenty weather. It's a simple, stylistic movie with everything you ever wanted to know about hypothermia—I highly recommend it.

Michelle has met amazing lifelong friends through SAR, and she is able to be a role model for her teenaged daughters and students. She invests over a thousand hours per year in SAR (not including dog training time), which eats into her family time and time to enjoy her art and music hobbies.

GERTIE'S GENIUS

Michelle's faithful partner is Gertie, and while a lady never reveals her age, perhaps Gertie wouldn't mind us knowing she is eight years old. She's from Homestead German Shepherds in Killam, Alberta. Gertie is an extra-high-energy dog who can search for up to twelve hours at a time and "loves every second of it," says Michelle. "She has an off switch and can hang around the house with the girls. Kyla and Kate were eight and ten years old when we got her. Gertie loves to travel and especially loves plane and helicopter rides," says Michelle.

Michelle had German shepherds when she was growing up. "I was always training them to keep them and myself entertained. I met Mike Ritcey and saw how effective the dogs were at finding people." She says that Mike Ritcey from KSAR has taught her most of what she knows about SAR dogs.

The breeder in Killam helped choose Gertie for Michelle based on the criteria for a search dog. Gertie was tested at puppy camp and passed. Michelle praises the excellent training she received from the RCMP dog trainers, both from the local handlers and at yearly validations.

CASE 38: TEEN MISSING
AVOLA, BC

On June 14, 2016, an autistic teen girl in Avola (near Wells Gray Provincial Park) left her home. The weather was unseasonably cool and wet for that time of year. She had taken a sleeping bag and some lighters with her. Wells Gray SAR and KSAR were called out to search for her.

> Subjects [on the autism spectrum] can present challenges to searchers, because they may not respond to searchers' shouts, might hide, or may have no fear of dangers. They are most commonly found in structures. Fortunately, since so many are found soon after they go missing, most are found alive.[79]

After three days of searching, Gertie found the missing teen one hundred metres away from her residence and very much alive.[80] Michelle says that she's never been prouder of her Gertie.

What Michelle loves most about being in SAR is her relationship and partnership with Gertie, getting out in nature, and knowing their hard work is for a good cause. She loves the adventures and helping families reunite. She's gained confidence and amazing friendships, and she's enjoyed the chance to help people, give back to her community and see remote parts of the province. Her future goal is to find balance.

Michelle is grateful to the Cooper Family Foundation for providing a new search-dog training facility in Kamloops that will be used by Search, Rescue and Detection Canines (SRD K9s) of BC, that will have their grand opening to the public in September 2022. "Their belief in what the dogs can do to support our community has been incredible. Nelly Dever and the Cooper family have been so great to work with," she says.

Michelle feels that SAR organizations need to find ways to support their volunteers. The administrative work is overwhelming, especially on top of a full-time job and family commitments.

On the morning of May 23, 2022, at the age of eight years old, Gertie was cut down by a high-speed hit and run driver. She was a very good girl and will be much missed by Michelle, her family and all of the KSAR members. She assisted in the search for missing persons Ryan Shtuka and Ben Tyner, who are still yet to be found; their cases are described in this book. She had more years of love, companionship and duty to offer to her humans and K9s.

ROGER BEAN—NORTH SHORE RESCUE, BC

Roger Bean, call sign Northshore 38, initially joined North Shore Rescue (NSR) more than forty years ago. Prior to retirement, his day job was with the Regional Parks as an operations supervisor. "I joined North Shore Rescue in 1979 and was with the team until 1994. I volunteered on the ski patrol on both Cypress Nordic and Manning Park Alpine. In 2015 I rejoined North Shore Rescue with the intention of training a SAR dog."

Like many of the NSR members, Roger was born and raised on the North Shore. He enjoyed skiing and hiking in the local mountains.

Joining SAR was a natural next step in educating himself on mountain travel and recreation. As a young member, he says he brought "enthusiasm and an interest in first aid. Currently, my specialty is as a SAR dog handler for wilderness search and avalanche rescue." Along the way, he met his wife through SAR: "She was the program assistant for the North Shore Emergency Management program."

Roger's favourite piece of equipment is his compass. "Because lost people are seldom on trails, most of our travel is off trail, and the compass helps to keep me on track, figure out where I am, and aids in assessing the terrain—batteries are not required," he says.

Meet Chloe

Roger describes his canine partner, Chloe, a Belgian Malinois as "a little bit edgy, hyperactive and driven."

He says the advantages of using dogs in a search situation are that "a dog greatly improves the chances of finding a non-responsive person, and it enables us to cover an area quickly and with good accuracy that would have taken multiple ground searches [and] much more time. The challenging part is living with such a high-drive dog. They don't make great pets."

Their training is a huge time commitment; Roger says it involves at least ten hours per week. "On each walk, we take some time to do a couple of quick training routines that can be obedience, article search, handler skills, fitness, etc. At least two days per week we will have a training session of several hours, working on SAR skills." He was most proud of Chloe when they passed their first full avalanche rescue validation."

Case 39: SAR Member Injured
Lake Lovely Water, BC

In a SAR career with too many call-outs to count, the most impactful and harrowing incident for Roger was during a training exercise up at Lake Lovely Water on August 5, 1989. One of his fellow members, Robert (Bob) McGregor, fell into the moat on Mount Dione in the Tantalus Range. Roger climbed down to Bob and spent several hours administering first aid and comforting him until they were able to evacuate him to the Squamish Hospital. Bob later died from his injuries.

Bob, a training officer for NSR, was only twenty-eight years old at the time of his death. His father said that "Bob was a great fellow and lived for hiking, skiing and climbing. He did a considerable amount of climbing in Peru and Bolivia at an early age and was excited when accepted by the North Shore Rescue group." NSR memorialized McGregor with a plaque placed in the Tantalus Range and named a rope rescue catwalk "McGregor Walk" after Bob.[81]

Roger is thankful for the community involvement that supports SAR. "You have heard the saying 'it takes a village to raise a child'—it also takes a community to find a lost person." He says that most people don't understand the depth of support local SAR teams get from their communities and how much that aids in finding the lost person.

The most heartwarming lesson that Roger has learned from his twenty years in SAR, "the one that always causes a lump in my throat," is that when a SAR call involves children, "supporters come out in full force. SAR members from other groups offering mutual aid come swarming in to help."

RYAN MORASIEWICZ

A corporate commercial litigation and outdoor/adventure lawyer in downtown Vancouver, Ryan Morasiewicz is married and has a young daughter. He's also been a member of North Shore Rescue since 2011. One of the first things he does when there's a call-out is Google map the meeting location to determine the drive time and which bridge is quicker to get to the North Shore.

Ryan, call sign North Shore 41, is coming up to a decade in SAR, and he's earned advanced certifications. He's a ground search team leader, an avalanche-response team member and a member of the BC Search Dog Association. His German shepherd, Neiko, was validated as a wilderness search dog in 2021. His foray into BCSAR started because he always felt at home in the outdoors.

Ryan grew up in Calgary, Alberta, and his parents took him to the mountains—Banff National Park, the Bow Valley, Kananaskis and along the Icefields Parkway—to hike or snowshoe almost every weekend. He moved to Vancouver to complete his undergrad degree, and soon after, he started hiking again. He began doing more advanced hikes and scrambles, and he also learned mountaineering.

One of his regular hiking partners ended up being a search manager for NSR. During their lengthy hikes, he told Ryan tales about recent rescues he was on. Ryan has a strong sense of community, and he thought joining SAR would be a great way to give back. However, he was unsure he would have the time to devote to SAR, given that he was a relatively young lawyer.

Ryan ran into the late, great Tim Jones on a solo snowshoe up at Mount Seymour one Friday afternoon. They talked about SAR, his situation and his NSR hiking friend. Tim invited Ryan out to a few Tuesday night training sessions to meet more people and see if SAR would fit into his life. He applied for that year's membership intake, was accepted, and nine years later he's taken on training a SAR dog.

Tim Jones was a paramedic on the North Shore and a NSR team leader. He died of a heart attack on January 19, 2014, on a trail on his way down from a rescue cabin on Mount Seymour. He was awarded the Order of BC in 2011 and an honorary doctorate by Capilano University in 2012.[82] There's also an annual Tim Jones Community Achievement Award, which is given to an outstanding sports or outdoor community volunteer who is an unsung hero.

Ryan brings special skills to the SAR table, including an acute visual and spatial memory; knowledge of all the public North Shore trails; a deep familiarity with the terrain, trails and off-trail areas; and an excellent GPS-like navigation sense.

"In my day job, I'm a lawyer, which can potentially be useful in some non-task situations or goings-on with the team as an entity as it does its various activities," he says. Ryan's outdoor and adventure law practice is the first of its kind.[83] They work with outdoor and adventure guides and tour operators, ski resorts, and gear and clothing manufacturers, retailers and distributors.

Since he joined SAR, Ryan does fewer personal hiking and mountaineering trips. Before SAR, he would be out three out of every four weekends doing a hike of twelve or more hours with a regular crew. He no longer does that because he gets so much outdoors and hiking time with SAR. In addition, he doesn't want to miss being available for SAR calls, which tend to occur on weekends. "I don't want to be too tired from a hike to be able to respond to a SAR call. I have to juggle other aspects of my life and can't overload it with too many 'outdoors' things," he says.

Ryan spends about 550 hours a year volunteering. These days he throws a substantial amount of time into search-dog training, and he has lessened his commitments to other aspects of the team as a result.

Neiko to the Rescue

Ryan's partner, Neiko, "is a very good boy! He has such a sweet, kind and caring disposition. He's quite affectionate and is fine with chilling and relaxing at home when he's not training and playing." However, when Neiko's on task or working on obedience, he's laser focussed on Ryan and on what they're doing. "Basically, he's the perfect dog, as far as I'm concerned," says his proud partner.

Neiko started out life in the RCMP dog program in Squamish, but he was rejected from that program after a year and a half of training because he was too friendly, then was transferred to the RCMP kennels in Innisfail, Alberta.

The Squamish handler sent an email to various validated search and avalanche dog teams, discussing Neiko and explaining that he needed a new home. Roger Bean forwarded the email to Ryan. After a quick chat with his wife, who was an enthusiastic "yes," Ryan emailed the RCMP handler.

After further discussions with other RCMP officers over the next few days, Neiko arrived from Innisfail, Alberta, to Ryan, and then Neiko's SAR training began with NSR. Ryan says, "I love seeing Neiko's personality come through and how much he enjoys our training and practices. He really does love the searching and tracking, as well as his toys and play sessions afterwards."

Some of the best advice he ever got from another dog handler was, "Dogs are horrible generalizers." What seems simple and intuitive to Ryan has sometimes been interpreted and acted on completely differently by Neiko. He finds it challenging to learn to think like a dog and to break everything down into components, work on those chunks, then try to put everything together. But Ryan loves the challenge, "Plus, I get to hang out and spend time with an absolutely amazing pup," he says.

CASE 40: HIKER INJURED
CROWN MOUNTAIN, BC

When Ryan thinks of one of his most challenging rescues, it's a Crown Mountain rescue that comes to mind. The overnight mission required the assistance of Squadron 442 of the Canadian Forces. This rescue was in "Episode 3: Peak Season" of *Search and Rescue: North Shore*, a series on Knowledge Network.

Ryan recounts the call for a severely injured hiker who had fallen about nine metres off a cliff on the backside of Crown Mountain on September 30, 2018. Another hiker who witnessed the fall called for help. Two SAR teams arrived at the subject's location around 1:30 a.m., and a helicopter was dispatched from CFB Comox.[84]

Out of concern for the subject's condition, they also called in assistance from Squadron 442 from CFB Comox. Ryan and four other NSR members, including two physicians and two ex–Canadian Forces members, hiked in with heavy medical and rope rescue gear, on top of their regular packs. They got to the peak around 1:30 a.m. at roughly the same time as Squadron 442's helicopter. The 442 Squadron's crew winched down and asked for NSR's help moving the patient to a better location to extract him.

NSR's team scrambled around the backside of Crown through a narrow cleft in the rock and rappelled fifteen metres (fifty feet) down to the subject, helped with the carry, then climbed back up so they could get away from the returning helicopter. It's an enormous helicopter with rotor downwash like hurricane-strength wind. "You don't want to be under it if you don't have to be," says Ryan.

The patient was successfully retrieved and brought to hospital. The NSR team hiked down the mountain for twenty minutes to a flat spot and had a nap for a few hours before their pick-up by helicopter at first light.

> Cellphone coverage can be unreliable in the backcountry, but if you can get a signal, it can help SAR locate you, if your phone has built-in GPS or a GPS tracking app. To conserve the battery, leave your phone off and power it up only when you need assistance, and then only during arranged check-ins.[85]

Of course, we only see the dramatic rescues in the media, but Ryan wants the public to know what else goes on behind the scenes at NSR. "Media will show the out-of-bounds snowboarder to elicit outrage. Not typically shown are the dementia walk-aways and the other searches that take up the greater percentage of our calls," he says.

> Every person with dementia is unique. There's a range of severity and changes in behaviour and cognitive skills. Dementia can cause difficulties with vision narrowing, causing the wanderers to move straight ahead until they get stuck.
>
> They may try to use the public bus or return to a place from their past. For example, if they were a fisher, they may try to find a dock or go to the water. They may look for a home they used to live at, or a favourite place. They might be found walking along roads or in buildings. They're unlikely to respond to shouts and don't ask for help. [86]

"I'm sure most people think it's almost all helicopter rescues, but that being said, the Knowledge Network series has probably shown a lot of people what else is involved," Ryan says.

He describes what he feels he's gained from being in NSR: "It's a great way to give back to the mountain community and help people (and their families) when they are at their worst. We bring people back to their loved ones. I volunteer and continue to do so for that reason—to help people."

ED MCROBERTS—HAYWARD, WISCONSIN

Edward "Ed" McRoberts first joined Sawyer County SAR of Hayward in 2010. His radio call sign is Sawyer County 417. He's trained in K9 handling, trailing and human remains detection, man tracking, search operations and management, and several other areas in the SAR field. "I am also a K9 evaluator for United K9s, previously for American Working Dog Association, and am currently apprenticing with law enforcement training services," Ed says.

Ed joined SAR after being inspired by his fiancée, now wife, who was the first K9 handler with the team. "Along with a desire to help others, and being a father and grandfather, I identified with several of the searches the team was called on," he says.

Ed has two SAR dogs. He describes Chaos as: "Quite the lady, prima donna if you will, and at the same time the quintessential sweetheart. She doesn't like to go out in the rain, and god forbid if she gets her feet wet ... but if you put her working vest on and scent her, she'll go through swamps and rivers and work herself to exhaustion to find the subject." says Ed. Chaos has a heart of gold, loves kids and is the matriarch of the two dogs.

Ed's other dog is Trouble, whose personality is "much like an adolescent human that always has that twinkle in her eye. She has a personality beyond most humans that I know. She's a snuggle bug, a sneaky girl and so much more," Ed says.

Ed has worked in the military service, law enforcement and security. "Officially, I retired as a cabinet maker and currently work part-time in the maintenance field," Ed says. He and his wife support each other as SAR volunteers. "There are days when you miss birthday parties or holiday gatherings, but I'm quite blessed to have a very understanding family." It's fortunate that his family is so generous, because in an average year he has ground SAR and K9 training, classes and call-outs. "Then include training done on my own with the K9s and man tracking, and it could easily be north of a thousand hours." says Ed.

CASE 41: TODDLER MISSING
DANBURY, WISCONSIN

A case that left an impact on Ed occurred in Danbury. Three-year-old Reena Mae Williams was found wandering the neighbourhood on August 14, 2012. A neighbour brought the child back home to her parents. This incident wasn't reported to authorities, like the prior six times that she had gone missing that year. A few hours later, the toddler was reported missing after disappearing from home for the second time that day.[87]

Ed's role in the search was that of a K9 handler, and this was when he was fairly new to the field. The dogs were utilized to find a possible scent trail of Reena. Sawyer County SAR worked with other agencies, including the FBI and Minnesota State Patrol air support.

Reena's body was found by divers the following day in a power dam canal twenty-three metres from her home.

"At the time, I had grandchildren around the same age, and the events, the entirety of this search, brought on a profound sadness at its conclusion," Ed says.

Reena's parents, Thomas Jay Williams and Jenna Elizabeth Danish, were both charged with a single count of child neglect resulting in death.[88] The maximum penalty of this crime is twenty-five years in prison and a hundred-thousand-dollar fine.

On November 24, 2014, Thomas Williams, who police said was high on synthetic marijuana at the time his daughter went missing, received five months in jail and three years on probation. Jenna Danish received one year of probation after pleading guilty to a misdemeanor child-neglect charge.[89]

Ed has gained a great deal from SAR in terms of experiences, knowledge and friends, "but most of all I have gained a family … SAR gets into your blood and becomes part of who you are." He hopes to continue a career as a K9 evaluator, but mostly he plans to continue to improve his skills and knowledge in all areas and advance within the team.

Nadine Conner—Wichita, Kansas

Nadine Conner, a professional dog trainer, says an acquaintance got her into SAR in 2010, and she started out working as a flanker. In 2011 she joined Great Plains Search and Rescue K9s (GPSAR K9s), which has fourteen K9 teams.

Nadine has three SAR dogs. Beast is a Texas heeler with a high search drive. A Texas heeler is a cross between an Australian blue heeler and a border collie. The crossbreed is known for its stamina, stubbornness and bravery. The Texas heeler likes water and tolerates both cold and heat. Dog number two is Carlee, a German shepherd, who is calm and collected in her work of searching for live subjects. Dog number three is Freck, a German shorthaired pointer with lots of drive. She is a ball of directed energy in her searches.

GPSAR K9s receives more call-outs for recoveries than live searches. For human remains detection (HRD) K9 training in the US, human body parts may be acquired for training. The parts are stored in dedicated freezers or left outside in secured boxes and allowed to decay. In Canada, where human body parts can't be purchased, human placenta is donated by midwives or mothers, dentists donate teeth with the roots still attached, hair is collected from hairbrushes, and human bones can be ordered legally.

The University of Texas and the University of West Carolina have body farms for archaeology students. Nadine attended the Forensic Anthropology Center at Texas State University (FACTS) under the tutelage of Dr. Ben Alexander to train her dog for whole-body finds. She says there's a section of the centre that is permanently set aside for K9 training. Nadine attends FACTS as a student in the Level III classes and as an assistant instructor for Level I.

"I think my favourite pieces of equipment are my canines. After that would be the Dogtra GPS collar that I put on them, or my SWAT boots that fit me so perfectly I don't even have to break them in," says Nadine.

Case 42: Blanco River Flood
Wimberley, Texas

Nadine recalls her first call-out on May 24, 2015, with her K9 Freck. During the Texas–Oklahoma floods, the Blanco River flooded. At Wimberley, the water level rose more than nine metres (thirty feet) in less than three hours, and a wall of over twelve metres (forty feet) of water crashed down on the town, taking out homes.

Nadine and Freck drove nine hours to get to the afflicted site for what was to be a five-day physically gruelling search that involved hundreds of volunteers. "It was rough on us and the dogs. Everything was a mess. The roads were washed out. It was hard going. The high velocity of the water decimated the bodies. There were areas of high interest for the dogs, and several of the missing were located. As of today, two are still missing," says Nadine.

Among the twelve bodies recovered were those of six adults and three children, members of two families who were staying together in one cabin. The house was built on telephone-pole-sized posts that snapped, and the house was swept away by the flood waters. Only one person survived, Jonathan McComb, and he sustained severe injuries. He lost his wife and two young children.[90]

Nadine says that the public may not realize that their organization relies 100 percent on donations. They buy their own gear, and they pay for training and travel expenses out of their own pockets. They do have a sponsor who provides dog food, and they receive grants from the state to pay for evaluations and certifications.

DOUG LESCH—FRISCO, COLORADO

*There is something about suffering through a night mission in a
snowstorm with people who are doing the same.*
—Doug Lesch

Doug Lesch is from Frisco, which is within Summit County. He
joined the Summit County Rescue Group (SCRG) in early 2017. His
county also has a Rapid Avalanche Deployment program—a group
organized by the sheriff's office that consists of avalanche workers
from SAR and the area's ski patrols. The program has members with
specialized skills in avalanche SAR, particularly those with avalanche
dogs. Doug's been a member of this program as a K9 handler since
2014. He's also a K9 handler with SCSAR.

Doug has been a ski patroller at Copper Mountain since 2011,
and the ski patrol community got him involved in working with avalanche dogs and ultimately into the SAR program. He joined SCSAR
to be involved in rescue efforts more frequently. When he first met
the ski patrol avalanche-dog handlers as a second-year patroller, "I
thought the world of them. I still do today," Doug says.

He knew he wanted to become a validated dog handler, but what
he learned through his mentors was that he also had to be a good professional rescuer. That required skills he wouldn't get without getting
involved in rescue on a bigger scale. He is still partial to working his
K9, but he has also learned that dogs are a tool. "While we love them
and they are an amazing resource, there are so many other skill sets we
need as humans to make us successful and respected as rescuers in the
field, volunteer or not," Doug says.

Doug began training with an experienced avalanche dog, Race, a
female yellow Lab, who belonged to John and Andrea Reller, who also
had another avalanche dog, Recco, at the time. Race lived and trained
with Doug during the week and went back to John and Andrea on the
weekends.

After a lot of hard work, Doug was certified as an avalanche dog
handler with Race. He then got Keena as an eight-week-old puppy and
returned Race to her primary handlers. Race continued as an avalanche
dog and worked with another handler, who became certified too.

Keena (age six) is a female black Lab. Keena means "brave" in
Celtic. She came from a breeder who specialized in competitive hunt-

ing dogs. However, Keena's mom had previously whelped two avalanche SAR dogs.

Doug visited the breeder several times prior to making the decision to welcome Keena into his life. He describes her as "very animated, with lots of energy, high drive, independence, high prey drive, very vocal and talkative, even for a Lab, and excitable. She has no 'off switch' unless she's in her kennel. She doesn't back down."

During simulations, Keena digs all the way down to the person hiding in the snow. "She doesn't want to give up her dog hole to the people with shovels," says Doug.

Keena and Doug recertify as an avalanche team every three seasons. Keena's been trained in air- and water-scenting, but they aren't certified in these areas. She's been exposed to human remains enough that she doesn't have a negative reaction to finding them. Doug says some dogs may tuck their tail in and cower in a negative reaction when they find human remains, if they haven't been exposed to the scent before.

Doug says that in the history of avalanche rescues in North America, there have been only a couple of live finds. That's why avalanche dogs and their handlers are brought in quickly by helicopter after an avalanche, within the short window of a person's survivability.

The dogs are trained with live volunteers, but they find deceased subjects in the snow. It's not known why avalanche dogs can find deceased people as if they were alive. What dogs can smell is complex. "Where we smell cake, a dog will smell eggs, butter, milk and all the ingredients in the cake," says Doug. He says bomb-sniffing dogs can smell all the chemicals that comprise a bomb, but they only indicate if all the chemicals are combined together.

Humans each have a unique scent, which we can smell too, but we also have a common scent that identifies us as a human being to dogs, says Doug. Even a deceased person buried under snow gives off volatile organic compounds (VOCs) that dogs can detect in the surrounding air.

In the spring of 2020, Keena and Doug went on a mission thirty-six hours after an avalanche occurred. The subject had a beacon and had been marked with a probe by his friends in case the batteries ran out, but Keena and Doug were needed to find the subject, even though there was no chance of survival. "We approached the incident with wanting to have as many options to locate the victim as possible—

beacon, probes and dogs," says Doug. The team helped locate the deceased subject, making the best use of time and resources since they were in an avalanche zone. Though the subject was known to be deceased, Doug and the rest of the team were successful in their efforts, however: "It's not always the case that a subject is found," says Doug.

Case 43: Injured Sledder
Janet's Cabin, Colorado

In the spring of 2018, Doug was out for dinner with John and Andrea Reller. Doug and his wife, Lindsay, took the couple out for dinner to celebrate his certification with Keena and thank them for all their help.

The couples were just sitting down at the restaurant when Doug was paged. Both couples try to balance life with SAR responsibility, so they decided to continue dinner. They were about halfway through their meal when Doug got a phone call from one of the team leaders on a mission, asking if he was available to help.

The mission involved an injured sledder with rib and chest injuries and potential associated medical problems at a backcountry hut. The subject had been sledding near the hut when he collided with a tree at Janet's Cabin, near the Copper Mountain Ski Resort, about nine kilometres from the trailhead. SAR members were needed to collect the patient at Janet's Cabin and transfer the patient to the bottom of the trailhead.

Because the terrain access to the hut was via snowshoes or skis, with some support at the bottom with snowmobiles, it would be a long slog in and out to collect the patient. They were looking for additional skilled members to help with the extrication.

Doug explained to the team leader that he was out to dinner that evening. Minutes later, John's phone rang with a similar request. At that point they explained to the team leader that they were out together with their families, but they would check in after dinner to see if they still needed help.

When dinner wrapped up around 9:30 p.m., Doug made the call to "check in," sheepishly hoping that they had all the SAR people they needed. The woman responded, "We need you guys, if you can come at all." Doug and John went home to collect their equipment, change into their SAR gear, and prepare for what they anticipated would be an all-night mission.

They arrived at the staging area after 10:00 p.m., and it was "snowing like crazy, a strong springtime snowstorm," says Doug. The initial team members, along with a paramedic to assess the patient, had already departed for the hut and were likely close, if not already there. Because of the potential medical issues associated with the subject's injuries, waiting until daylight for a medical helicopter to evacuate him wasn't the best option.

John and Doug left on a snowmobile from the trailhead to the backcountry access gate away from Copper Mountain Ski Resort. They knew the trail was relatively well packed, as this was a common out-of-bounds ski area. They also knew there were teams ahead of them that had used the trail, so there should be a good track. Their special operations sheriff's office sergeant was out in front of them on snowshoes, working his way to the hut.

John and Doug went as far as they could on the snowmobile, about eight hundred metres, then donned skis and skins—synthetic strips attached to the bottom of skis for traction—to continue uphill toward the hut.

The snow was accumulating quickly. They were past halfway when the trail left the trees and moved into more open areas, and then it became a whiteout. They were unable to see the trail, or anything outside of a few feet in front of them. They found the sergeant, who had also lost the trail and was concerned about finding his way to the hut in the blinding conditions. "We gathered together and hunkered down under some larger spruce trees to try to shelter from the snow and the wind and regroup on what we were going to do," says Doug.

Even in that moment, in the middle of the night, lost in a snowstorm where they had no idea which way to go, Doug wasn't worried. "I felt completely comfortable and at peace," he says. The three men came up with a plan to keep working toward the hut. "We probably made it to within a mile or even less of the hut," says Doug. There was a short, steep climb out of the drainage bottom to get to the hut, but at this point they were still in a complete whiteout.

They stayed in place again—wet, cold, but still trying to get ready to help with the evacuation. They built a fire intended not just for themselves, but also for rescuers who were leaving the hut to reach them with the patient to gather and dry themselves off. The three huddled around the fire, "content, comfortable, waiting to support the next phase of the mission. Not really knowing the time frame [of] when the team from Janet's Hut [would make] it to us," says Doug.

When the rescuers with the patient in tow arrived from where they'd been sheltering comfortably at Janet's Cabin, the somewhat rested and strong skiers, John and Doug, took over to ski the patient out. They hoped it would be a downhill ski, but that was not at all the case. Between the slope that was too gradual for them to be able to use gravity as their friend, the new snow, and a melt-freeze crust, they broke through the crust under the weight of the sled and themselves. "We ended up having to drag the akja [rescue toboggan] out to waiting snowmobiles," says Doug.

After an uphaul to the snowmobiles and a short ski back to the trailhead, they arrived shortly after six in the morning, at sunrise. Doug had to work that day on ski patrol at Copper Mountain, so he tried to catch some sleep in the lower patrol room before the day started.

This mission is one he will never forget. "To be honest, it sucked, yet it was so much fun. It was physically and mentally exhausting, but I was doing it with people I trust and want to be stuck under a tree within a blizzard," Doug says. He still jokes that there are few people he would rather "be stuck in the middle of a snowstorm with, in the middle of the night, than those guys, because of their experience, abilities, attitude and commitment."

"I like being part of our SAR program, to be involved in a puzzle that we can help solve. To be able to help someone who cannot help themselves. I do it for the comradery and the community it creates amongst others with similar values," Doug says.

SAR in Colorado is at a turning point, he says. "We are seeing more and more people recreating and accessing the backcountry. Our call volumes are increasing, and our members are having to balance life, jobs and their volunteer commitments." He continues, "I see commercial recreation industries relying on volunteer SAR programs as part of their emergency plans, while not all do so, and [while] many are supportive and active in their own rescues, it is an added burden on these teams."

As a consequence of the increased demand for SAR support, Doug says there are mental health and fatigue concerns arising in his communities, and they are going unaddressed. His main concern is about the long-term impacts this will have on team members in this volunteer industry. "It is something that is coming to light more and more. The cumulative stress that rescuers experience can take a toll," Doug says. There are programs out there to support members who suffer stress, PTSD and Complex PTSD, but he feels that more awareness is key that what they experience on duty impacts them. Doug's concerns echo other Colorado SARs.

The state has twenty-eight thousand rescue volunteers who respond to thirty-six hundred call-outs each year. With eighty thousand people moving to Colorado per annum and 90 percent of them saying they will use the outdoors, the number of call-outs will continue to increase and overwhelm rescuers.

9. Mountains

Talking about incidents helps. Internalizing them haunts you.
—Skee Hipszky

Skee Hipszky—Colorado Springs, Colorado

Istvan "Skee" Hipszky joined the El Paso County Search and Rescue (EPCSAR) team when he was eighteen years old; that was forty-eight years and thirty-five-hundred missions ago. Skee is the longest-serving member of EPCSAR's approximately seventy-person-strong mountain SAR crew. He attends about a hundred incidents and does more than 120 hours of training each year. EPCSAR began in 1966 as the Wilderness Wanderers, a four-by-four club specializing in rock rescue and first aid. The Wilderness Wanderers became the El Paso County SAR in 1970.

Skee's first mountain rescue was at the age of sixteen, even before he joined SAR, when he was on a climb and one of the six climbers in his party fell from Windom Mountain. The climber landed thirty-three metres down scree (small loose stones covering a slope on a mountain) and had head injuries. Skee and the rest of the climbers carried him down to a clearing where a Bell helicopter with a sked flew him out for care.[91] The injured climber survived to climb again.

Skee is a retired life-support instructor; he taught CPR, advanced cardiac care and pediatric care in a hospital to doctors, nurses and other medical personnel. He gives Hug-a-Tree presentations to kids, in which they learn about what to do if they get lost. Skee was awarded the Pikes Peak Red Cross Hometown Hero first responder award in 2014. He received an award from the American Red Cross for saving the life of a man who was struck by lightning in 1996 by performing CPR on him.

Skee racks up about two thousand volunteer hours per year with SAR, the most out of all the volunteers interviewed for this book. He attributes his high volunteer hours to being an on-call mission coordinator. To decompress, he enjoys nature photography, and he occasionally takes on wedding photography gigs. He has a passion for flying

Colorado Ski Patrol prepares to evacuate an injured skier. Shutterstock 46271764

glider planes, although he doesn't have time for flying these days. Skee is an FAA-certified drone pilot. EPCSAR has two drones with FLIR (Forward-Looking Infrared) that can be used at night.

His wife, Ginger, is the weather forecaster for the team. She uses the weather cams on the top of Pikes Peak, weather apps and radar to give the team up-to-date weather information due to the quick-changing conditions on Pikes Peak, especially in winter.

Case 44: Rock Climber Fall
Eleven Mile Canyon, Colorado

Now sixty-six, Skee was only eleven years old when he started technical rock climbing. On Labour Day weekend in 1982, Skee and another member from EPCSAR, Ann, had just finished a climb and stood watching two others climb nearby. "I said to Ann that the one climber shouldn't be where he was, as he was going to fall. Just as I said the word 'fall,' the man fell," Skee recalls. Patrick "Pat" Pennington (age seventeen) of Colorado Springs fell thirty metres from a cliff and landed on a rock ledge.

Skee had locked his keys in his truck, so Ann hitchhiked into the nearest town to call for help. In the meantime, Skee improvised a rescue team, including Pat's friends and Boy Scouts who were camping in the park. They carried the unconscious Patrick down from the ledge.

Skee performed mouth-to-mouth resuscitation on the badly injured boy. Fort Carson sent in their military UH-1 (Huey) helicopter with four crew members aboard, including the pilot, co-pilot, medical technician and crew chief.[92] It was the kind of helicopter that was used in the Vietnam War. Pat was loaded into a sked—rescue stretcher—on the side of the helicopter.

Skee asked the pilot if he could come to assist with Pat's care. There was already a medic on the crew, and the pilot was concerned about the weight of the chopper, so Skee stayed on the ground. The pilot saved his life, even though he didn't know it at the time.

The helicopter was just out of sight when Skee and Ann heard a crash and saw smoke. Skee had managed to get his keys out of his truck by then, and he drove at top speed to the crash site. The helicopter was on the ground, fully engulfed in flames. Skee jumped into action and used a door from the downed helicopter as a heat shield, grabbed the nearest casualty, and dragged him out of the fire. Ann shouted to get back because the oxygen tank would blow up as soon as the fire reached it.

Pat, who they had just rescued from his fall down a cliff, was crushed under the helicopter's engine. He, along with Major Richard C. Bulliner, Captain William S. Inklebarger, PFC Mark R. Welch and SSgt Gregg A. Penn, all died. There were no survivors.

Skee says there was a thunderstorm and the chopper likely got caught in a downdraft or microburst. The pilot lost control, and the blades of the helicopter struck the top of a tree.[93] The helicopter slammed into the canyon wall, turned upside down and crashed to the ground, where it burst into flames, likely from the fuel igniting.

The area was extremely busy with people over the holiday weekend. "It was a miracle no one was where the helicopter went down at the time," says Skee. He can still picture where all the medical supplies were ejected from the helicopter upon impact on the ground.

Skee and Ann went back to Ann's place and wrote down everything they remembered for the National Transport Safety Board (NTSB) for the investigation that would come. Meanwhile, the

EPCSAR heard of the crash and feared the worst—that Skee or Ann were on the helicopter when it crashed, since they were overdue from their climb. They launched a team to Eleven Mile Canyon to see if their compatriots were safe. They were greatly relieved to find that Skee and Ann were alive and well.

Christopher Van Tilburg, MD
Hood River, Oregon

Dr. Christopher Van Tilburg has been a member of the Hood River Crag Rats for nearly twenty-five years. The group has fifty members and responds to an average of thirty call-outs each year. The Crag Rats, established in 1926, claim to be the oldest SAR organization in North America. The Crag Rats cover Mount Hood and the Columbia Gorge areas, and they're certified in high-angle, avalanche and crevasse rescue by the Mountain Rescue Association.

They only accept applicants who are experienced mountaineers, skiers and outdoors people, as they have no time to train members in these core skills; rather, they give them mountain-rescue experience. A prerequisite is that applicants have already climbed Mount Hood and Mount Adams.[94]

Christopher is an active rescuer and medical director of Portland Mountain Rescue, Clackamas County SAR and Pacific Northwest SAR in Oregon. He joined SAR because of his "Part love of outdoors, part love of rescue, part wanting to help someone. I grew up in a household with a strong commitment to community volunteering."

He is an author of more than a dozen books on outdoor adventure. His most recent book is the thoroughly engaging *Search and Rescue: A Wilderness Doctor's Life-and-Death Tales of Risk and Reward*. He's currently writing a book on the impact of COVID on his practice of medicine.

Christopher works as a doctor at an occupational and travel medicine clinic, at a hospital emergency room and at a ski resort clinic. He's also a public health officer and a medical examiner. He's been an expedition doctor and a cruise ship doctor.

Being a member of SAR is jarring to the family when there are call-outs at midnight, Christopher says. "It's disruptive to leave work early or go to work after being in the mountains all night, but it's tremendously rewarding to save a life and interact in the outdoors in a way [that] very few people experience and with colleagues who are a unique brand of person."

Skis are his favoured pieces of SAR equipment. "One, I love skiing, and two, it's the most efficient and safest way to travel in the mountains."

Case 45: Climber Missing
Snow Dome, Oregon

On October 27, 2020, twenty-seven-year-old Austin Mishler from Bend, Oregon, was on a solo climb when he was reported missing on Mount Hood—Oregon's tallest peak. Austin was an experienced climber and a wilderness guide. He had recently summitted five peaks in about two weeks' time.[95] Two days later, after air and ground searches were conducted, his body was discovered in a crevasse at 2,865 metres on the north side of the peak, in the area known as the Snow Dome.[96] Austin had suffered a fall, landing on a jagged ridge of ice in an icefall east of Horseshoe Rock at the top of Snow Dome. The recovery of his body was conducted as a joint Crag Rats and Portland Mountain Rescue (PMR) mission, with the Crag Rats leading.

Christopher says that in these circumstances, "We're not in crisis mode." Rescuers during a recovery aren't under the same time pressures, like when they have a critically injured or hypothermic subject and every minute counts.

The rescuers were divided into four teams. Team 1A and 1B were assigned to the technical work on Snow Dome. Teams 2A and 2B were to assist by carrying loads to the bottom of Snow Dome and helping with the evacuation below timberline. All the teams departed Cloud Cap Inn at 4:20 a.m. on November 2, 2020.

Christopher led the Crag Rats in team 1A, and they reached the area where Austin lay on the icefall at around 9:00 a.m. A rescuer placed anchors and rigging about one hundred metres above the icefall, and a rescuer descended on belay to the body. Once he reached the location and set his own anchors, his line was used as a fixed line for other rescuers to descend.

Austin's body was raised and moved to the edge of a larger ice mass, where it was transferred to a longer system that was anchored several hundred feet above. The initial fixed line was converted to a sliding guideline to direct the body horizontally across the slope, and it was then raised to the top of Snow Dome. There, rescuers packaged the deceased in a body bag, then secured the deceased in the sked, which was lowered to the bottom of Snow Dome. They reached the Timberline Trail for the handoff to Teams 2A and 2B around four that afternoon.

Teams 2A and 2B, Pacific Northwest SAR (PNWSAR) and Clackamas County SAR received the body on the trail and transported it back to Cloud Cap. The Crag Rats and Portland Mountain Rescue (PMR) returned to Cloud Cap around 5:00 p.m. PNWSAR arrived at Cloud Cap with Austin's body at approximately 6:30 p.m.

The recovery was exhausting and highly technical, and they had barely enough members to cover the challenging call-out. On the plus side, they had the night before to plan the complex steps that would be required, which rescuers don't usually have the luxury of doing ahead of time.

CASE 46: INJURED HIKER
GORTON CREEK CANYON, OREGON

In January 2021, the Crag Rats had three call-outs in the last two weeks of the month. From January 14 to 17, four Crag Rats joined the Mountain Rescue Patrol at Mount Rainier National Park.

The first rescue was on January 16, when they had a mission high on the formidable peak of Mount Rainier starting at about four in the afternoon. They assisted in the rescue of three climbers who were cold, injured and stuck on the Muir Snowfield at 2,480 metres. The temperature was minus three Celsius, with winds gusting to sixty-four kilometres per hour; sunset was at 4:50 p.m., so they would soon be in darkness.[97] The last time the Crag Rats had responded to a call on Mount Rainier was back in 1929, and that was for a body recovery on the Ingraham Glacier.

The second rescue was on January 18, when the Crag Rats rescued two lost hikers in upper Warren Creek Canyon near Warren Lake. The hikers were located with their cellphone's geolocation and successfully rescued.

The third call-out occurred on January 23, when they responded to an injured hiker in Gorton Creek Canyon—a box canyon. A box canyon has steep side walls and ends in a vertical cliff. Box canyons are extremely hazardous for all aircraft, both rotary and fixed-wing, to maneuver and land in, especially if there are obstructions like tall trees in the area. Flying into a box canyon at night greatly adds to the inherent high level of risk.

Morgan Bailey (age forty-three) of Milwaukie, Oregon, was exploring the burned-out area near Eagle Creek when he took a wrong turn and got lost. He fell fifteen metres off a cliff, sustained injuries and became hypothermic. He spent the next three days scrambling over cliff faces, until two hikers found him, bleeding and cold. Morgan was dressed lightly for the weather, had few supplies, and hadn't left a trip plan or informed anyone where he was going or when he would be back.[98]

At dusk, the Crag Rats responded—along with the Cascade Locks Fire Department (CLFD) and PNWSAR—to the remote, steep, narrow canyon, away from any trail. The CLFD and Crag Rats reached Morgan, who was unable to walk. They gave him medical care and transported him across a rocky stream in the canyon to a small clearing.

It was dark when the US Coast Guard helicopter arrived at the confined area. "There was a downdraft from the helicopter, putting the entire group at risk," says Christopher. The helicopter hoisted the patient and transported him to hospital. The low temperature that night in the Columbia River Gorge was approximately 1.1 degrees Celsius.

Morgan spent four days recovering in hospital. His right arm was broken, his T10 and T11 vertebrae fractured, and he had rhabdomyolysis.[99] Rhabdo is a serious condition that occurs through a combination of injury to the muscles, overexertion and dehydration. Death of muscle fibres occurs, and their contents are released into the bloodstream and can cause kidney failure.

In his book *Search and Rescue,* Christopher often talks about the risks that rescuers face every time they go out on a call. "There's no right or wrong, there's only risk assessments," Christopher said in an interview.

The Crag Rats once entered an avalanche zone to recover a deceased person who'd been buried under an avalanche. I asked, "Couldn't you have waited until spring when the snow melted to do the recovery?"

"It depends on how hard the family pushes," he explains. Families in grief often urge searchers to keep looking, even when conditions are too harsh for them to continue. Families just want their loved ones returned, and they may not be in a place where they are thinking about the potential harm or death of rescuers. That's when authorities, search managers, and incident commanders must step in and say "no" for the sake of the safety of the SAR members, as tough a call as that may be—especially in small communities, where everyone is connected to the subject and their family.

Christopher is passionate about SAR. "I love volunteering, I love the camaraderie, and I love interacting with the outdoor world in a way very few people experience and with a focussed mission. We go to locations at times that no one would otherwise go." He would like the public to know that SAR members "are all volunteers and sacrifice our personal time, money and well-being to rescue people."

When his work feels overwhelming, Christopher decompresses by talking things through with colleagues while they're on recreational outings together.

MIKE CHERIM—NORTH CONWAY, NEW HAMPSHIRE

Mike Cherim is a mountain guide and the owner of Redline Guiding. He joined Androscoggin Valley Search and Rescue (AVSAR) in 2013, where he does above-the-treeline team rescues in the winter. AVSAR has fifty members who are all specialists in above-treeline SAR. AVSAR receives grants for equipment from the Outdoor Council, as well as free parking passes for the national forests. Mike has an excellent blog at redlineguiding.com, in which he discusses outdoor topics, such as *22 Winter Alpine Travel Tips*.[100]

CASE 47: OVERDUE CLIMBER
MOUNT ADAMS, WASHINGTON

On February 15, 2015, Kate Matrosova, thirty-two, an experienced climber from New York, who once summited Denali Mountain, Alaska, with an elevation of 6,190 metres, was determined to summit seven peaks—one on each of the seven continents. She came to the White Mountains and set out to do a solo traverse of the Northern Presidentials. Her plan was to carry the minimum of gear and dress lightly as she traversed twenty-five kilometres. A weather report warned of an arctic front; the temperatures were forecast to drop to minus seventy-three degrees Celsius with extreme winds.[101]

Kate didn't descend to the valley before the brutal winds and cold came, as she had promised. She pressed her personal locator beacon (PLB) and sent an SOS. When a PLB is activated the manufacturer of the beacon picks up the signal and contacts authorities with the GPS location and the identity of the beacon owner. Unfortunately, after sending the SOS, Kate put away the PLB in her pack and turned it off, which made it difficult to track her exact location. If Kate had left the PLB on, it would have led the SAR team to her much more quickly. However, she left the antenna up and sticking out of her pack, so they did get a faint signal.

"It was too dangerous that night," says Mike. According to the Mount Washington Observatory, located at an elevation of 1,914 metres, the temperature that night dropped to minus thirty-seven Celsius, and the winds blew at 196 kilometres per hour from the north. However, it would be much colder and windier on the mountains, where Kate would be completely exposed to the elements and at a higher elevation. The peak of Mount Adams is 3,743 metres, but Kate likely didn't make it to the summit in those severe conditions. Rescuers went up to get a fix on her position from the activated PLB despite the high-risk conditions; however, they didn't find her.

The following morning, the wind subsided somewhat and searchers went up again to look for Kate on a parapet near where her PLB had gone off. "I knew it would be a recovery," says Mike. She couldn't have survived the extreme weather overnight dressed as she was and with minimal gear.

"The wind was 108 miles per hour [174 kilometres per hour] and the temperature minus twenty [minus twenty-nine Celsius]. We hiked up Adams on the north side of the mountain to the treeline. We were slammed into the rocks. One of us crawled on hands and knees using an ice axe," says Mike. "It was sunny but cold. I got frostbite around my cheeks," Mike says.

Mike was on a rock outcropping when he saw someone in a silver puffer jacket fifteen metres below him. He thought it was a fellow SAR member, but it turned out to be Kate, lying on her side. Mike thinks she fell from where he was standing. Two of his fellow SAR members reached her from below where Mike stood, confirming that it was Kate.

"It was my first death. I felt a strong sense of empathy. It could've been me or somebody I know," says Mike. That night the temperature dropped to minus thirty-seven Celsius again, and the wind was up to 227 kilometres per hour.

Miles Randell—Squamish, BC

Miles Randell, a retired SAR member, is a paramedic and educator on the SARMed team in Squamish. He currently works for a subscription-based air ambulance service, TEAAM Aeromedical, that serves industrial clients like logging, tree-planting, guiding, railway, oil and gas companies, which don't fall within the SAR and BC Ambulance mandates.

SARMed courses aren't mandatory for BCSAR members, like the Red Cross First Aid courses are, but members are encouraged to take SARMed classes to get certified in first aid for outdoors scenarios.

Case 48: Skier Cardiac Arrest
Whistler, BC

This incident at a ski hill changed the way rescuers look at resuscitation of subjects in the cold. A twenty-four-year-old female landed head-first into a tree well. Her companions quickly pulled her out. She suffered a cardiac arrest, so they started CPR right away. By the time Miles and the rest of the SAR team arrived, two hours had elapsed. His team took over and did advanced life-saving procedures, including putting a tube down her throat to help her breathe.

A helicopter took her to Vancouver General Hospital, where she was put on extracorporeal membrane oxygenation (ECMO), a treatment originally used for premature infants, which pumps blood through an artificial lung and back into the bloodstream. This treatment is also used to treat severe cases of COVID, when patients' lungs are badly damaged.

She was rewarmed slowly, as her core body temperature was only seventeen degrees Celsius. Normal body temperature is thirty-seven degrees. She'd been without a pulse for four hours. She required defibrillation twice to get her heart started. Amazingly, she made a complete recovery.

Hypothermia turned out to be her saviour, not her enemy. Miles says that her brain being chilled before she had a cardiac arrest protected her from brain damage and death. This rare phenomenon is called severe accidental hypothermia with cardiac arrest.

CASE 49: DIABETIC IN DISTRESS
CHILLIWACK, BC

The Great Storm of 1996 (aka Snowmageddon) found Miles in the middle of several epic rescues. Over four days, from December 26 to 30, 1996, more than 1.5 metres of snow fell on the Lower Mainland, closing the highway between Vancouver and the Fraser Valley. The volume of snow grounded most flights at Vancouver International Airport and kept BC Ferries in port. It was the worst storm seen in seventy-five years, and Chilliwack was the epicentre of it.

Miles was with the Central Fraser Valley SAR at that time, and they got a call-out for an unconscious diabetic trapped in her car on the highway. A snowplow escorted the team's rescue four-by-four to get them through the snowdrifts on the highway. Theirs was the only rescue car left in the area.

"The highway was a war zone of hundreds of abandoned cars," says Miles. They had to stop where a semi carrying milk had slid sideways and blocked traffic from moving in both directions. Drivers were trapped in their cars.

Miles clambered over the drifts to get to the car with the diabetic patient. He found the woman and treated her. The team got her into the cab of a front-end loader for transport to the hospital.

They kept the rescue truck running as they dug people out from their snowbound cars, but eventually the truck froze and stalled. They found a farmhouse, and as they rescued people from their cars, they took them to the house. The family hosted and fed them and found places for them to sleep. They stuffed 176 people into the farmhouse while they waited for rescue for forty-eight hours. They slept on tables, couches, in the basement, wherever they could find space. Being farmers, they had plenty of food in their freezer and pantry. The SAR group also moved the horses into the barns so they wouldn't freeze to death.

Miles's friend and mentor Tim Jones, a station chief with BC Paramedics, sent snowcats and the military to the farmhouse to bring supplies. A railroad ran in front of the house, so BC Rail sent a train to rescue people en masse, with the medical cases going out first. The medical evacuees filled up the train, so it returned a second time to pick up the rest of the stranded motorists.

Miles is happy to help those in need after thirty years of volunteering. He would like to see a hybrid model of paid and volunteer services, because the purely volunteer model is not sustainable, in his opinion. "There's always a need for volunteers and paid professionals with advanced skills," he says. He gives the example of paid technical mountain guides, such as free climbers or base jumpers, who can get to subjects stuck and injured on mountain cliffs faster than a SAR team can. Locations like Whistler, Squamish, Golden and Revelstoke hire professional mountain guides in emergencies. Parks Canada hires pro mountain guides as visitor safety specialists in Banff and Jasper national parks, for example. Hiring a pro equals lives saved, in Miles's opinion.

In the future, Miles would like to see intensive courses offered at an indoor training centre. He's seen one in Germany that has a helicopter hanging from the ceiling to practice getting in and out of a helicopter, or even longline rescues; a pond area; a cold area and other simulated environments to practise rescues safely.

ALYSSA KARPA—COLORADO SPRINGS, COLORADO

Alyssa Karpa joined the El Paso County Search and Rescue (EPCSAR), the second busiest SAR in Colorado, nearly four years ago. SAR "quickly became a part of my life," Alyssa told me.

She is now an EMT, and the program was free to her as a SAR volunteer. The EMT experience led to her pursuing a nursing career. "SAR takes over your life in a good way," says Alyssa.

She graduated from the nursing program in May 2022 and started her first nursing job in June 2022. "It's not been easy to work, study, as well as do SAR," she says. Her employers were supportive, and she's chosen jobs that are flexible so she could still go out on SAR call-outs.

The fifty to eighty members receive up to 250 calls a year, but like all SAR groups not all call-outs result in full-blown missions. In 2020 there were fewer call-outs for her group, but Alyssa says the ones they got were more intense. Alyssa says they had only 130 missions that year, but some that lasted for days on Pikes Peak. By comparison, in 2021 they had 237 calls and 117 missions that came out of those calls, but, as Alyssa indicates, the number of missions doesn't indicate the complexity or length of a rescue or recovery. The group has several members that age out every year, and they start a new class every year, bringing in about fifteen new members-in-training.

EPCSAR receives no funding, except what they raise themselves and some grants, which are available through the ID cards the state sells for outdoors people. Their fundraisers are races—a 5k, a 10k and a marathon up Pikes Peak. Races were virtual during the pandemic.

Case 50: Hikers Injured
Pikes Peak, Colorado

On August 12, 2020, Alyssa and over twenty other members of her team were called to the top of Pikes Peak, at an elevation over 4,300 metres, to rescue some injured hikers. The man had called for help with his cellphone. Rope teams rappelled down to a man and an injured woman.

Alyssa was the first one to reach the woman, who had ankle and head injuries. The man was mildly hypothermic. The woman was moved to a litter, where she stayed for fifteen hours. Alyssa spent the night on the ledge with her at 4,115 metres. Anchors were put into the cliff, and Teller County SAR team came to assist. At sunrise a helicopter arrived to evacuate the injured woman. The man was able to get to the top on his own with the help of SAR the day before. Alyssa was on the call from three in the afternoon on August 12 to three o'clock on August 13. "It was very rewarding," she says.

Alyssa has attended many body recoveries in the wilderness. She copes by "keeping detached." This professional detachment serves her well on calls like the following. During a blizzard, she went by snowcat to do a welfare check on a couple. Upon arrival, she found the woman slumped against the door of her home and hypothermic. Her husband was covered by snow in the yard and deceased.

The husband had gone out in the blinding snowstorm to turn on the generator, and he got lost on the way back to the house. If a guide rope had been tied between the house and where the generator was, it would've saved his life.

Alyssa had to keep repeating the sad news to the elderly woman, because she was hypothermic and kept forgetting what had happened. The woman began to calm down as she warmed up, and she showed Alyssa an album of pictures of her grandchildren until the ambulance arrived four or five hours later.

Mike Conway—Whistler, BC

The more I talk through tragic circumstances, the more I feel the negative energy leave my body. I've had to go down a crevasse for a recovery. Talking through it helped.
—Mike Conway

Michael "Mike" Conway joined the Whistler Search and Rescue Society in 2014, during a recruitment drive. WSAR, which was started in 1972, responds to the rugged terrain adjacent to one of the busiest ski resorts in North America. It has a two-year member-in-training program, which includes doing the Ground SAR program through the Justice Institute of BC.

Mike has completed avalanche (AST 1) certification and has taken many in-house courses, like rope training, first aid, and helicopter operations. During pandemic restrictions, in-person training hasn't always been possible, which has hampered the members from progressing in their training.

Mike says he joined WSAR for a number of reasons: "The satisfaction I get from helping people injured or in trouble, gaining of skills, collaboration of knowledge, and adventures that come with training and rescues." He's a physiotherapist by profession and already had basic first aid coming into SAR. He has a high level of fitness, having completed triathlons, Ironmans and adventure races. However, he says that the major skills he brought to the group were his "enjoyment of the outdoors and competency with some of our rescue methods in regard to biking, snowmobiling and skiing—but the truth is, my most applicable skills were gained with weekly SAR training."

Mike says that in the application interview, they asked questions to see if he was likely to stay in Whistler for the long-term—if he had a business, a home, and if he was planning to live there permanently. SAR invests a lot in training in each member, so they want to be as sure as possible that members will stay. Being a ski resort town, Whistler has a transient population and housing is extremely expensive and in short supply. All the members that came in with Mike's cohort have stayed.

Mike, a father of young children, says that his call-outs sometimes result in him leaving a dinner or other engagement. But his family is understanding and supports his role as a SAR member. He says, "There is some flexibility amongst the thirty-two members, so I do not attend all the calls, which is helpful."

Mike estimates that sixty hours of volunteer work each year, in addition to the time dedicated to his practice and family, provides a healthy balance. In the long-term, he feels this should prevent burn-out. Mike tells me that Whistler SAR's member retention is said to be one of the best in the province, with the average retention now getting close to approximately twenty years.

Case 51: Injured Skier
Callaghan Valley, BC

On January 5, 2021, WSAR was called out to the Callaghan during day five of a full-blown coastal snowstorm, where almost two metres of snow fell in ninety-six hours. The call was attended by twelve WSAR members and three employees from Canadian Wilderness Adventures with snowcats. Two skiers were returning from Hanging Lake when one skier injured his knee.

Mike says that what turned an old-school SAR call into one that demanded every skill and tool in the shed, was that the injured subject had a rare genetic condition called Hyperkalemic Periodic Paralysis (HyperKPP), which affects only one out of 250,000 people. It's so rare that it's classified as an orphan disease. When a person with Hyper-KPP becomes cold or fatigued, they become temporarily paralyzed. In this rescue, the subject was paralyzed from the neck down, unable to move but able to speak in a weak voice.

WSAR set off at 7:00 p.m., snowmobiling and using the assistance of a snowcat to groom and build a road, including building a bridge of snow over a creek to where ski touring—backcountry Nordic skiing—could begin. Ski touring with ten snowmobiles was made more difficult with the heavy first aid, hypothermia and transport devices, including a toboggan and an evacuation mat. The sheer depth of snow and the obstacles of tree wells made for slow going. Mike says that the snow depth was endless, so if anyone fell into the snow, it would be a bottomless free fall.

The skier accompanying his injured friend was studying to be a mountain guide with the Association of Canadian Mountain Guides (ACMG). The ACMG program is rigorous, requiring advanced first aid and extensive training in both skiing and alpine guiding. He didn't know that his companion had a potentially life-threatening condition before they went skiing together. When the man became injured and paralyzed, the guiding student built a snow cave for them to hunker down in while they waited for help. He wrapped his friend up to keep him warm, laid him on skis to keep him off the cold snow, and provided GPS coordinates for SAR to locate them.

The subjects were located by navigating to the GPS coordinates at about ten that night. Both subjects were hypothermic and needed warming up. WSAR had a charcoal heater with them to help with that. The uninjured subject was guided out on skis, while the injured skier was packaged in a hypothermia "burrito" package, put on a toboggan and slid out. Roughly twenty-five belays were used to lower and navigate the patient out through deep snow and dense trees. The snow continued to fall so thickly that their snowmobile tracks going into the area were covered over by the time they made their return trip.

They arduously pulled their paralyzed patient on the toboggan and got him to a snowmobile by 12:30 a.m. The snowmobile got him to the ambulance by 1:00 a.m.

Mike found the connection and collaboration between all the rescuers and teams involved extremely satisfying.

CASE 52: SKIER LOST
WHISTLER MOUNTAIN, BC

On December 15, 2016, Mike was on a team of WSAR members who searched for a skier out-of-bounds on the backside of Whistler Mountain in the Cake Hole area down to Cheakamus Lake. This is an area where people often get lost. They ride the ski lift and head down the back of the mountain, where countless perils can await them. By the time the skier was reported missing, it was too dark to search. The team had to wait for first light.

Mike and his team found the man lying by the Cheakamus River, where he'd endured the minus seventeen Celsius temperature overnight. "I'll never forget the paleness of his skin and the discoloration of his eyes," says Mike. The man was barely conscious and as close to death, without actually being deceased, as Mike had ever seen someone. The subject's body was so stiff that he couldn't move—his joints were frozen in place. The rescuers were unable to move his arms and legs.

North Shore Search and Rescue waiting for a helicopter while rescuing a skier with a broken leg. Shutterstock 1652436403

The team moved the subject carefully, so as not to move any of the cold blood from his extremities toward his heart—to do so could cause a cardiac arrest. He was taken by helicopter to the hospital, where his body temperature was thirty degrees Celsius (normal body temperature is thirty-seven degrees Celsius).

The subject was released that night and made a full recovery. His home country's consulate sent WSAR a letter of commendation for rescuing their citizen.

Mike says he's gained too many skills to mention from being in WSAR, some of which include navigation, snow science, avalanche management, rope rescue techniques, helicopter operations, patient transport and first aid. He won't leave SAR until he can no longer do call-outs. Members have to age out or resign before they will bring in any new members. He says he would like to try being a SAR manager someday, but his group has five SAR managers at this time.

Don't be afraid to call for help—and do it early, rather than later. The sooner you make contact, the better.
—Mike Conway

JAIME BERNARD—NEW HAMPSHIRE

Jaime Bernard is the vice-president of the Pemigewasset Valley Search and Rescue Team (PemiSAR). He and his family moved from the Merrimack Valley in Massachusetts to Thornton, New Hampshire, to enjoy hiking.

Jaime joined PemiSAR in 2017 to help people. He's a licensed nursing assistant and currently a physical therapist at a nursing home. He's made good use of his medical experience within SAR. He attends about twenty missions a year and puts in 250 to 300 volunteer hours annually.

"A lot of what I own is ancient, literally held together by tie wraps and superglue, including my pack. I adore the old classic gear. Equipment was made to last back then." His favourite piece of SAR equipment is a Lowe Alpine 115-litre backpack that's massive but goes down to 90 litres or less by adjusting the straps. "It allows me to pack all of my essential gear and leaves plenty of room to pack for others, including a patient's needs. It's so large, my friends gave me the trail name Costco," Jaime says.

He's enjoyed seeing PemiSAR blossom into a healthy place with eighty members. They receive New Hampshire Council grants for training and gear, such as new radios and GPS. The members pay modest membership dues and must attend three missions and one training session annually to maintain membership in the group.

They have a lot of fun together. "It's my family," he says. He's proud to wear their distinctive "slime green" shirts. Jaime maintains internal peace and is a spiritual person, an approach that helps him to cope with the stressful nature of some of the SAR incidents he encounters.

Case 53: Missing Hiker
Lincoln, Massachusetts

In late June 2019, PemiSAR was called out to search for Christopher Staff, age seventy, who had set out to complete the Pemigewasset Loop trail in a day—a fifty-kilometre trek with twelve mountain peaks. Christopher started the loop at about one in the morning on Monday, June 24. His plan was to return by 9:30 p.m. that evening. When he didn't arrive on time, his wife, Catherine ("Catha"), called authorities.[102]

This was the first time Christopher had hiked the trail. He was spotted on the trail by other hikers until he veered off the trail three-quarters of the way along, only eight kilometres from the end. Jaime was one of the thirty searchers who scoured the Pemigewasset Wilderness for five days, focussing on the Bonds area.

Knowing that Christopher was out in the open for that length of time with no shelter or food, they thought he may be deceased. The search was called off Friday afternoon, and they were packing up when word came that hikers had found him on the trail, sitting on a log. Upon hearing the news, Jaime returned to the trailhead and was one of several rescuers to drive up the trail by ATV to get Christopher. In his state, Christopher said that it seemed like it took hours for the crew to reach him.

Jaime said that considering what Christopher had gone through, he was in excellent physical and mental condition. Jaime attributes his survival to his will to live.

Jaime and his team appreciated the thank-you cake that Christopher sent from Icing on the Cake in Newton, Massachusetts, where Christopher is the owner and baker.

CHRISTOPHER STAFF'S SURVIVAL STORY

"Two years later, it's still with me. It will be with me the rest of my life," Christopher Staff, seventy-two in 2021, says. His voice sounds emotional on the phone, even years after his ordeal near the Pemigewasset Loop trail in New Hampshire where he fought for his life.

The veteran hiker of forty years got off trail in the darkness. He got disoriented—depleted of salt and electrolytes from drinking too much water, a condition called hyponatremia, not to mention being exhausted from hiking for nineteen hours. He entered a dream-like state that helped him get through his ordeal calmly. "The days floated by."

On day two, he walked away from his backpack, which had everything he needed in it, like bug spray, food and water. He doesn't remember why he left it behind, but likely he was in a fugue due to pushing his body past its limits. He stayed close to the river, which was rushing like a rapid. "I had two hundred mosquito bites on my back," Christopher says. He crossed the river at one point because he thought he saw someone waving at him, but there was no one there, and the mosquitoes were twice as thick on the other side. He had many hallucinations over those five days. He saw helicopters searching for him overhead, and they were real, but he wasn't visible to them on the ground, as he was in thick brush.

On day five he felt like it would be the end of him if he didn't get out of there. "I had to go," he says. He followed the river downstream and came to an area that looked like it had recently been used for a picnic. He followed a trail up to an intersection and found a trail sign. He couldn't believe his luck. Two hikers came along, and he asked them, "Which way to civilization?" They pointed down the trail, said he was about a mile (1.6 kilometres) from the parking lot, and carried on their way, but it was actually over eight kilometres away.

"I couldn't walk," says Christopher, even though the hikers had given him walking sticks. He was unable to tell them he needed help. Another hiker came along and recognized that Christopher was in trouble. He had his kid run ahead to get help.

Soon a rescuer came and put mosquito netting around Christopher, who was so relieved to have that protective layer. Christopher walked three kilometres with the help of the incredible SAR team, and then an ATV, with Jaime on it, met them and carried him out from there. "I had no idea the extent the searchers went to searching for me," he says.

"It was the best day of my life. Fantastic," says Catha, about the moment when they brought Christopher back to her. He spent two days in hospital, having fluids put slowly back into him. He had lost nearly 13 kilograms, going from a slender 67 kilograms to 54 kilograms in five days. Thankfully, he suffered no long-lasting physical effects.

Christopher received counselling for the first month after the traumatic event. "I still have PTSD myself," says Catha. She believes it helped him feel able to talk about his experience.

Christopher says, "I'm still a hiking person and want another crack at it." He goes on short solo hikes of eight to ten kilometres in the Blue Hills outside of Boston. Catha makes sure he tells her where he's going and for how long.

10. Mounted Search and Rescue

*Horses find people. They have a keen sense
of death an danger. —Dr. Norm Brazel*

Norm Brazel—Douglasville, Georgia

Norman (Norm) Brazel, Ph.D., co-founder, president and incident commander of West Georgia Mounted Search and Rescue (WGM-SAR), joined ranks with the group in 2010. The other co-founder is Norm's wife, Brenda, a naturopathic doctor and the base commander for WGMSAR. Norm and Brenda live 40 kilometres away from WGMSAR's base, and they travel up to 240 kilometres or more to conduct searches in Georgia, Alabama and Tennessee. So deep is their commitment to SAR, they're willing to travel wherever they're needed. However, there are some requests that WGMSAR turns down. "We don't do swamps," said Norm.

Norm aided the FBI with recoveries and searches for evidence, including those related to serial-killer cases. He was certified in tracking, CPR, first aid, communications, General Mobile Radio Service (GMRS) systems, Emergency Radio System and SAR's own radio band. "Radios allow us to keep in constant communication with our riders and law enforcement. They give us instant locations of our people and coordinates with our search maps," he said.

WGMSAR has twenty-five members, including sixteen riders, the majority of whom are women, and thirteen horses. They train in all weather "except tornadoes," said Norm. They don't train at night, even though horses can see at night, because it's unsafe for the riders.

Sadly, Norm passed away on January 9, 2022. He is remembered fondly as a kind man with a big heart and a devoted member of his community.

How Horses Find People

"Horses have keen senses as prey animals," said Norm. He explained that horses have two types of vision—monocular and binocular. "They

Horses are valuable to search and rescue as they are prey animals and more sensitive to sounds and scents than dogs, which are predators. All Canada Photos 2H6YJN4

have miles of range of vision. Their sense of smell and hearing is better than canines, who are predatory animals." Horses also have an uncanny sense of direction.

In the field, SAR horses and their riders are sent out in teams. They have a 75 percent recovery rate, according to Norm. On occasions when K9 teams have failed to find subjects or human remains, horses have been able to find them, according to Norm.

Search Horses vs. K9s

The advantages of using mounted teams are numerous. Searching with the benefit of that additional height gives the riders a better perspective of the area. A mounted team is faster than searchers on foot. Horses can withstand extremes of temperature, whereas dogs can only search for thirty minutes in hot temperatures before they need rest. Horses can search for up to seventy-two hours at a time.

Horses also carry all the gear the searchers need, leaving them less fatigued and their hands free to use equipment like GPS. A dog handler often has their dog on leash, and they need to carry their pack and rewards for their dog. They also require a flanker or two to navigate for them, as they are focussed on the dog and not on a compass.

Horses are non-threatening, whereas some subjects—such as children, people with dementia, or people with cognitive differences—find searchers and K9s threatening and will even hide from them.

In July 2018, Norm and four other mounted searchers were looking for an eleven-year-old girl who'd run away from her aunt's home unclothed. Her aunt had recently adopted the girl and it was believed that she was upset by the change in homes. Searchers looked for the distressed child for three or four hours with no luck, and the K9 teams had come in and searched for her for thirty minutes in forty-degree-Celsius heat. Norm brought some of the girl's clothing in his saddlebag, along with water. Many of the searchers on this mission were women.

They found her next to a tree, and she was covered in bug bites. The women dismounted and dressed the girl, who happily rode back doubling on Norm's horse.

TYPES OF HORSES USED IN SAR

"These aren't show horses. We even have a mule," Norm said. Horses suitable for mounted SAR are sturdy, experienced trail horses and should be over four years old. They need to be able to carry weight, line up with other horses and stand still.

A SAR horse needs a good temperament. The horse needs to be able to react to differences in the environment, like when it comes across a deer or something else unexpected. The rider also needs to learn to read the horse's reactions, such as ear movements or looks, said Norm.

"Horses are herd animals and won't leave the herd, but we need a horse to leave the herd when we want it to," said Norm. A rider should be able to mount and dismount from either side, and the horse should be able to be led by someone else. The horse must be able to pull weight, such as a log, and willing to cross a creek, stop on command and not spook. The horse must be willing to load into a trailer within ten minutes and unload within five minutes.

CASE 54: MISSING MALE
KENNESAW, WEST GEORGIA

In March 2014, WGMSAR was called out to assist with a search for Chase Massner, twenty-six, a war veteran who had recently returned from Iraq. Chase disappeared after spending a night at his friend Brad Clement's house in Kennesaw following an argument with his wife, Amanda.[103]

Amanda reported Chase missing when she couldn't reach him on his cellphone.

Brad told a detective that he was cooking breakfast, then went to wake up Chase, but Chase was nowhere to be found; however, Brad's story kept changing over time.

A search was organized that included K9 teams and Norm's Mounted SAR team. The K9 teams failed to find any sign of Chase, but Norm said, "Our horses reacted to an area at his best friend's house. It was the brand-new cement porch. I reported to the police that that was where he was buried." At the time, the police didn't pursue the information.

Chase's family continued to search for him. They put up posters offering a $5,000 reward for information leading to his location. Still, there were no leads as to what happened to Chase. Brad moved away just months after Chase went missing. With no new information, interest in the missing-person case dwindled.

Then, acting on a tip, police returned to Brad's former home with cadaver dogs in the summer of 2017. They had enough of an indication from the dogs to use a backhoe to dig up the porch. On August 1, 2017, they found Chase's body, wrapped in plastic and duct tape, under the cement slab, exactly where the horses had indicated.[104]

Brad became the main suspect of his friend's murder. Chase's autopsy showed no obvious trauma or assault that could've caused his death. However, the toxicology report showed drugs in Chase's system that could've caused an accidental overdose death, specifically, heroin and methamphetamine.

Brad was charged with one count of concealing a death and one count of making a false statement. He entered the Alford plea—acceptance of guilt of a crime by a person who claims innocence in the activity. When you enter an Alford plea, the judge sentences you as if you did plead guilty and are subject to a conviction.

Brad's sentence was fifteen years—eight years in prison, seven on probation, plus a fine of one thousand dollars.[105] Brad, thirty-eight years old in 2022, is serving his sentence at the Georgia State Prison in Reidsville.

CASE 55: ABDUCTED WOMAN
DARDEN, TENNESSEE

On the morning of April 13, 2011, Holly Lynn Bobo, a twenty-year-old nursing student, was dragged from her home by a man wearing camouflage. A neighbour heard Holly screaming and called her mother, who called 911, saying someone had taken her daughter. Holly's brother, Clint, saw the man take her into the forest.

WGMSAR were among the approximately ten thousand searchers that looked for Holly on the most expensive investigation in the Tennessee Bureau of Investigation's history. Norm and his mounted teammates assisted the FBI in the search of over a hundred homes, fields, woods and farms. "There was one owner who wouldn't let us cross his land. I suspected him," says Norm. Norm reported his suspicions, but the FBI didn't get a search warrant for the property of Zachary "Zach" Rye Adams at the time. That initial search, though extensive, didn't turn up any sign of Holly.

Nearly three years later, ginseng hunters came across a skull in the woods in Decatur County, not far from Holly's home. The skull was confirmed to be Holly's. Zach Adams and his friend, Jason Autry, were charged with kidnapping, drugging, raping and murdering Holly.[106] Jason pleaded guilty to solicitation to commit murder and facilitation of an especially aggravated kidnapping. He was sentenced to eight years in prison.

Zach Adams was found guilty of first-degree murder, for which he received a life sentence without parole, especially aggravated kidnapping, for which he received a twenty-five-year sentence, and aggravated rape, for which he received another twenty-five-year sentence. He is held in maximum security at the Morgan County Correctional Complex, near Wartburg, Tennessee.[107]

Zach's brother, John Dylan Adams is in maximum security at the Riverbend Maximum Security Institution, in Nashville, Tennessee. For the crimes he committed against Holly he received a thirty-five-year sentence for especially aggravated kidnapping and a fifteen-year-sentence for first degree murder to be served concurrently. He will be released on November 1, 2048. He will be sixty years old at the time of his release.[108] Shayne Austin, Jason's cousin, who was also involved, died by suicide in February 2015.

At the trial, Jason said that Zach had asked him for help. Zach drove to the river, with Holly wrapped in a blanket in the back of his pickup truck. They were going to throw her into the river, but Holly made a sound and moved. Zach got a pistol out and shot Holly. The two loaded Holly back into the truck and drove away, according to Jason. It was after that failed murder attempt that the three men must have killed Holly, then hid her body in the woods in Decatur.[109]

On September 14, 2020, Jason, then forty-six, was released from prison after waiting for trial for five years. On December 3, 2020, he was charged with being a felon in possession of a firearm, and there was evidence that he was dealing in and using meth. Jason claims that the reason he was in possession of a gun, was that he was hunting a deer in a field in Benton County. He says he ran, then fell down, where the authorities found him lying on the ground wearing pyjama pants with a rifle nearby.

Jason Autry is currently in the Metropolitan Detention Center in San Diego, California. The charges against him had a maximum sentence of up to ten years in federal prison, followed by three years of supervised release and a fine of $250,000. If he qualified as an armed career criminal under federal law, the mandatory minimum sentence is fifteen years and up to life imprisonment. His release date is currently listed as "unknown."[110] There is no parole in the federal system.[111]

Tennessee is a state that still has the death penalty for first degree murder. Riverbend Maximum Security Institution, where John Adams is incarcerated, is where Tennessee's death row prisoners are held and where executions are carried out as recently as February 2020, usually by lethal injection, though the prisoners may opt for death by electrocution.

When Zach walked past Holly's family in the courtroom, he told them he was sorry for what he'd done. This show of remorse is perhaps one of the reasons he was spared the death penalty.

Ray Elliston—Appleton, Ontario

Raymond "Ray" Elliston of Appleton, a hamlet forty kilometres west of Ottawa, is a retired army officer. He is the mounted team leader of Rideau Mounted Search and Rescue in Smith Falls, Ontario. Rideau MSAR has four mounted members and twenty ground SAR members. Ray grew up around horses, since his grandfather was a teamster who drove horse wagons. Ray began riding seriously after retiring in 1998.

In 2004 Ray got Tyr, a two-year-old Suffield Mustang gelding. Tyr, now twenty, loves people, children and attention. He is comfortable working alone or with other horses. He is patient and can be left tied unattended for long periods without becoming restless.

In 2012 Ray established the mounted SAR team, and it took him two years to get it certified. The number of horse-and-rider teams grew to seven; however, in 2017, the Ontario Provincial Police (OPP) minimized their use of volunteer SAR teams, and they lost riders as a consequence of underutilization.

In one of their training simulations, one MSAR team was requested to search for a subject hidden approximately one hundred metres into the bush, while another team dealt with two "injured" subjects. The horses were spaced about twenty metres apart when entering the bush. The horses alerted, and the riders gave the horses their heads, meaning they relaxed the reins and let the horses go where they wanted to. Ray says horses are naturally curious animals and will investigate smells and noises. In this case, the horses on the team tasked to look for the "injured" subjects turned and converged one hundred metres into the bush, right in front of the two subjects.

Horses are people-friendly animals; they are particularly good with young children and the elderly with dementia, says Ray. Children are wary of strangers and may hide from rescuers, but when a horse is involved, "they want to come out to see the horse," he says. In one documented case, Ray says that a despondent woman who may have caused herself harm was approached by a searcher on horseback. The horse became a topic of conversation, and the team was able to save her from self-harm.

Case 56: Elder Missing—Ottawa, Ontario

On September 27, 2018, eighty-five-year-old Jose Rey went missing in an area near Dunrobin. He was wearing light blue pants and a short-sleeved shirt with light green stripes. Jose shuffled when he walked; he was hunched over and hard of hearing. The man had also wandered away a year prior to this incident and was found only 150 metres away.

Rideau SAR was tasked to assist. On day two of the search, the City of Ottawa Police asked Ray's Mounted team to assist with four riders, including himself. The Ontario Provincial Police (OPP) helicopter thought they had found Jose well beyond his house, which backed onto a trail system in the woods. His body was recovered off a trail just three hundred metres from his house; he had sunk into the wetland bog to where just his head and shoulders were above the water. As it turns out, one of the horse-and-rider teams had come within fifty metres of the subject in the thick brush. SAR members struggle with these near misses terribly in cases such as this when the outcome is so tragic.

Ray says that horses are primarily used recreationally in Ontario, except for the Amish, who use them on their farms and for transportation on their buggies.

The SAR horses that Ray and his team use aren't trained in air scenting because of the time involved in training horses to do that.

His horses have a high public profile because they ride in parades and provide communications and security for events.

"Outside of the horses themselves, my personal favourite piece of equipment is the surveyor's vest that we all wear," says Ray. The vest has multiple pockets and suspension points to carry their OSAR-VA (Ontario Search and Rescue Volunteer Association) ID, map, compass, whistle, watch, GPS, radio, flashlight, notebook, pens and pencils, extra batteries, tally counter (same as a step counter), flagging tape, surgical gloves, toilet paper, snacks (for horse and rider), gloves, self-closing plastic bags, space blanket, fire-starters and parachute cord.

11. Plane Crashes

Society is a jigsaw puzzle, and I happen to fit in the
right place with SAR.—Richy Till

RICHY TILL—SUNSHINE COAST, BC

Richard "Richy" Till, call sign Sunshine 08, is on the reserve list of the SCSAR, after serving for twenty-five years. Being on the reserve list means that when there is a large incident or extra members are needed, he's called in.

Richy is nostalgic for the early years of SAR, when members were recruited from the community because of their reputation for being outdoors people. "Now, members may have no significant outdoors background. Under current procedures, all members require extensive training, certification and recertification. In the beginning, members were recruited because they knew the bush and the mountains," he says of the dramatic change in the profile of SAR members.

Richy was recruited after someone lost something on the beach and he found it for them. Someone said he should join SCSAR, so he showed up and joined. He was a mountaineer, climber, caver and hiker; he had experience in mountain rescue as an outdoor educator with the Sechelt Nation and he worked for the exploration industry. He had skills in mapping and had worked for Outward Bound at Keremeos, BC.

He grew up in the UK, where he started his climbing and other outdoor interests at the age of seventeen. He received a Duke of Edinburgh award, which encourages leadership, volunteerism, skill building, physical fitness and adventuring in the wild, amongst other qualities. At twenty-three years old, he moved to BC.

He has a strong preference for rain gear amongst all the SAR equipment available to him. "For those out in the field we rely on good clothing. On the coast here we need good rain gear. Our searches tend to be in the dark and in bad weather," says Richy.

Case 57: Plane Crash
Thormanby Island, BC

Richy says that the most significant inter-agency and memorable incident that ever occurred on the Sunshine Coast was a plane crash on Thormanby Island. The small island has the best sandy beaches on the Sunshine Coast. There's a water taxi that will take you to the popular destination in the summer.

On a foggy day, November 16, 2008, Thomas "Tom" Wilson, boarded a Pacific Coastal Airlines flight with six other passengers, who were his colleagues and close friends. Their pilot, Peter McLeod, said to the passengers, "Guys, we are going to have to do some low-level flying because of the weather conditions. If anyone has a problem with that, I will let you off."

"The cabin was silent when he made that offer. None of us felt like flying, but none of us spoke up," says Tom. Perhaps their silence came from the same place as the pilot's decision to fly in poor visibility conditions—from a sense of conscientiousness and pressure to do their job and not let down their employer?

Tom fell asleep in the middle of the flight, which left Vancouver at about ten that morning. Twenty minutes later, he was awakened by a horrible noise, which he described in the prologue of his memoir, *Moments of Impact*: "I bolted awake to the loud sound of something bashing into our aircraft ... As treetops began ripping into the underbelly of the plane, he applied full power to the engines and pulled back on the stick ... A split second later, we slammed into the rugged side of a mountainous island at full throttle."

Tom lost consciousness when the twin-engine, amphibious Grumman Goose hit the ground. The seaplane had fuelled up in Vancouver, so it had full tanks of aviation gas (avgas) for its journey to Toba Valley's hydroelectric project after a stop in Powell River.

The plane burst into flames and exploded when it crashed to the ground from an altitude of between thirty to ninety metres. The plane had been flying at low altitude to maintain visual reference to the ground, but the fog was too thick for the pilot to see the mountain. With a full passenger load and nearly full gas tanks, the plane was likely too heavy for him to pull up in time to avoid hitting the mountain or to bank forty metres to the right, which would've saved seven lives.

The Grumman Goose, the same kind of amphibious plane owned by Pacific Coastal Air, that slammed into a hill on Thormanby Island due to thick fog, killing seven people including the pilot, leaving one survivor badly burned. Photo: Greany J. Malcolm

When Tom regained consciousness, he was soaked in avgas and on fire. The Transportation Safety Board of Canada (TSBC) report said he was "thrown clear." The impact and the fire instantly killed the pilot and the other six passengers. Tom found himself "in the middle of nowhere. I had no skin on my hands or face. I held my hands up and stared in horror. The skin on my fingers had popped off as if it was a cooked sausage."[112]

The military's 442 squadron flew from Comox to the crash site, after Pacific Coastal Airlines reported the flight an hour and a half overdue, by following the backup SPOT satellite GPS. The SPOT device burned in the crash, but the data it sent before the crash "helped to narrow the search area and reduce the search time to find the aircraft. The fact that the wrong data were consulted caused an initial delay in reporting the missing aircraft."[113] The airline had initially taken the data from the day before, so it appeared to them that the flight had already arrived at Toba Inlet.

The emergency locator transmitter (ELT) was too badly burned to operate, so it was unable to send a signal for rescuers to track. There had been no time for the pilot to send a Mayday call over the radio.

Tom says that hunters on the island heard the crash and reported it. The intense fire and smoke gave rescuers a clear indication of where to look for survivors.

Sunshine Coast SAR was tasked with guiding the other agencies to the crash site, including BC Parks, the TSBC, the RCMP and the coroner. When SCSAR arrived, they looked at the wreckage, which covered a large area, and didn't think there could be any survivors.

Tom was in excruciating pain from burns on his face, hands, stomach and back. He feared he wouldn't be found, so he made a harrowing trek over cliffs and followed a creek for two and a half hours to the shoreline of South Thormanby Island, hoping for rescue for many hours. "It was the longest four and a half hours of my life," he said.

The Canadian Coast Guard Auxiliary, now RCMSAR Station 12, launched from Halfmoon Bay and found him. They transported him back carefully in their Zodiac. From there he was taken by ambulance on the twenty-kilometre trip to Sechelt Hospital and flown by helicopter to Vancouver General Hospital's burn unit. He was transferred from there to the burn unit at the University of Alberta Hospital, closer to his home in Fort McMurray.

Tom survived what the TSBC deemed an "unsurvivable" crash, but it came at a high price. He spent two weeks in a glass room in isolation. His severe burns made him open to potentially life-threatening infections. He was in hospital for four months.

Peter McLeod was an experienced pilot with over twelve thousand flight hours, approximately eight thousand of them spent flying seaplanes. Despite his impressive number of hours, he was known to take off in less-than-ideal flying conditions, when other pilots would choose to stay on the ground and wait for the weather to clear.[114]

Peter was the only pilot to take off from the Vancouver International Water Aerodrome (CAM9), and it was under a Special VFR (SVFR) clearance. This means he asked permission from the tower for takeoff since the conditions were below the minimum visibility. During his pre-flight briefing, he was told to skip Powell River and go straight to Toba if the visibility remained below the minimum for landing.[115]

The pilot had other choices, such as turning around any time after takeoff when the visibility got worse and going back to CAM9 or landing on the endless runway of the Pacific Ocean to wait out the fog.

Tom doesn't blame the pilot, even though he suffered many hardships as a result of the accident. He says he received no compensation from Pacific Coastal Airlines for his severe physical injuries, loss of income or emotional scars. He suffered from PTSD and developed addictions to cope with the emotional pain in the years that followed. He says the physical healing was the easy part in comparison to the emotional healing. Writing his book was a key part of his healing and recovery.

The TSBC report mentions that the pilot requested Instrument Flight Rules (IFR) training from the airline, who denied his request, stating they were concerned that it would encourage their pilots to fly in minimal visual conditions. The TSBC found that there was pressure placed on the airline and its pilots by Kiewit, their client at Toba Inlet.

The TSBC said that the pilot's pre-flight briefing to the passengers was abnormal. Have you ever heard a pilot come on over the intercom and ask you to decide whether you want to fly that day, as if you were part of the flight crew?

Tom came back to the Sunshine Coast on the sixth anniversary of the crash to thank the Halfmoon Bay crew, SCSAR and the other agencies for saving his life, and to place a yellow cross with the names of the people who lost their lives at the crash site.

Among the people he met with was Richy Till. It was an emotional reunion for Tom. He hugged everyone and wept. The Halfmoon Bay Coast Guard took Tom out to the crash site. Tom spent the entire day afterwards with the rescue teams and had dinner with them. He was told by the rescuers that he was the first person they've rescued who has come back to thank them.

It took Tom eight years before he could talk about the crash, but after he wrote his book, he spent four years as a motivational speaker, talking about the crash all over the world. He feels that the crash was something that he's been able to grow from, and it's made him realize the preciousness of life. "I feel more mortal now than ever," he says.

Richy's absolute joy is to find lost children. "Children lost in the woods receive high priority; the response is faster, and we call in mutual aid right away."

Children present a challenge to searchers, as they tend to hide and stay silent when they are being searched for. Like frightened animals, they find somewhere to squeeze into where they feel safe. Some children will respond to a family "safety word" if the family has one. Searchers have to look in all the nooks and crannies and try to reassure the missing child that they aren't in trouble.

MARK MIRAGLIA—ANCHORAGE, ALASKA

In 1994 Mark Miraglia was invited by a friend to join the Alaska Mountain Rescue Group (AMRG). He says, "I consider myself a rope geek, and it sounded like fun." His background includes mountaineering, glacier travel, ice climbing and rock climbing. His career title is telecommunications facilities maintenance foreman, and he's a union electrician.

Mark is a SAR incident manager. This team responds at the request of the Alaska State Troopers to assist or take over management of multi-day searches anywhere in the state.

Mark has recovered close to two dozen bodies in his SAR career. "It is difficult to deal with, especially when it is someone you know or the body is horribly damaged."

He stresses the importance of being able to remain calm and rely on using his brain. "As Arnor Larson of the British Columbia Council on Technical Rescue used to say, 'A little bit of knowledge is light in the backpack.' Working as part of an incident management team, maintaining a 'cool head' amidst chaos is primary."

CASE 58: PLANE CRASH
YENTNA GLACIER, ALASKA

One recovery operation that was extremely challenging for Mark was an aircraft crash on the Yentna Glacier in June 2000. Well-known and beloved local pilot, author, teacher, Iditarod Trail Sled Dog racer, and rescuer Don Bowers, fifty-two, a native of Fort Smith, Arkansas, was a Vietnam vet who served in the US Airforce. His sister, Ann Bowers Kinder, says that Don flew a Lockheed C-130 Hercules, which is a four-engine turboprop military transport aircraft meant to carry troops and equipment into challenging environments and war zones. C-130s can carry up to 42,000 pounds of cargo, including tanks and helicopters.[116] Ann says that Don's missions involved "hot landings," during which he was being fired upon, and "short landings" into extremely tight landing areas, so he was a highly experienced and capable pilot.

Don went on to fly in the Arctic and wrote a non-fiction book about his experiences, *Flying Your Airplane to (And In) Alaska*. Don also wrote a non-fiction book on his other passion, Iditarod Trail Sled Dog racing, a 1,100-mile gruelling race in Alaska, called *Back of the Pack*.

Don took off from Talkeetna in a Cessna 185E Skywagon owned by Hudson Air Service Inc. and operated by the National Park Service. The six-seater taildragger—meaning the plane lands on the two large front wheels, and the back wheel is small—was built in 1966 and equipped with both skis and wheels. There were three volunteer rangers aboard when they took off at 5:10 p.m. bound for the Kahiltna Glacier base camp, located at a heady elevation of 2,200 metres.

The rangers were going to Denali Mountain to patrol and assist any climbers in need. Denali is the highest mountain peak in North America, with a summit elevation of 6,190 metres. Denali is the third most prominent and third most isolated peak on Earth, after Mount Everest and Aconcagua.

The passengers were Cale Schaffer (twenty-five) of Talkeetna, a mountaineer and EMT, Brian Paul Reagan (twenty-seven) of Anchorage, who worked for the Alaska Natural History Association, and Adam Kolff (twenty-five) from Boulder, Colorado, who had recently returned from Peru, where he worked for a non-profit environmental group. Adam had climbed the Andes, Himalayas, Rockies and the Alaska Range, and he'd also done a 241-kilometre traverse of Mount St. Elias.[117]

The Kahiltna base camp manager reported that Don didn't telephone the base camp prior to takeoff. If he had, he would've been advised not to fly there, since one aircraft was already waiting on the ground due to low clouds. At noon, a few hours prior to the flight, a ranger, who later was one of the passengers in the accident, called her. The manager told the ranger not to bother coming, since the weather had been "up and down" during the day. Whether or not this information was passed along to the pilot wasn't documented.

The base camp manager heard the radio conversations between Don and another pilot flying in the area who, after departing base camp, returned to remain overnight at the camp. The manager said she tried to contact Don over the radio, but he didn't hear her. The ranger radioed the ranger station to report that their flight was returning to Talkeetna. There were no other communications from the airplane.[118]

Missing from the NTSB reports, but reported by *The Anchorage Daily News*, was that ranger Cale Schaffer, who was a passenger on the flight, radioed the Park Service ranger station in Talkeetna to say his group wasn't going to make it to Kahiltna and they were coming back. Don radioed the Kahiltna base camp that he'd lost visibility, but he saw a break in the clouds to the west. His new plan was to fly his way out and turn back to Talkeetna. "He, like the other Talkeetna pilots who ferry climbers and tourists to McKinley all summer, had done this safely hundreds of times. Sometimes it meant working on the edge, but that is what Bowers's earlier career as a US Air Force pilot had trained him to do."[119] Taking off in poor visibility and not properly checking weather reports is what flight instructors would call complacency and dangerous airmanship, if that's indeed what Don did.

Likely, poor visibility disoriented the pilot and wind shears spun the plane around like a weathervane, except that the flaps were lowered to the twenty-degree position. Flaps are located on the back of the wings of the plane, and they work in unison. Before a pilot lands a plane, they gradually lower the flaps. The twenty-degree position is the first flap setting in preparation for landing.

Don may have made a last-minute, desperate decision to do an emergency landing onto the snow. Because the plane was outfitted with skis, it was the safest option at that moment. He was flying the plane blind into the storm and could only hope that he was going to touch down in a safe spot.

As he tried to land the plane, he flew it into a sheer cliff face. The plane split apart and ignited during the crash—burning all aboard. Don died of blunt-force trauma from the impact of the crash.

There was nothing SAR could do for them but recover their remains. "When we arrived, a black bear was circling the aircraft. The heli had to chase the bear away," says Mark. "We found all four bodies still seated in the aircraft and charred. This mission affected me for weeks after. I felt a need to learn the names of the deceased to put my mind at ease. We didn't consider psychological first aid back then like we do now," he says.

The NTSB found that the probable cause of the crash was Don's continued flight into known adverse weather conditions and subsequent inflight breakup. The weather conditions consisted of low cloud ceilings, turbulence and thunderstorms. The NTSB found that the flight was inadequately overseen by the company management.[120]

CASE 59: THREE MISSING HIKERS
BEAR MOUNTAIN, BC

Mark was the contact for a search for three men who had climbed a gully route to the top of Bear Mountain in the winter and went missing near Chugiak. "One was a local who had climbed the route before, and the other two were Wounded Warriors [a non-profit charity that assists veterans in the US and Canada] from Colorado and Florida. Both had summited Denali Mountain. These were experienced climbers, although they had no avalanche transceivers, only ice axes and crampons," he says. The last known contact with the three was at 10:30 p.m. on February 2, 2021.

Alaska Mountain Rescue Group (AMRG) was called out by Alaska State Troopers at 5:10 a.m. on February 3 to search for the hikers—Thomas Devine (fifty-four) of Chugiak; Matthew Nyman (forty-three) of Denver, Colorado; and Edward Watson (fifty) of Miami, Florida.[121]

Mark's SAR group used a software program called D4H for mission management, as do many SAR groups throughout North America. Using the D4H communications portal, the mission control team can email and text members and groups, such as avalanche or technical rescue specialists, giving updates as to the location of the subject, ETAs on equipment or transportation, or other critical information.

Mark's job on this mission was to message field teams from his laptop in town as directed by either the incident commander or the operations section chief. "The only time I'm a hasty-team leader nowadays is on the technical team. I do have the most experience in technical rescue, so that is the role I'm assigned," he says. A hasty team is usually a pair of fast and fit members who arrive first at the search area and do a quick and efficient search to the likely spots where a subject(s) might be found, such as along the trail and other places. A hasty team could be on foot, e-bike, snowmobile, ATV, UTV, or dirtbike, or the K9 teams could be called in first as the hasty team to conduct a preliminary search.

Pings from the hikers' cellphones and Apple watches gave valid GPS coordinates to locate them. Their vehicle was found at a trailhead. Once on scene, hasty teams headed up the gulley, following the GPS coordinates. As they climbed up the gulley, they came upon avalanche debris. They located the first subject buried in snow and deceased. The two other subjects were found buried in snow shortly afterwards and were also deceased. None of the three climbers had avalanche beacons.

An Alaska State Trooper helicopter was used the next day to fly AMRG avalanche advisors and Chugach National Forest Avalanche Information Center personnel to the area near the crown of the avalanche to assess the conditions that had led to the avalanche and prepare the preliminary accident report. The avalanche threat continued, and the public was warned to stay away from the area.

Mark says that when he's in the field as a searcher, "it seems to take forever to be deployed to the field." For example, if a team member is the first on site, they have to wait until a team leader or search manager arrives, and then they can only proceed when the search plan is put together. For an incident manager, the initial information is often "scarce, incorrect or misleading." It can be frustrating waiting for the requesting authority, such as the RCMP or sheriff, to give them the full information about the case.

As the case proceeds, working in the Incident Command Post (ICP), Mark wants more information from the field teams than he typically gets. "The field teams, once they have the subject, are sometimes overwhelmed by the ICP requesting updates continually before the field team has a chance to get that information." Whether he's in the ICP or the field, he finds that people do not use proper radio protocol, compounding miscommunications. "They do not give precise information in a short, concise format," he says. Reminders for "no chatter" can be frequent on a search if there are unnecessary conversations over the radio. Teams should give "please stand by" messages if they are busy with aiding the subject.

Mark enjoys incident management because "you get to see the whole picture, which is pretty cool, whereas in the field you are only aware of a small portion of the mission." There have been times when a village searched for days with no result, and the state troopers requested that the Alaska Incident Management Team (AIMT) SAR group take over. "We have to start from scratch. Typically, these end with no success. But working as part of a well-tuned incident management team is rewarding when you come in and take over a poorly run mission and do have success," he says.

Mark stays in SAR for the comradeship, a sense of giving back to the community, and the enjoyment of teaching technical rope rescue. He's not sure when to retire. "I'm no longer as physically fit at seventy years of age as I was five years ago. I will move to the incident management side."

He hopes that AMRG trains for succession with new, younger members who are able to take over the roles of the senior members as they retire. "We need to build back up after about a year of no personal training due to the COVID pandemic," he says.

In Alaska, the state troopers are responsible for SAR statewide, with the exception of the national parks. "We respond around the state, anywhere except above ten-thousand-foot elevation due to living near sea level and acclimatization issues that could arise on a mission," he explains. They don't get adequate helicopter support for missions, since the single Trooper helicopter in Southcentral Alaska has primarily a law enforcement role. "One time, after being dropped off on a mountain ridge, the Trooper helicopter had to deploy for a law enforcement mission, and we were left having to pack two six-hundred-foot ropes and other gear down the mountain," says Mark.

Funding is an issue that Mark doesn't see changing. "I've been with AMRG for twenty-six years, and it has always been a bit of a struggle."

He'd like the public to "be prepared for your endeavour, know your limitations, leave a trip plan, [and] realize [that] your accident might put others at risk and that help might not arrive as soon as you would like."

12. Ropes

The families of SAR members are the real heroes.
—Alan Hobbler

JAMES SEELEY—SOUTH CARIBOO, BC

James Seeley is one of the two remaining founding members of the South Cariboo SAR (SCSAR). He is SCSAR's search manager and has other certifications. SCSAR began twenty years ago, when it was recognized that the South Cariboo didn't have a registered SAR team. All requests for assistance were being handled by volunteers who had no certified training or leadership. A request went out through the local media to organize and form a SAR team based in 100 Mile House. At the beginning of 2001, a group of interested volunteers was selected and formal training began.

When James joined the original SAR team, he was a firefighter with Vancouver Fire Rescue Services. He's always been interested in SAR. "Growing up in North Vancouver, I hiked the mountains, fished the rivers and became aware of the need for trained people to respond to wilderness rescue incidents."

"Within the fire service, I was a high-angle rope rescue team member, haz-mat, fire boat operator and auto extrication [specialist], skills which all enhanced my rescue knowledge and technical abilities," James says.

James relocated to 108 Mile Ranch, preparing for retirement, and he commuted to Vancouver for work, four days on and four days off. When he moved to the Cariboo, he spent a great deal of time training local volunteer firefighters in the Medical First Responder program. This led to his desire to become a more dedicated volunteer in his local communities.

With all his background in personal wilderness recreational activities, including alpine skiing, ocean kayaking and remote area fishing, combined with his rope rescue skills and his medical training as a firefighter, James soon became an organizer and team leader within the SAR team. "After five years of commuting back and forth, I was

Rope Technician certification for SAR members takes two courses, Rope Technician I and II, with twenty hours of supervised practice, two weekends of training, and a knowledge test, which requires studying a 250-page manual for each course. All Canada Photos 49287

offered a chance to work part-time for British Columbia Ambulance Service in 100 Mile House, and since I was already instructing WCB first aid part-time for Thompson Rivers University in 100 Mile House, I resigned as a firefighter after thirty years [and] dedicated myself to working and training within the local community."

The annual number of call-outs SCSAR attends is between fifteen and twenty. The area they cover is vast, remote and extremely technical. Most of the people who venture out are well-prepared and experienced, only requiring help when things go very wrong. "We train for two to three hours each Wednesday night all year and also spend the odd day on a weekend doing rope, swiftwater or first aid," he says.

The "rescue" side of things is where his interest lies, due to his firefighting and paramedic careers, so once a subject is found, the question is how they should get them back to safety. He easily spends three to four hundred hours a year volunteering with the call-outs and training.

One of their SAR members designed and fabricated what they call a litter wheel, which is a heavy-duty rubber all-terrain wheel built into a steel frame that fits underneath any of their basket stretchers. This allows SAR members to walk alongside and wheel the injured subject to safety, instead of having to carry them manually. "Imagine the difference in carrying a 250-pound [113-kilogram] load versus just balancing, pushing and pulling the load. The overall ergonomics of this activity-saving device makes it my favourite single piece of SAR equipment," James says.

Case 60: Canine Rescue
Hendrix Creek Falls, BC

James was enjoying a round of golf with his sister and brother-in-law on a cloudless sunny day on the afternoon of July 5, 2007, when he got a call-out.

"She's stuck where?" he says he replied to the local area SAR manager, who then repeated: "The dog fell over the cliff at the Hendrix Creek waterfalls and is stuck down the canyon."

When James arrived at Hendrix Falls, he found the pitiful pooch, Sheila, a female black Lab, perilously perched on a narrow ledge. James peered over the thirty-metre precipice into the rugged canyon below. He knew this was going to be no ordinary rescue.

One of the team members came over to him and, in a low voice, asked, "Bitten off more than we can chew?"

James replied, "Nah, nothing to it." But that was "not exactly what my stomach was telling me."[122]

Sheila had been on the ledge for about six hours without water in the oppressive heat. Her owner had no idea how she'd fallen, as she was off leash at the time.[123]

James and his buddy planned to go down to the dog, rig a web harness and haul her up. The rope lines were rated for a load of four-thousand-plus pounds. The harness, the carabiners and the webbing for the anchors were rated for technical loads of several thousand pounds. "But when you're going to hang your ass over a hundred feet [thirty metres] of vertical descent, that rope doesn't look very thick, and the stitching on the harness looks awfully suspect," says James.

> With a brave face, but serious pucker factor, my partner looked at me and gave me the nod: "Well, I guess you have to trust the equipment."
>
> "You nervous?" I asked.
>
> "Oh, yeah."
>
> "Well, how scared do you think that poor dog is right now?"
>
> "Guess we better get going, eh?"
>
> "You first."
>
> Over the edge and down approximately thirty feet, we descended to the dog ... She was perched on a three-foot-wide sloping ledge about four feet long and had managed to cling to this for hours, waiting for help. Sixty feet below, the water coursed through the rugged canyon, upstream three hundred feet away, the waterfalls roared in our ears.
>
> Trev held the dog's collar while I rigged a web harness for the trembling canine. After clipping the dog to my harness and the haul line ... we started our ascent, slowly, the poor dog limp with fear in my arms, bit by bit and finally over the edge at the top.
>
> The owner was in tears, our team struggling with their emotions as well.[124]

The local RCMP gave the team an award for rescuing Sheila. It made their whole team feel great and really gave them strong motivation to further develop their specialty teams. They prefer that people do what that dog's owner did and call for help, rather than trying to rescue their pets themselves in such a dangerous situation—a leash wouldn't hurt either.

James's greatest personal gains within BCSAR are the lasting friendships and the respect that he has within his team. The fact that he helped to organize and develop an excellent group of volunteers is a proud memory for him. "I will continue to assist in whatever manner that I can; however, age is starting to be a factor. The main reason I continue is to be a mentor and assist in team member development," he says.

"I really like the concept of the financing program that BCSARA is working on," he says. "A steady budget for training is going to be the biggest help to all teams across the province."

James feels that SAR teams across the province need dedicated financial aid, because a lot of teams need help establishing a building for training and equipment storage, vehicles for SAR responses, specialty equipment, personal gear and more.

He says, "Currently, we get an income tax break from the federal government, a pittance—really, it's an insult, considering the time and effort we all go through to certify and maintain our specialty training, such as swiftwater, rope rescue and avalanche response." Members must log at least two hundred volunteer hours per year to quality for the income tax benefit.

There are a lot of personal expenses for any SAR volunteer, like the cost of good PPE and associated gear, especially during the pandemic. Then there's the time and expense of travel for certifications and training, as well as the loss of wages or vacation time of missing paid work.

James hopes the public sees and hears about SAR services across the province and learns one simple rule, the Boy Scout motto: Be Prepared. He warns that when venturing into the vast recreational wilderness, you need to prepare for weather, the terrain and the unexpected. He says, "Know your limits and leave a trip plan with someone. Things [can] go wrong really quick on even the simplest outing. Educate yourself and be ready to help yourself, because up here in our area, like most of the province, SAR response is going to take a while, due to travel and terrain."

ALAN HOBLER—KAMLOOPS, BC

Alan Hobler is a single dad of a young son and caretaker to his mother, who has Alzheimer's. He works for BC Parks in the Thompson region and has a passion for working in remote areas of the province. He's served for ten years at Kamloops Search and Rescue (KSAR) and is one of only ten level-II SAR managers in the province, so he often gets pulled into searches from all over the province. He is certified for swiftwater rescues, and he used to participate in salmon counts with the Department of Fisheries and Oceans.

Alan says he was on a first date when he got a SAR call-out for a car that had gone over a cliff, and it involved a fatality. His date went with him, waiting in the car until five in the morning. She later became his wife.

After a while, though, she began to resent the calls that pulled him away and the fact that he carried the burden of what happened on calls when he came home. He also had SAR training and executive meetings to attend. "Indirectly, SAR had a bearing on the breakup," he says. However, he now has a new partner who is accepting of his relationship with BCSAR.

Alan says the helicopter is probably the most versatile equipment they have access to. Helicopters can do quick searches of difficult, high-probability areas, give quick transport of SAR crews and transport patients. However, he finds helicopters limited in advanced search techniques. "Bringing in air SAR who are trained in air searches and have trained spotters is more effective. There are specialized helicopters like the HETS and Vernon heli-winch that make difficult extractions easy," he says.

Kamloops SAR is one of the first teams in BC to use unmanned aerial vehicles (UAV), commonly known as drones. They use advanced drone technology for wildfires, and they realized there might be an application for SAR. "We have been using them ever since," Alan says. They can do high-definition imaging, similar to Google Earth but in real time and in much higher definition. "This allows us in command to plan our searches with much better mapping and ground information than using just maps or older satellite imagery," he explains. UAVs can fly at night when helicopters can't. Used with a FLIR (forward-looking infrared) camera, a drone can be effective for searching high-hazard areas at night, such as avalanche terrain or lakes with thin ice. "We have had success using them exactly like that," says Alan.

There are other pieces of equipment that are critically useful. GPS has revolutionized SAR management. They can now map exactly where teams have gone in the field to exactly where they are expected to be. "In the past it was very hit and miss. When we started using GPS tracks, we realized how off some teams were, causing gaps in coverage and search areas. Areas we thought were searched well would have areas completely missed," says Alan.

Case 61: MVA—High Bar, BC

The most spectacular and terrifying rescue Alan has ever seen happened at High Bar on April 6, 2014, at three in the morning. Excessive speed was a factor in the accident. A call came in for a rescue for a one-ton Dodge truck that missed a hairpin curve and drove off a cliff. Two people were in the cab and five were ejected from the back of the truck, including one in a wheelbarrow. People ejected from the back of the truck walked to a house, where they called for help. Alan was the manager of the SAR rope team when the page came around five in the morning.

The situation was so urgent, with the truck teetering 152 metres over the cliff edge on an outcropping, that the air ambulance en route to the site wanted to land on the road and pick up the SAR rope team and fly them to the scene. The rope team decided to drive there together, though, as they would need all their members for this rescue.

When Alan and his team got there, the fire department, RCMP, air ambulances and police were waiting for them. They looked to the rope team like they were going to solve this most urgent problem. The most relieved was a BC Ambulance paramedic who had spent hours in darkness calming the two subjects that had gone over the cliff. (The paramedic later suffered PTSD from the extreme stress of the call, and that was a contributing factor in his suicide a month later.)

The man had been ejected from the truck and was clinging to life. The woman was inside the rocking truck, which could fall to the bottom of the cliff at any moment. Alan was surprised that they were still alive.

The team divided into two, with one team setting up the ropes and the other deflecting the rocks that came loose to prevent them from hitting the subjects and the rescuers. It took several hours to bring both subjects, in their early twenties, up from the cliff on stretchers. It was Alan's proudest moment of his rope team when they pulled the subjects to safety. The young woman lost her leg from the accident, but considering the alternative, she was fortunate to have the KSAR rope team at the ready. For Alan and his team, it was a twelve-hour call-out.

> Solo subjects account for 67 percent of incidents. A group of two accounts for 19 percent of incidents.
>
> Solo subjects have a higher fatality rate than groups.[125]

Alan finds SAR thrilling, especially when it comes to putting all the pieces of the puzzle together. "I love the good calls and bad calls. You wear those bad calls. Reality sets in. It's not a hobby, because someone's life depends on you. If I didn't get out of bed when the call comes and answer that phone, the outcome would be different."

He finds new technology helpful, such as when KSAR was chosen for a pilot drone project for BCSAR in 2017. One of their many successful finds with the drone was for a group of seven out-of-bounds skiers and snowboarders at Sun Peaks ski resort. Alan knew an area where thrill-seekers tend to get lost, so he started the search there. The fact that the surroundings were cold and the subjects moved to keep warm made it easier for the thermal cam mounted on the drone to find the subjects. However, if it had been summer, perhaps Alan would've called in a helicopter or a spotter plane to search the area.[126] He would love to get his hands on a submarine drone for some searches they have to perform under bridges.

> Snowboarders are well-dressed for the conditions, carry food and water, tend to be in good shape and 26 percent will self-rescue. When they get lost, it's because of a wrong turn, missing trails, whiteouts, blizzards, darkness, getting separated from their group.[127]

From a prevention point of view, Alan has one thing he wants to say to the public—"wear a PFD when you are out on the water." He says that 80 percent of drowning deaths are preventable, if people would just wear their life jackets and make sure their kids do as well. "Hearing a mother scream when her kid gets pulled out dead, I've heard that scream enough times."

13. Swiftwater

There were moments of tears, hugs, anger, and genuine em-
pathy all while tied together and anchored on a log that was
jammed into the canyon walls. Those are the moments that
although the outcome is unfortunate, it is why I am a member
of SAR and will continue. —Adam Laurie

Nick Rivers—Parksville, BC

On December 14, 2020, Nick Rivers of Arrowsmith Search and Rescue (ASAR) captured the attention of the nation when he rescued a man from certain death at Little Qualicum River on Vancouver Island. The man had fallen into the rushing river between two waterfalls, and he was clinging to a log. He was only four to five metres above a waterfall and was in danger of being swept over.

Nick harnessed up and was lowered on a rope twenty-six metres down into the roiling water, upstream of the subject. On his first attempt, Nick missed the man and ended up downstream of him. The man couldn't hold on to the log anymore and let go. Nick used all his swiftwater skills and strength and, guided by the team above to a more sheltered area close to the cliffside, was able to catch the man as he was swept downstream, got a harness on him, and dragged him to the river's edge. Thirty SAR members on the cliff pulled them both to safety, and the man was rushed to hospital to be treated for hypothermia, which was so severe that he was unable to speak. Nick was so exhausted that he had to be carried as well.[128] Nick said that it was the most technical rescue he's ever done.

Arrowsmith SAR has fifty-two members, and they get about fifty-eight call-outs a year—a number that Nick says is increasing as more people take to the outdoors.

Nick joined ASAR in 2010, straight out of high school, and he joined the board the next year. He was president of ASAR until 2020, then became the vice-president and training officer in 2021. His certifications include team leader, swiftwater technician, level-two rope

Swiftwater Search and Rescue has had the most fatalities among SAR incidents; however, there is such a high level of safety measures and risk assessments applied, fatal incidents are rare. When any kind of SAR member injury or death occurs during a mission, an inquiry takes place and rules and practices are reassessed to make operations safer. All Canada Photos JH6B6C

rescue, level-two search manager, Project Lifesaver instructor, public safety lifeline leadership, code-three driver instructor, and lost-person-behaviour instructor. He puts in over twelve hundred volunteer hours per year with ASAR.

Nick runs an auto and marine repair and fabrication company, and he has a family business, Brigadoon Golf Course, in Parksville. He says he has no time for a personal life.

Case 62: Driver Trapped in Car
Lantzville, BC

Before the Little Qualicum Falls incident, Nick says the most technical rescue that he was ever involved in was rescuing a woman, Karena Donnelly, when her car was swallowed up by a sinkhole. During the night of January 28, 2018, Karena was driving home in pouring rain when the road ahead suddenly washed out. Her car fell twenty metres down a muddy slope, rolling as it went, landing upside down and trapping her inside. The car filled up with water. Karena used her cellphone and called her friend for help.[129]

Nick came by boat from another call-out related to the flood. "Every fire truck and police car [was] there," says Nick. The rest of the road was in danger of caving in on top of Karena's car at any minute. "I always end up in the hot seat," jokes Nick. He harnessed up and rappelled into the dark, clambering over rocks, avoiding falling debris.

He reached the car and was afraid the rocks would tumble down and bury them alive. Karena thrust her hand out of the car, holding her cellphone. Nick tucked the phone in a pocket before pulling her out of the back window. Karena wore a dress and high-heeled shoes—not the kind of attire appropriate for scrambling over rocks and roots, so he carried her to the ropes, harnessed her in, and she was pulled to safety.

By the next day, forty-five more metres of the road had fallen away. Karena's car was buried under nine metres of rubble.

Case 63: Hiker in Crevasse
Little Mountain, BC

This time Nick found himself not in churning water but in a tight crevasse, extracting a badly injured man wedged in between the rocks on October 8, 2020. The man had fallen into the deep crevasse the night before while hiking Little Mountain on Vancouver Island. He broke both of his legs in the fall.[130]

In the morning, a group of hikers heard him calling for help. Nick says that at just half a metre wide, the crevasse was too narrow for their standard stretcher, and there was just room for himself and another rescuer. They turned a stretcher vertically above the patient and tied ropes around him to lift him out. He was airlifted to hospital.

Nick is extremely proud of the new hall that ASAR is building. ASAR started in 1956, and this will be their first hall. They fundraised $890,000 of the $1,300,000 construction costs. The rest of the building costs were funded by a twenty-five-year mortgage from a local credit union.

Adam Laurie—Chilliwack, BC

Adam Laurie, call sign Chilliwack 50, became a member of Chilliwack SAR (CSAR) in 1999. When he had some time to devote to volunteering, he looked at something within emergency services, like the fire department. He's always been interested in adventure, survival, technical rescue and anything to do with water—"the faster moving, the better." He volunteered at Manning Park with the ski patrol, and he was looking for another volunteer organization that would encompass all his interests. It was his wife, Sandi, who suggested they go to the open house that CSAR hosted. She too toyed with the idea of applying to the group. When they got to the event, Adam took one look at the whitewater rescue raft, learned about their swiftwater team and was hooked.

Adam had lived in California for several years as a child, and that's where his addiction to water sports started—"from playing in the ocean at Pebble Beach to the rivers in Kings Canyon to sitting in my first kayak." He says, "I have one of the greatest careers in the world, being a swiftwater rescue instructor."

The couple applied to CSAR, but then they learned they were going to have a baby. Adam was accepted into CSAR, but Sandi's turn would have to wait. Adam was balancing a job in construction with being a new father and a new member of Ground SAR, all at the same time.

He was told early in his SAR career that SAR always comes last, after your family and your work. But Adam admits, "Although times and call volumes have changed over my twenty-one years, it was and continues to be a challenge to balance the time and commitment that SAR requires." His daughter, who is in her twenties, was actually involved in his SAR activities; she played a "subject" in practice rescues throughout her childhood. She graduated with a diploma in the recreation, fish and wildlife program at Selkirk College in Castlegar, BC.

SAR led to an early important career change for Adam. "One of my SAR teammates was a paramedic and suggested that I apply to the BC Ambulance Service. This led to a nineteen-year career as a paramedic, which I just retired from in 2020."

Adam's new career is director of operations with Rescue Canada, a training, equipment and rescue service provider. Their clients are emergency services, government agencies, occupational and resource management contractors, adventure guide university programs and the general public. Adam instructs all levels, including some specialty swiftwater courses as well as rope rescue, helicopter safety and rescue, raft and boat courses. He also teaches for the Justice Institute of BC as a paramedic instructor and GSAR team leader.

Within CSAR, he is the team leader and oversees the training for swiftwater. His other roles are rope rescue team member, organized avalanche response team leader, Sea-Doo operator, medic and SAR manager.

He started as a rookie in swiftwater and is now a leading expert who teaches and works with many SAR teams across the province, as well as the RCMP Underwater Recovery Team. "It opened the doors to new friendships, as the river is a place where bonds are forged like steel—they last forever, regardless of the places we go or changes we make," Adam says. He will soon be moving to Manning Park and changing SAR groups.

Adam also works as a raft guide, and he loves to play recreationally in the rivers. The water is a major source for his personal growth. "The river has a way of just draining all the 'bad' and replacing it with a Zen state," he says.

Adam says the greatest challenge facing many SAR members, especially in smaller groups, is that they wear so many hats that it's difficult for them to maintain currency in each area. Each specialty—for example, swiftwater rescue—takes twenty hours of training to stay current. He sees that changing in the future, when there will be smaller, more specialized groups within SAR organizations.

Another challenge he mentions is that members always have their rescue hat on. Even when he's not on a SAR call, Adam says it's hard to turn off the instinct to jump in and assist. He's often been at the Chilliwack River, seen tubers get into trouble and gone to their rescue. He says there was once a woman stranded on a gravel bar who had a look of despair. He threw on his PFD and swam over. She told him, "I think I am stuck, and I don't know what to do." After a brief conversation, she hopped back in her tube, and with her paddling, Adam towed her back across the river to the trail side.

When hiking the Chief in Squamish about a year ago, Adam and his wife noticed two frightened hikers holding onto the rock and asked if they were okay. They said, "This is the first hike we have ever done; we never leave the city."

Adam and his wife helped them off the top of the Chief by placing one foot in front of the other for them until they got them down off the face and back down into the trees. "I think all members are ready to jump in when needed. It is just what we do." SAR is why Adam has the career and lifestyle he has. "I can't thank the team and organization enough for the investment.

His favourite SAR equipment is his swiftwater kit, which includes his dry suit, PFD, helmet, water shoes and throw bag. "The gear has given me the ability to test my own perseverance and resilience when faced with stressful and high-risk situations," says Adam.

Case 64: Family in ATV Accident
Foley Lake, BC

On May 4, 2020, a couple took their three children in a side-by-side ATV to Foley Lake for a fun off-road trip. They wore the mandatory helmets and seat belts. As they drove down the Foley Creek Forest Service Road, the ATV wheels hit slippery mud, and it rolled down a fifteen-metre embankment and landed in five metres of water.[131]

The parents and one child escaped and crawled up onto the embankment. Bystander Joy Pringle bravely jumped into the water and tried to reach the other two children, a nine-year-old girl and a ten-year-old boy, who were still strapped into the sunken ATV.

Joy who was camping nearby at the time, put her own life at risk by diving down several times, trying to reach the children. She was unable to get farther down than the wheels of the car. Joy's friend, Hannah Reinholt, wrapped up the survivors, keeping them warm before they were taken by the SAR boat to a helicopter and then to hospital.[132] Adam, along with his SAR team and divers, recovered the bodies of the drowned children.

Adam went through a tough few months after that call and was diagnosed with PTSD. He feels that without his teammates and the SAR organization's support, he wouldn't have recovered. "My psychologist was next level, and the results were mind-blowing. Through my sessions, I learned so much about my mental health, how I respond, and I now have an even stronger resiliency plan," he says. Adam has a plan to follow after every SAR call, and he wishes every SAR member did as well. He thinks the debriefing that is incorporated at the conclusion of every call is important.

CASE 65: DRIVER MISSING
CHEHALIS LAKE, BC

- 50 percent of searches are over within three hours and ten minutes.
- 81 percent of searches are over within the first twelve operational hours.
- 93 percent of searches are over within the first day.
- The average search is sixteen hours long.
- 8 percent of searches go beyond a day; in these searches, the subject is often truly in peril.
- Time negatively correlates with survival.[133]

Over the Canada Day long weekend (July 1 to 4) in 2016, twenty-six searchers from the Kent Harrison SAR, Chilliwack SAR, Mission SAR, Central Fraser Valley SAR and the local RCMP searched everywhere—ground, shoreline and air—for a missing male. His disappearance started when he was camped with his friends and family about thirty kilometres along the Chehalis Forest Service Road. He and a friend left to get firewood on July 1, but their car broke down three kilometres away from the campsite. His friend went back to camp to get another car. When he came back, the subject was missing.[134]

The search included areas of the lake that flows into the Chehalis River and the Chehalis Canyon. The canyon is so treacherous, with its forty-six-metre walls, that it could only be covered by helicopter or by walking along the top of the canyon and peering down.

On July 4, the subject was spotted by his girlfriend and a male friend at the water's edge at the bottom of the canyon. They tried to climb down to him. The girlfriend fell, was injured and got trapped on the canyon wall about fifteen metres above the river. The male friend successfully hiked down without injury, but he was stranded on the opposite side of the water.

Along with other members from Chilliwack SAR, Adam travelled up to the site and planned the rescue and recovery of the subjects. Adam and two other swiftwater members were flown into the canyon and did a hover exit onto extremely tight quarters. Once on the ground, they climbed up the canyon, located the male friend and confirmed that he was okay and in a safe location. They continued up the canyon and found the deceased subject.

They couldn't see where the girlfriend was from their location, but other SAR members had voice contact with her from the top of the canyon. They removed the deceased subject from the water and placed him in a body bag before moving upriver. Adam swam the deceased man down the river to the staging area. The helicopter was waiting and completed the recovery.

They ascended back up the canyon and left one member with the male subject. Adam and another member climbed up the canyon wall to assist the girlfriend. They requested that a second helicopter return to Chilliwack Airport to pick up CSAR's three-metre inflatable whitewater raft. They knew this would be the best way to remove the girlfriend out of the river canyon.

After a quick assessment, they determined that she only had minor injuries and was quite cold. The next hour was one that Adam will never forget. He was thankful for his years as a paramedic, as he knew that as soon as he reached her, she would ask about her boyfriend.

With the news that her boyfriend was dead, she began to grieve. They were over fifteen metres up the canyon wall on a cliff, so it posed some challenges. "There were moments of tears, hugs, anger and genuine empathy, all while [we were] tied together and anchored on a log that was jammed into the canyon wall. Those are the moments that, although the outcome is unfortunate, it is why I am a member of SAR and will continue," says Adam.

The human connection and bond, regardless of the outcome of the task, is what Adam thinks all SAR members seek. "After about an hour of consoling, listening and talking with the girlfriend, the other two members arrived with the raft," he explains.

Adam lowered the girlfriend down to the other members with an improvised rope rigging, and then he rappelled to the canyon floor. They all climbed into the raft and travelled the short distance down the canyon to the helicopter staging area. The weather was rapidly deteriorating, and they were losing light. They did a hot load into the helicopter and quickly flew out of the canyon to the main staging area and ambulance. A hot load means that the pilot didn't turn off the engine of the helicopter. Usually, the engine is turned off for safety reasons.

"The grip that the subject had on me the entire time, from the raft to the helicopter and in flight, will stick with me forever. Probably her worst day, but in my mind one of the most successful responses I had ever been on," says Adam.

CASE 66: DRIVER MISSING MVA
MANNING PARK, BC

On February 28, 2017, Pat Gaudet went missing in his semi-truck and trailer, which was fully loaded with wood chips. It took two days of searching to find him. Hope SAR (HSAR) found him by pinging Pat's cellphone repeatedly.[135] He was trapped in his truck, which was suspended perilously from where it had plunged over thirty metres down the embankment on the hill at Rhododendron Flats on Highway 3.

Once they had found Pat, the question was how would they get him out? The thirty members of HSAR needed Chilliwack SAR to conduct the rope rescue. Other agencies assisted, including police, ambulance, tow truck contractors, other SAR groups and a mechanic.

CSAR mustered at their base and drove forty-five minutes to the scene. Paramedics were already there when they arrived, but due to the risk, they couldn't get to Pat. Adam and his team built a rope system, then he and two other members made their way down the embankment. The truck was held in place by tow vehicles. HSAR was opening the cab with the Jaws of Life. The only way they were going to be able to get Pat out was through the bottom of the truck.

When Adam got to Pat, he did a quick assessment. He had been hanging upside down, pinned by the steering wheel, for two days in snowy weather. (Adam appears in a video debrief of the dramatic rescue, which shows the enormous effort and scale of the rescue.)[136]

After climbing back up to consult with the paramedics, Adam administered as much treatment as possible, including warming, medications and fluids, while the complex extrication was carried out. Adam says it was one of the most difficult extrications he'd ever been a part of, even though when he was a paramedic, he had seen his share of trapped subjects in cars, semis and recreational vehicles. "I kept trying to talk to the patient and keep his spirits up. These connections stick with you. I think sometimes I am the lucky one that gets to meet these people when they are at their worst and attempt to provide a calming presence," he says.

The crews did an amazing job of removing the vehicle from all around the subject part by part—the dash, the seat, the back of the cab; however, he was still trapped. They lifted and rotated the cab to give the crews better access, but it took the removal of the transmission, which weighed over 225 kilograms, to get the final crumpled pieces removed to get him free.

It took over ten hours to get Pat out of the wreckage and onto a stretcher for the rope rescuers to ready him for the pull up the embankment. All the crews on scene assisted in pulling him up the slope and getting him into the back of the ambulance. It was a physically and emotionally draining call and a very slow decompression of the task on the drive back to Chilliwack. Pat was still alive when they got him to the ambulance, but he passed away from his injuries in hospital several days later.

As you can see by the kind of rescues Adam has assisted on, where he's had to use every skill and tool at his disposal, not only has SAR guided him in his overall career path, but also, he's developed exceptionally close friendships and a "brotherhood" that will last his lifetime. For him, SAR was a calling. Adam believes he will probably be involved in SAR for as long as he can, as it is so integral to his lifestyle. "When exploring and having adventures in the backcountry with my wife, it is a huge advantage to have SAR skills, experience and knowledge," he says.

Adam confesses that even SAR has mishaps, despite their experience and training. In his early SAR years, he was once dropped by helicopter up a creek to search for a missing person. After a few hours of shoreline searching, his team headed back to their vehicle, but they were unable to find it. "Yes, SAR gets lost too! With the help of the helicopter and using our compass skills, we discovered that our actual location was very different from what our command and we had thought," Adam admits. A few more kilometres of bushwhacking through six-foot-high stinging nettles and a few hundred metres of elevation gain and they made it back.

He attributes his success and every SAR member's success to the support of family back at home. "I can only imagine what goes through my wife's mind when she only knows I am 'on a call' but has no idea what I am doing, the seriousness or risk of it, and the potential mental impact. I personally could not do what I do without her!" he says.

14. Still Missing

When they said, "We'll see you," it sounded like they pronounced a death sentence on my child. They said goodbye, then everyone was gone. —Heather Shtuko

CASE 67: MALE MISSING
SUN PEAKS, BC

Heather Shtuko is a mother of three. She has two daughters—one is sixteen and the other is twenty-one—and a son, Ryan, who went missing four years ago. The lovely blonde woman spoke with me by video from her cozy home in Alberta during the Christmas holidays in 2020. She said that she doesn't know the pain of having a child die, because she's the mother of a missing child. While she is resigned that after thousands of hours put in by volunteers, he might not be found at all, she still "hasn't got to the point of grieving for Ryan." She feels caught between letting go and having hope.

On Saturday, February 17, 2018, Ryan went missing after two that morning when he left a house party alone to walk the short distance to where he was living at the ski resort.

There were gusty winds and blowing snow that night. The avalanche risk was moderate below the treeline and considerable at the treeline and alpine levels. The Arctic wind blew away the cloud cover overnight, and the temperature of minus ten Celsius dropped to a bone-chilling minus twenty-two by Sunday morning.[137]

Heather and her husband, Scott, got the call that every parent dreads, telling them that Ryan was missing. They drove from Alberta and arrived at Sun Peaks around 9:30 on Saturday night. When they pulled in, they saw that the RCMP were there with their dog units, and SAR was there too. In fact, twenty-three members of Kamloops SAR and other SAR groups were assembled for the search.[138]

On Sunday morning, Heather saw the SAR base camp set up and expected that the search would continue until their son was found. However, an RCMP officer and SAR manager Alan Mole came to their hotel room later that day. Heather and Scott were squeezed in

A red ribbon represents missing or murdered Indigenous women and girls, such as those who disappeared along the Highway of Tears. All Canada Photos 2H5PKJM

their room with five friends who had driven from Alberta to join them. She describes the shock of the situation:

> They told us they didn't find him. Alan was devastated. He had children too. I could see he was pained. They said they did all the tasks they could, and until there was something new or a change in the environment, there was nothing more that they could do, given the outside temperature.
>
> The worst was when I was told Ryan could have got locked into an outbuilding, unable to get out. When they said, "We'll see you," it sounded like they pronounced a death sentence on my child. They said goodbye, then everyone was gone.
>
> Monday the nineteenth came, and there was no one searching for my son. My friends became my search party.

Heather appreciated Alan's honesty as the SAR manager, but there was no time to mentally prepare. "It was a little jarring. We were in shock and paralyzing grief. In those moments when they said they were not going to come back until a new lead or weather change, we didn't fully understand. We didn't know until the next day that we would be on our own," she says.

The first seventeen to twenty-four hours are the most critical in a rescue, because the odds of finding the subject alive drop steeply after that time period. After fifty-one hours, there's a moderate probability of finding the subject alive, but after a hundred hours, there's almost no likelihood of finding the subject alive in the wilderness.[139]

A bulletin was put out by the RCMP with Ryan's details. BCSAR came back a week later to search again, but there was still no result.

Two busloads of volunteer searchers came from Alberta to help. Scott looked through every snowdrift in the town with a bobcat for ten hours a day for a month and half, searching for Ryan's body or any evidence related to his son's disappearance. He found nothing.

Their search continued every day from February 19 to June 17, 2018. They paid all the expenses to bring in avalanche dogs and handlers from the Canadian Search and Disaster Dogs Association and then Canadian Avalanche Rescue Dog Association to search for Ryan. They wanted to bring in an Alberta SAR group at their own expense as well, but EMBC was unwilling to allow an interprovincial search. In April, they brought another busload of Alberta volunteers to search.

On April 7, 2018, ten KSAR members returned to Sun Peaks to search the area after they got a tip from an employee at a bar working the coat check, who believed they'd seen Ryan. Unfortunately, still no trace of him was found.[140] On May 11, 2018, thirty-six KSAR members assisted again with additional searches.[141]

After June 2018, Heather and her husband went home, but they continued to return every month, spending four or five days at a time searching. With COVID restrictions, it was difficult for them to return as frequently.

Heather believes that Ryan is at Sun Peaks. Three scenarios of what might have happened to him have been presented to her by the authorities:

1. He wandered away—the best of the worst-case scenarios and the one that she believes in her gut that happened.
2. He overdosed on party drugs.
3. He was hit by a drunk driver.

Perhaps, a combination of these three scenarios happened, but there's been no physical evidence found to prove any of the above—no blood, no hair, no clothing, no tire tracks or vehicles with dented bumpers; nothing at all has been found.

Heather is positive, in that intuitive way only mothers possess, that they will get closure on what happened to their son. She also feels at peace that they have explored every possible avenue they could to find him.

She is grateful for all the effort that BCSAR and the SAR groups and individual volunteers have put into the search for Ryan. "We as a family were so very grateful for the call to action that all of them took to help find our son. We used donations and free accommodations donated to us to help offset any costs," says Heather. However, she wonders why they only spent one day searching for Ryan in the critical period when he first went missing, when searches for other missing people last longer.

Heather wants to make it clear that she doesn't begrudge any family who receives an initial search that goes longer than Ryan's did.

For illustration purposes only, she mentions Ben Tyner, who went missing in the Merritt area the following January. BCSAR searched for Ben for a week following his disappearance. However, Ben was last seen two days before it was known that he was missing, so it was possible that he had already been missing within that critical window of twenty-four to forty-eight hours before the search even began.

HEATHER'S PURPOSE

Heather says that after the official search was over, she didn't know what to do, and there was no one to tell her what to do next to keep searching for Ryan, so she learned everything herself. She wants parents and the loved ones of missing children to consider her as a resource.

> *My purpose is to help other parents who have lost a child.*
> —*Heather Shtuko*

She and other parents and family members of missing children and loved ones started a non-profit group called the Free Bird Project. They reach out if assistance or support is needed. "I absolutely will assist any family going through this type of tragedy. But I am humble enough to know that I am only one person," says Heather.

Wings of Mercy is a resource that uses drones to help look for lost people after the publicly funded organizations suspend a search. The drones can even look for degradation of colours as people age. "Ryan's hat was red, so they adjusted the camera to look for a red hat that has been outside for a long time," she explains.

Heather also wants people to know about the Canadian Benefit for Parents of Young Victims of Crime for parents of missing children under twenty-five to assist them financially while they look for their children. The benefit provides parents with payments of $450 per week for a maximum of thirty-five weeks over two years.

Social media has been a fantastic tool for Heather for podcasts, to coordinate other resources for searches, and to receive supportive messages that bolster her family's spirits. However, social media can be a double-edged sword, she warns, as she also receives negative comments and judgements.

Ryan's case gives a glimpse into how confusing and frustrating it must be for families of missing persons to navigate their way through both public and private SAR resources. It's concerning that there are groups and individuals that may not be properly trained and certified who mean well but can interfere with the proper authorities when they show up to search with equipment and dogs. Untrained or improperly trained volunteers can destroy important evidence and put themselves and other searchers or bystanders at risk. There are also private groups that prey on families and charge them a considerable amount for their search and rescue services.

All Heather wants to hear is, "We found him." There is a fifteen-thousand-dollar reward for information leading to finding Ryan.

Case 68: Rider Missing
Merritt, BC

Ben Tyner of Wyoming was reported missing on January 28, 2019, in the Nicola Valley, when his horse was found wandering on a logging road near Highway 97. Ben, who was working as the manager of Nicola Ranch, was last seen two days earlier.

The weather from January 28 to January 30 was mild for winter in that area, hovering around zero to two degrees Celsius. By Friday, February 1, the high was up to six degrees during the day, with a low of plus three. In a terrain of flat, rolling hills, there wasn't the threat of avalanches that is present at ski resorts or in mountainous backcountry terrain.

But by Sunday, February 3, there was a sudden cold snap, and the temperature at night dropped to minus eighteen. The search was suspended Monday, February 4, after a week of searching, due to the extreme weather in the Merritt area.

The search for Ben included RCMP, SAR teams, spotter planes, search dogs, drones, and volunteers on snowmobiles and horseback and in vehicles and helicopters. In total, 215 SAR members responded from Nanaimo, Hope, Shuswap, Nicola Valley, Princeton, Vernon, Kamloops, Central Okanagan, Chilliwack, Comox Valley, Coquitlam, Grand Forks, Kent Harrison, Mission, North Shore Rescue, Ridge Meadows, Oliver/Osoyoos, Surrey and Logan Lake.

In March 2019 the RCMP declared the case "a suspicious disappearance."[142] The three-year anniversary of Ben's disappearance was on January 26, 2022. The RCMP have now stated they believe that Ben was the victim of a homicide. The family is offering a reward of thirty thousand dollars for any information leading to the location of Ben and to the arrest and conviction of the person(s) responsible for his death.

Case 69: Hiker Missing
Strathcona Park, BC

Beverly Pick spoke with me from her cottage in Gatineau, Quebec, to share the details about how her son, Rick Grey, became a missing person.

In April 1994, Beverly's twenty-two-year-old son, Rick Grey, left his home on Quadra Island, BC, taking the short ferry ride to Campbell River and then hitchhiking to Strathcona Provincial Park on Vancouver Island for a solo hike.

Rick had told his landlady that he was going for a hike for a couple of days. Unfortunately, she didn't report him missing for two weeks. Rick had written out his trip plan on a park pamphlet and put it in the box at the park entrance. This impromptu trip plan was found by police in early May after they received the landlady's call that Rick hadn't returned. Valuable time and evidence had already been lost since he'd started on his trip on April 14 or 15.

"The buddy system was Mom's rule," Beverly said. Rick was an experienced and skilled outdoorsman, but she says that she "would've turned him over my knee" for not going hiking with a friend. Beverly lived in Masham, Quebec, at the time that Rick went missing. She flew to Vancouver Island to look for her son.

Beverly recalls Campbell River SAR, Gold River SAR, a fire department and an RCMP helicopter carrying out the search for Rick for four days. A private SAR kept on searching for a couple more days, then three more times over the summer and fall. The search yielded Rick's sweatpants, sweater and towel at the high-water mark near the main highway bridge crossing Elk River, and there was tissue-like material in the river. The evidence was submitted to the RCMP, but no conclusions were made. His backpack was never found.

Rick may have fallen through thin spring ice on the Elk River, but a woman who had met him briefly a couple of times in 1993 thought she recognized him getting on a bus at the Kelowna bus station. She was interviewed by authorities, but the man she spotted couldn't be tracked down.

Beverly remains hopeful that Rick is in that "one percent group who may have hit his head and can't remember who he is and is out there somewhere." She is a "mother without closure." Beverly stayed on Vancouver Island, where a private SAR hired her as a general manager. After eighteen months, she returned home to her family and eventually started a private SAR team in Wakefield, Ontario. She's now retired.

Afterword

The interviews for this book were extremely interesting, and I loved meeting the SAR members from all over North America. However, they were incredibly emotionally draining, and not just because of the time-zone changes. I booked only two phone or video calls per day, each one lasting between an hour and ninety minutes, because that was as many as I could manage. There were days when I had to take three interviews—those weren't easy days. I have a vivid imagination, so the scenes I heard would replay in my mind.

I have shielded my readers from the most disturbing incidents and details and will never share them, which may be hard to believe considering the raw and graphic nature of some of the stories included here. I feel it's important that the public is aware of what SAR members experience when on an incident, but I intend to balance that desire by acknowledging the sensitivities of the surviving family members.

I rested in between interviews and processed what I had just heard, regardless of whether the outcomes were positive or negative. I was swamped with interviews for months, and I had little time to turn those interviews into written words. Three notebooks were filled with notes. There were 386 deaths that I encountered while researching this book, not including fourteen cold cases.

Sometimes as I fall asleep, I feel haunted by the stories of these people and the terrible ways in which they died or disappeared. However, I'm left with the hope that after readers have digested the challenging contents of this book there is a chance that they have learned something of value and a life might be saved, or a missing person found.

There were sixty-nine thousand people evacuated due to natural disasters, like fire or flood covered in this book. The evacuation stories had me relive the intensity of the wildfires of 2007, when I interviewed people from the interior of BC who lost their homes. I lost my professional boundaries and felt connected to the people of those communities who lost everything to the flames. I cried with them, raised money and brought food donations to them. They have rallied and rebuilt their lives since then.

After five months, the interviews tapered off, then I revisited the notebooks. I did my best to verify the cases the interviewees told me about by searching online archives for media stories, many of which contained few details—no names, maybe a target year, season and location. For the most part, that was successful, but there are some stories that never appeared in the media or were such old cases that no trace in the archives could be found.

Next, I contacted the families of the deceased subjects and the survivors wherever possible to let them know that the story of their loved one or themself would be included in the book if I had their blessings. It was satisfying to piece together stories, some that happened as long as forty years ago.

The cases in this book are not representative of the usual call-outs SAR members get. There are call-outs that are stood down (cancelled) before members even get to the staging area. Many are to go and get someone who called 911 on their cellphone and needs SAR to go and help them, so there's no searching involved. Most of my interviewees are senior SAR members who were chosen by their group to represent them. They drew on a lifetime of experiences in SAR when they presented their most memorable cases. That's why the incidents in this book are the tough cases, the tragic and the miraculous, the surprising and the puzzling ones.

I don't like to generalize about the personalities of the SAR members, as the people I interviewed are all unique individuals. However, they do share common passions and traits. It makes sense that SAR teams would look for new members who are similar and will complement the teams. I found that they love to solve puzzles; like to work in teams; and are loyal, highly intelligent, self-sacrificing, meticulous natural leaders who want to help people.

I hope the advice that these outdoor experts offer will land where it's needed and there will be far fewer recoveries for SAR to do in the future. Most at risk statistically are young adult males who go hiking, or out-of-bound skiing or snowshoeing on their own. Perhaps part of the solution would be getting this demographic involved at a younger age in programs like AdventureSmart, Hug-a-Tree, and Survive, a youth SAR, university and college SAR outreach or an education program that has yet to be developed.

Skee Hipszky, a nearly fifty-year veteran of SAR, says, "Extreme skiers and snowmobilers are on the number-one hit list for avalanche deaths." A SAR education program for these two groups of high-risk outdoors players may reduce the number of fatalities, but that would need funding to develop.

The other problem for the majority of SAR groups is lack of funding for essential equipment. They spend a lot of time fundraising, when ideally, they could instead spend more time on training and development. Perhaps some of the SAR teams with extra equipment in storage could help support teams that don't have enough basic equipment, like radios and sleds. The Yukon SAR comes to mind as a ground team in dire need. Perhaps there are a few members from each province and state who could put together an inventory of equipment available for SARs in need.

I enjoy interviewing SAR members and want their heroic acts to be appreciated by the public. I also want members of the public to be educated about outdoor safety so that they don't become cautionary tales, rather they become role models and mentors.

References

98.9 Rewind Radio. "Search and Rescue Teams Locate Two Women in Tumbler Ridge Area." 989 Rewind Radio. October 10, 2017. 989rewindradio.com/2017/10/10/search-and-rescue-teams-locate-two-women-in-tumbler-ridge-area.

AccuWeather, Manning Park, BC, October 9 and 10, 2020. accuweather.com/en/ca/manning-park/v0x/october-weather/2290369?-year=2020.

Adams, Annette, Ph.D., et al. "Search is a Time-Critical Event: When Search and Rescue Missions May Become Futile." *Wilderness and Environmental Medicine* 18, no. 2 (June 1, 2007): 95–101.

Alexander, Howard. "Dangerous Rescue after Pick-up Goes over Cliff Near Clinton." *Kamloops News*, April 6, 2014.

Amendt, Jens, et al. "Helicopter Thermal Imaging for Detecting Insect Infested Cadavers." National Library of Medicine. September 2017. pubmed.ncbi.nlm.nih.gov/28889866.

Anderson, Andrea. "The Searchers: Whitewater Area Mounted Search Team and Rescue Uses Horses to Help with Searches." *The Gazette*." October 12, 2014. newspaperarchive.com/janesville-gazette-oct-12-2014-p-1 and newspaperarchive.com/janesville-gazette-oct-12-2014-p-12.

Appalachian Trail Conservancy. 2022. appalachiantrail.org. https://appalachiantrail.org/explore/hike-the-a-t/thru-hiking/2000-milers.

Associated Press. "Authorities: Missing Hiker Is Found Dead in Sandia Mountains." September 20, 2020. apnews.com/article/missing-persons-mountains-new-mexico-archive-albuquerque-85eceece68b-1908cf09080561e71417f.

—. "Missing Nursing Student's Body Is Identified." September 9, 2014. nytimes.com/2014/09/10/us/holly-bobos-remains-found-in-tennessee.html.

—. "Pikes Peak Avalanche Kills One, Rescuers Battle Snowdrifts." April 26, 1995. apnews.com/article/55adb1ea99b065896b0d885f8edf22d7.

—. "Tennessee Convict Pleads Guilty in Holly Bobo Murder Case." September 14, 2020. toronto.citynews.ca/2020/09/14/tennessee-convict-pleads-guilty-in-holly-bobo-murder-case.

Associated Press and NBC Bay Area staff. "Missing Couple Found Alive After More Than a Week in Inverness Area." Updated on February 23, 2020. nbcbayarea.com/news/local/north-bay/missing-couple-found-alive-after-more-than-a-week-in-inverness-area/2239245.

Bailey, Ian. "Pilot of Fatal Sunshine Coast Crash Known to 'Push the Weather.'" *The Globe and Mail.* September 22, 2010. theglobeandmail.com/news/british-columbia/pilot-of-fatal-sunshine-coast-crash-known-to-push-the-weather/article1213813.

Baker, Paula. "Truck Driver Found Alive after 100-Foot Fall Down Embankment near Manning Park." Global News. Updated March 3, 2017. globalnews.ca/news/3284383/truck-driver-found-alive-after-200-foot-fall-down-embankment-near-manning-park.

Bass, Dale. "Tracking Sisters—Mark by Mark." *Kamloops This Week*, January 2, 2014.

BBC News. "MH370: Private Company Plans to Resume Plane Search. January 3, 2018. bbc.com/news/world-asia-42550118.

—. "Reisending Rescue: German Caver Johann Westhauser Surfaces." June 19, 2014. bbc.com/news/world-europe-27922781.

BC Local News, "RCMP Still Looking into the Nicole Hoar Disappearance: Hopes for Public Help in the Highway of Tears Investigation." July 15, 2020. bclocalnews.com/news/rcmp-still-looking-into-the-nicole-hoar-disappearance.

BCSARA. Alternative Support Model for Ground and Inland Water Search and Rescue in British Columbia. Proposal. December 2015. bcsara.com/entries/Robert-McGregor.

—. Search & Rescue Volunteer Memorial. 2013-2021. bcsara.com/service/sar-volunteer-memorial.

—. Wall of Honour. 2013-2021. bcsara.com/service/wall-of-honour.

Beltran, Veronica. "Nine Years Since the Disappearance of Madison Scott: RCMP Continue to Investigate." May 28, 2020. ckpgtoday.ca/2020/05/28/nine-years-since-the-disappearance-of-madison-scott-rcmp-continue-to-investigate.

Blevins, Jason. "Colorado's Volunteer Search and Rescue Teams Are Overwhelmed and There Are Fears It's Going to Get Worse." *Colorado Sun*, February 28, 2020. coloradosun.com/2020/02/28/colorado-search-and-rescue-overwhelmed-underfunded.

Blumberg, Jess. "A Brief History of the St. Bernard Rescue Dog." March 1, 2016. smithsonianmag.com/travel/a-brief-history-of-the-st-bernard-rescue-dog-13787665/?fbclid=IwAR1oPYqzyMhVRJqmwyHwmvG6Iv3cTq1FvU83l5xp-Cl7gs22fug2hzSjdfQ.

Brasch, Ben. "Case of Missing Iraq War Vet from Cobb ends with Conviction." *The Atlanta Journal-Constitution,* December 17, 2018. ajc.com/news/local/man-sentenced-death-formerly-missing-iraq-war-vet-from-cobb/S1bTCDtHwZMB9z51xSdORJ.

Briones, Michael. "Arrowsmith SAR Crews Extricate Man Who Fell Down Deep Crevasse Near Little Mountain." October 8, 2020. pqbnews.com/news/arrowsmith-search-and-rescue-rescue-man-who-fell-down-deep-crevasse-near-little-mountain.

Brown, Molly. "4 Killed in McKinley Crash." *Anchorage Daily News.* June 21, 2000.

Bruinn, A.K. and Marcel Poitras. *Three-Dog Nights: The Search and Rescue of Annette Poitras.* 2018.

Bryceland, Jack, Mary and David Macaree. *103 Hikes in Southwestern British Columbia.* 5th Edition. Greystone Books. Vancouver/Toronto. 2001.

California Department of Forestry and Fire Protection. *Cal Fire Investigators Determine the Cause of the Camp Fire.* May 15, 2019. fire.ca.gov/media/5121/campfire_cause.pdf.

CBC Archives. "B.C. Digs Out from Huge Blizzard." 1996. cbc.ca/archives/entry/1996-bc-digs-out-from-massive-blizzard.

CBC News. "Cody Legebokoff Sentenced to Life on 4 Counts of 1st-Degree Murder." September 16, 2014. cbc.ca/news/canada/british-columbia/cody-legebokoff-sentenced-to-life-on-4-counts-of-1st-degree-murder-1.2768118.

—. "Drowning video angers family and search and rescue inquest: Fellow volunteers 'complacent' alleges Sheilah Sweatman's brother.'" Nov 21, 2021. www.cbc.ca/news/canada/british-columbia/drowning-video-angers-family-at-search-and-rescue-inquest-1.1251421.

—. "Girl, 9, and Boy, 10, Identified as Victims of Deadly Off-Road Vehicle Crash near Chilliwack." May 4, 2020. cbc.ca/news/canada/british-columbia/atv-crash-chilliwack-bc-foley-lake-children-killed-1.5554690.

—. "'I Held on with Everything I Had': Rescuer Recalls Daring Operation to Save Man Who Fell into Raging River." December 14, 2020. cbc.ca/news/canada/british-columbia/little-qualicum-falls-rescue-video-bc-1.5840907.

—. "Investigators Head to Site of BC Plane Crash That Killed 7." November 17, 2008. cbc.ca/news/canada/investigators-head-to-site-of-bc-plane-crash-that-killed-7-1.772600.

—. "Missing BC Mother and Child Found Safe Near Powell River." October 25, 2012. cbc.ca/news/canada/british-columbia/missing-b-c-mother-and-child-found-safe-near-powell-river-1.1293298.

—. "Missing Girls from Driftwood Area Found Safe." August 31, 2020. cbc.ca/news/canada/sudbury/driftwood-cchrane-missing-girls-1.5706388.

—. "Remains Identified as Missing Florida Woman." November 17, 2004. cbc.ca/news/canada/remains-identified-as-missing-florida-woman-1.465951.

—. "Rock Slide Near Lions Bay Kills Erin Moore, 7, on Hike." Last updated December 23, 2014. cbc.ca/news/canada/british-columbia/rock-slide-near-lions-bay-kills-erin-moore-7-on-hike-1.2881775.

—. "Search for 2 Missing Hikers Near Keremeos Continues." June 24, 2015. cbc.ca/news/canada/british-columbia/search-for-2-missing-hikers-near-keremeos-continues-1.3126040.

—. "Tim Jones, North Shore Rescue Team Leader, Has Died." January 19, 2014. cbc.ca/news/canada/british-columbia/tim-jones-north-shore-rescue-team-leader-has-died-1.2503178.

—. "'We Won't Give Up,' Mother Says as Search for Missing Son in BC Continues." November 27, 2020. cbc.ca/news/canada/newfoundland-labrador/josie-naterer-missing-son-1.5819066#:~:-text=%26%20Labrador-,'We%20won't%20give%20up%2C'%20mother%20says%20as,175%20kilometres%20east%20of%20Vancouver.

Canadian Press. "Man Dug Out of Avalanche on Cypress Mountain in West Vancouver Saturday." March 4, 2017.

Channel 21 News. "Search ends in tragedy: Bend climber's body found in crevasse on Mount Hood." Government Camp, Oregon. October 29, 2020. ktvz.com/news/bend/2020/10/29/air-and-ground-search-underway-for-missing-bend-climber-on-mount-hood.

Chauvin, Pierre. "Skier Would Likely Have Died Overnight, RCMP Believe." *Whitehorse Daily Star.* December 3, 2015. whitehorsestar.com/News/skier-would-likely-have-died-overnight-rcmp-believe.

Chun, Diane. "Shands Group Remember Couple During Memory Walk." *The Gainesville Sun.* November 5, 2004. gainesville.com/story/news/2004/11/05/shands-group-remember-couple-during-memory-walk/31674494007.

Coquitlam Search and Rescue. "Three Dog Night: The Rescue of Annette Poitras and Three Dogs from Eagle Mountain, Coquitlam." November 24, 2017. coquitlam-sar.bc.ca/2017/11/three-dog-night-rescue-westwood-plateau/.

—. "Trail Safety for Dog Walkers." December 4, 2017. coquitlam-sar.bc.ca/2017/12/trail-safety-for-dog-walkers.

Corrie. "Steve Flynn of Blackcomb Helicopters Wins Medal of Bravery." *Helicopters.* January 17, 2008. helicoptersmagazine.com/steve-flynn-of-blackcomb-helicopters-wins-medal-of-bravery-670.

Cox, Kevin. "Couple Missing from Shoreline in Cape Breton." *The Globe and Mail.* October 20, 2004. theglobeandmail.com/news/national/couple-missing-from-shoreline-in-cape-breton/article1142903.

Crawford, Robyn. "Bodies of Lil'wat Nation Mushroom Pickers found in BC, Ending Search." October 30, 2020. CKNW. Global News. globalnews.ca/news/7431900/bc-mushroom-pickers-found.

CTV News. "'It's Filling Up with Water!': Woman Rescued from 20-Metre Sinkhole Shares Terrifying Story." January 30, 2018. vancouverisland.ctvnews.ca/it-s-filling-up-with-water-woman-rescued-from-20-metre-sinkhole-shares-terrifying-story-1.3782656.

—. "Searchers Find Missing 46-Year-Old Man in Kejimkujik National Park." July 3, 2019. atlantic.ctvnews.ca/searchers-find-missing-46-year-old-man-in-kejimkujik-national-park-1.4492101.

—. "Seriously Injured Hiker Rescued after Falling Off Crown Mountain." September 4, 2018. bc.ctvnews.ca/seriously-injured-hiker-rescued-after-falling-off-crown-mountain-1.4079380.

Daflos, Penny. "A BC First: Heat-Seeking Drone Used in Search-and-Rescue Mission." CTV News. February 21, 2017. bc.ctvnews.ca/a-b-c-first-heat-seeking-drone-used-in-search-and-rescue-mission-1.3295797.

Darnell, Tim. "Chase Massner Death: Clement Pleads Guilty Monday, Sentenced." *Patch*. December 17, 2018. patch.com/georgia/marietta/chase-massner-death-clement-pleads-guilty-monday-sentenced.

Dauphinee, Denis. *When You Find My Body: The Disappearance of Geraldine Largay on the Appalachian Trail*. Camden, Maine: DownEastBooks, 2019.

Dremman, Sue. A lost Palo Alto Couple. A Miraculous Rescue. Here's What Happened to Ian Irwin and Carol Kiparsky: How a Valentine's Hike Turned into a Journey of Survival. *Palo Alto Weekly*. December 4, 2020. https://www.paloaltoonline.com/news/2020/12/04/a-lost-palo-alto-couple-a-miraculous-rescue-heres-what-happened-to-ian-irwin-and-carol-kiparsky.

Department of Corrections Washington State. *Security Levels*. https://www.doc.wa.gov/corrections/incarceration/classification.htm#:~:text=Monroe%20Correctional%20Complex.

Emergency Management BC. *Ground Search & Rescue, 3rd Edition*. March 2017. New Westminster, BC: Justice Institute of British Columbia.

—. *Provincial Search and Rescue Operating Guidelines*. January 2022. https://www2.gov.bc.ca/assets/gov/public-safety-and-emergency-services/emergency-preparedness-response-recovery/embc/volunteers/sar_safety_program_operating_guidelines.pdf.

—. BC SAR Rope Rescue Manual. Section 2: Rope Rescue Technician I. Province of BC. January 29, 2018.

—. "Weekly Incident Situation Report." February 27 to March 5, 2017.

—. "Weekly Incident Situation Report." February 18–24, 2019.

Everitt, Bill. "Hiker Struck by Falling Rock." *Penticton News*. October 21, 2014. castanet.net/news/Penticton/125284/Hiker-struck-by-falling-rock.

Farrell, Jim. "Cave Tragedy Recalled." *Edmonton Journal*. October 21, 1991.

Federal Bureau of Prisons. "Jason Autry." www.bop.gov/inmateloc.

Feinberg, Jennifer. "Trapped Trucker Succumbs to Injuries." *Hope Standard*.

March 6, 2017. hopestandard.com/news/update-trapped-trucker-succumbs-to-injuries.

Ferguson, Mary. "Olson Wanted to Sell Information to Media, Parents of Victims." UPI. January 15, 1982. upi.com/Archives/1982/01/15/Olson-wanted-to-sell-information-to-mediaparents-of-victims/6698379918800.

Find A Grave. "Patrick "Pat" Pennington." n/d. findagrave.com/memorial/35030043/patrick-roger-pennington.

Floyer, Joyce and Keith Robine. *Avalanche Skills Training Handbook.* Revelstoke, BC: Avalanche Canada, 2018.

Friscolanti, Michael. "People Say There Were No Casualties. There Are Two Now." *Maclean's.* May 7, 2016. macleans.ca/news/canada/people-say-there-were-no-casualties-there-are-two-now.

Gagne, Ty. *Where You'll Find Me: Risk, Decisions, and the Last Climb of Kate Matrosova.* Conway, NH: TMC Books LLC, 2017.

Gallaher, Bob. "More than a Year Later, Family of Missing Korean War Veteran Keeps Searching." Weau 13 News. January 10, 2021. weau.com/2021/01/10/more-than-a-year-later-family-of-missing-korean-war-veteran-keeps-searching.

Gaye, Jeff. "4 Wing Responds to Rescue Call." *The Courier: News and Publishing.* August 8, 2017.

Global BC TV News. December 24, 2020.

Golgowski, Nina. "Parents Charged over Death of Toddler Found Drowned in Canal Hours after Neighbor Discovered Her Wandering the Streets." *Daily Mail.* September 23, 2012. dailymail.co.uk/news/article-2207674/Reena-Mae-Williams-Parents-charged-toddler-drowned-canal-hours-recovered-wandering-streets.

Government of BC. "Emergency Coordination Centre Incident Summaries." February 27 to March 5, 2017.

—. "Emergency Coordination Centre Incident Summaries." May 1–7, 2017.

—. "Emergency Coordination Centre Incident Summaries." October 2–8, 2017.

—. "Emergency Coordination Centre Incident Summaries." December 30 to January 5, 2019. www2.gov.bc.ca/assets/gov/public-safety-and-emergency-services/emergency-preparedness-response-recovery/embc/ecc-incident-summaries-2020/weekly_incident_summary-12302019-01052020.pdf. December 2 to December 8, 2020. www2.gov.bc.ca/assets/gov/public-safety-and-emergency-services/emergency-preparedness-response-recovery/embc/ecc-incident-summaries-2019/weekly_incident_summary-12022019-12082019.pdf. December 9 to December 15, 2020. www2.gov.bc.ca/assets/gov/public-safety-and-emer-

gency-services/emergency-preparedness-response-recovery/
embc/ecc-incident-summaries-2019/weekly_incident_summa-
ry-12092019-12152019.pdf.

—. "Emergency Coordination Centre Incident Summaries." February 12–
18, 2018. gov.bc.ca/assets/gov/public-safety-and-emergency-ser-
vices/emergency-preparedness-response-recovery/embc/ecc-inci-
dent-summaries-2018/
incident_summary_-_feb_12_-_18_2018.pdf.

—. "Emergency Coordination Centre Incident Summaries." April 2–8,
2018. gov.bc.ca/assets/gov/public-safety-and-emergency-ser-
vices/emergency-preparedness-response-recovery/embc/ecc-inci-
dent-summaries-2018/
incident_summary_-_april_2-8_2018.pdf.

—. "Emergency Coordination Centre Incident Summaries." May 7–13,
2018. gov.bc.ca/assets/gov/public-safety-and-emergency-ser-
vices/emergency-preparedness-response-recovery/embc/ecc-inci-
dent-summaries-2018/
incident_summary_may_7-13.pdf.

—. "Emergency Coordination Centre Incident Summaries." July 9–15,
2018. www2.gov.bc.ca/assets/gov/public-safety-and-emergency-ser-
vices/emergency-preparedness-response-recovery/embc/ecc-inci-
dent-summaries-2018/incident_summary_july_9-15_2018.pdf.

—. "Emergency Coordination Centre Incident Summaries." July 23–29,
2018. gov.bc.ca/assets/gov/public-safety-and-emergency-ser-
vices/emergency-preparedness-response-recovery/embc/ecc-inci-
dent-summaries-2018/
incident_summary_-_july_23-29_2018.pdf.

—. "Emergency Coordination Centre Incident Summaries." July 30 to
August 5, 2018. gov.bc.ca/assets/gov/public-safety-and-emergen-
cy-services/emergency-preparedness-response-recovery/embc/
ecc-incident-summaries-2018/
incident_summary_july_30-aug_5_2018.pdf.

—. "Emergency Coordination Centre Incident Summaries." September
7–13, 2020. gov.bc.ca/assets/gov/public-safety-and-emergen-
cy-services/emergency-preparedness-response-recovery/embc/
ecc-incident-summaries-2020/embc_weekly_incident_summa-
ry-09072020-09132020.pdf.

—. "Emergency Coordination Centre Incident Summaries." August
23–29, 2021. gov.bc.ca/assets/gov/public-safety-and-emergen-
cy-services/emergency-preparedness-response-recovery/embc/
ecc-incident-summaries-2021/embc_weekly_incident_summa-
ry-08232021-08292021.pdf.

—. "Mushroom Picking." n/d. gov.bc.ca/gov/content/industry/crown-land-water/crown-land/crown-land-uses/mushroom-picking.

—. "Wildfire Season Summary." 2017. gov.bc.ca/gov/content/safety/wildfire-status/about-bcws/wildfire-history/wildfire-season-summary.

Government of Canada. "Canada's Missing." May 25, 2022. *www.canadasmissing.ca/index-eng.htm*

—. "National Search and Rescue Program." publicsafety.gc.ca/cnt/mrgnc-mngmnt/rspndng-mrgnc-vnts/nss/prgrm-en.aspx.

—. "Public Safety Canada." December 9, 2013. cdd.publicsafety.gc.ca/dt-pg-eng.aspx?cultureCode=en-Ca&provinces=1%2C2%2C3%2C4%2C5%2C6%2C7%2C8%2C9% 2C10%2C11%2C12%2C13&normalizedCostYear=1&dynamic=false&eventId=401.

Governor General of Canada. "Decorations for Bravery." gg.ca/en/honours/canadian-honours/decorations-bravery.

Government of Western Australia. "Vergulde Draeck." n/d. museum.wa.gov.au/maritime-archaeology-db/roaring-40s/vergulde-draeck.

Graham, Kathleen. "Kathleen on Teamwork." March 2020. youtube.com/results?search_query=ahnvbSRqDOw.

Hasegawa, Regan and David Molko. "Night-Vision Goggles Lead to Historic Overnight Rescue on North Shore." CTV News. December 24, 2020. bc.ctvnews.ca/night-vision-goggles-lead-to-historic-overnight-rescue-on-north-shore-1.5244245.

Hennig, Clare. "Weekend Rescue Prompts Search-Crew Warning to Mushroom Pickers Seeking Bumper B.C. Crop." CBC News. June 5, 2018. cbc.ca/news/canada/british-columbia/missing-mushroom-picker-rescued-spike-in-pickers-1.4692820.

Hill, Andrea. "Emergency Crews, Family and Friends Search South Saskatchewan River for Missing Teen." *Saskatoon StarPhoenix*. July 17, 2017. thestarphoenix.com/news/local-news/emergency-crews-searching-south-saskatchewan-river-for-missing-17-year-old-boy.

Hopes, Vikki. "Fatal Ultralight Crash in Abbotsford, Highway 1 Westbound Has Reopened." *Abbotsford News*. November 18, 2013. abbynews.com/news/update-fatal-ultralight-crash-in-abbotsford-highway-1-westbound-has-reopened.

Hopper, Tristan. "Couple Walks Out of B.C. Backcountry Just as Families Were Saying 'Their Last Goodbyes.'" *National Post*. June 29, 2015. nationalpost.com/news/canada/ontario-couple-walk-out-of-b-c-backcountry-in-surprisingly-good-condition-just-as-rescuers-were-about-to-give-up?fbclid=IwAR0Mg-X-UoALUmTZdQo-cLn6fAKrdwheIp DNSgg_x0MqMVF4okP9A5YJhDek.

Howard, Scott. n/d.

Hui, Stephen. *105 Hikes In and Around Southwestern British Columbia*. Vancouver: Greystone Books, 2018.

Igor Sikorsky Historcal Archives. "Jimmy Viner." September 22, 2012.
   sikorskyarchives.com/
   Jimmy_Viner.php.

Jang, Brent. "B.C. Foster Mother Fears Missing Boy Was Abducted." *The
   Globe and Mail.* September 4, 2002. theglobeandmail.com/news/
   world/bc-foster-mother-fears-missing-boy-was-abducted/arti-
   cle1026061.

Jensen, Chris. "Anatomy of a Search: When Hiker Called for Help, N.H.
   Rescuers Braved Monstrous Storm." *New Hampshire Public Radio.*
   January 1, 2016. nhpr.org/
   post/anatomy-search-when-hiker-called-help-nh-rescuers-braved-
   monstrous-storm.

Jiwa, Salim. "Prince George murder: The Life and Death of Jill Stuchenko."
   Digital Journal. October 31, 2009.

Jones, Whitney. "Holly Bobo Case Already Most Expensive in Tennessee
   Bureau of Investigation History." WKMS. April 30, 2014. wkms.
   org/post/holly-bobo-case-already-most-expensive-tennessee-bu-
   reau-investigation-history#stream/0.

Kamloops This Week. "Runaway in Avola Found, Is Safe." June 17, 2016.
   kamloopsthisweek.com/news/update-runaway-in-avola-found-is-
   safe-1.23232564.

Kelly, Ash and Denise Wong. "North Shore Rescue Postpones Search
   for Surrey Hiker Caught in Avalanche." City News. Last updated February 20, 2019. vancouver.citynews.ca/2019/02/19/
   north-shore-rescue-hiker-avalanche/.

Knowledge Network. *Search and Rescue: North Shore.* "Episode 3: Peak Season." knowledge.ca/program/search-and-rescue-north-shore/e3/
   peak-season?gclid=Cj0KCQiA2uH-BRCCARI-
   sAEeef3l2mZerYV-m04fBdvItnT1-80IpExItoa4zaY1q4KjfCAK-
   LZIlnSMwaAoH2EALw_wcB.

Kobin, Billy. "Family's Quest for Missing Veteran with Dementia Leads
   Search to Kentucky." *Louisville Courier Journal.* March 18, 2020.
   courier-journal.com/story/news/local/2020/03/18/tony-dan-
   tzman-missing-possible-sighting-california-man-waddy-ken-
   tucky/5054986002.

Koester, Robert J. *Lost Person Behavior: A Search and Rescue Guide on Where
   to Look—for Land, Air and Water.* Charlottesville, VA: dbS Produc-
   tions, 2008.

Komo News. "Missing DOT Employee's Body, Truck Found in Deep Sater
   Near Hood Canal Bridge. Peninsula Daily News. May 24, 2016.
   peninsuladailynews.com/news/missing-dot-employees-body-
   truck-found-in-deep-water-near-hood-canal-bridge.

Komo Staff. "Crews Recover Truck, Body of DOT Worker Who Drove off Hood Canal Bridge." Komo News. May 26, 2016. komonews.com/news/local/crews-recover-truck-body-of-dot-worker-who-drove-off-hood-canal-bridge.

Landrigan, Kevin. "Lone Hiker in Pemi Wilderness Found, Hospitalized after Four-Day Search." *New Hampshire Union Leader.* Updated July 13, 2019. unionleader.com/news/environment/lone-hiker-in-pemi-wilderness-found-hospitalized-after-four-day-search/article_5fcbc773-cf28-5236-b16d-dc142849c5dd.html.

Lerten, Barney and, Jordan Williams. "Search ends in tragedy: Bend climber's body found in crevasse on Mount Hood." KTVZ. October 29, 2020. ktvz.com/news/bend/2020/10/29/air-and-ground-search-underway-for-missing-bend-climber-on-mount-hood.

Little, Simon and John Copsey. "Tragic End to Search for Missing Ontario Snowshoer on B.C.'s North Shore Mountains." Global News. January 15, 2021. globalnews.ca/news/7578108/search-for-woman-on-north-shore-mountains-continues.

localnews@mwcradio.com. "Body of Missing Man Found." August 12, 2016. wtaq.com/2016/08/12/body-of-missing-man-found.

Luperon, Alberto. "Controversial Key Witness in Holly Bobo Murder Arrested on Gun and Drug Charges." December 4, 2020. lawandcrime.com/live-trials/live-trials-current/holly-bobo-zachary-adams/controversial-key-witness-in-holly-bobo-murder-arrested-on-gun-and-drug-charges.

Maclean, Rachel. "Rat's Nest Cave Rescue Takes Place Overnight to Free Man Stuck on Tour." CBC News. April 26, 2016. cbc.ca/news/canada/calgary/rats-nest-cave-rescue-overnight-1.3554220.

Manning Provincial Park. Park Trail Map. 2020. manningpark.com/wp-content/uploads/2020/08/Green-Park-Map-2020.pdf.

McClam, Erin and Erin Calabrese. "Texas Floods: Eight People in Wimberley Vacation House Are Missing." NBC News. May 26, 2015. nbcnews.com/news/us-news/texas-floods-eight-people-wimberley-vacation-house-are-missing-n364636.

Merritt Herald. "Tyner Case Remains Cold." January 29, 2020. merrittherald.com/tyner-case-remains-cold/.

Mertz, Emily. "Fort McMurray Triplet Killed Fleeing Fires was Daughter of Deputy Fire Chief." *Global News.* May 5, 2016. globalnews.ca/news/2680870/horrific-crash-on-albertas-highway-881-sparks-blaze.

Menzies, Michael. "RCMP Helicopter, Search and Rescue Help 17 ATV Riders Lost Near Wolf Lake." Lakelandconnect.net. May 26, 2020. lakelandconnect.net/2020/05/26/rcmp-helicopter-search-and-rescue-help-17-atv-riders-lost-near-wolf-lake. May 26, 2020.

Mesh, Aaron. "What It's Like to Get Lost in the Columbia River Gorge." *Willamette Week.* February 23, 2021. wweek.com/outdoors/2021/02/23/what-its-like-to-get-lost-in-the-columbia-river-gorge.

Meuse, Matt and Maryse Zeilder. "'A Great Tragedy: Bodies of 5 Missing Hikers Recovered Near Lions Bay, B.C. CBC News. Last updated April 10, 2017. cbc.ca/news/canada/british-columbia/lions-bay-search-resumes-hikers-found-and-recovered-1.4062976.

Miles, Kathryn. "'When You Find My Body': The Last Days of Gerry Largay." *Globe Magazine.* August 24, 2016. bostonglobe.com/magazine/2016/08/24/when-you-find-body-the-last-days-hiker-gerry-largay/DcaZf6RcojOTN2LNsOXm0K/story.html.

Mishler, Austin. Facebook page. facebook.com/photo?fbid=10220434662840321&set=a.1636164747690.

Mount Washington Observatory. February 2015. mountwashington.org/uploads/forms/2015/02.pdf.

Nassar, Hana Mae and Ellen Coulter. "Body of Missing Cache Creek Fire Chief Located." CityNews 1130. May 28, 2017. citynews1130.com/2017/05/28/body-missing-cache-creek-fire-chief-located.

National Park Service. "Appalachian: Footpath for the People." May 10, 2019. nps.gov/appa/index.htm.

National Post. "Surviving the 'Unsurvivable' Plane Crash: Tom Wilson Woke up Soaked in Fuel. He Was on Fire." April 27, 2015. nationalpost.com/news/canada/surviving-the-unsurvivable-plane-crash-tom-wilson-woke-up-soaked-in-fuel-he-was-on-fire.

National Transport Safety Board. "Aviation Accident Data Summary." ANC00GA071. Talkeetna, Alaska. July 16, 2001. accidents.app/summaries/accident/20001212X21135.

Nielsen, Mark. "Verdict Draws Applause from Victims' Families." *Prince George Citizen.* September 11, 2014. princegeorgecitizen.com/legebokoff-trial-archive/verdict-draws-applause-from-victims-families-3713798.

NIVISYS. "Night Vision Goggles Approved for Civil Aviation." *Helicopters Magazine.* December 10, 2008. helicoptersmagazine.com/night-vision-goggles-approved-for-civil-aviation-1279/.

North Shore Rescue Facebook page. Post on rescue at Suicide Creek, December 24, 2020.

Northshorerescue.com.

Northword Magazine, "Risk and Rescue in a Northern BC Cave." August 4, 2010.

Oxley, Dyer. "Wife of Missing WSDOT Worker Issues Statement as Search Continues." Last updated May 18, 2016. My Northwest. mynorthwest.com/294292/search-crews-looking-for-wsdot-worker-who-may-have-gone-over-hood-canal-bridge.

Pardo, Annalisa and KRQE Staff. "Body of Missing Hiker Found in the Sandia Mountains." KRQE News. Last updated September 21, 2020. krqe.com/news/albuquerque-metro/body-of-missing-hiker-found-in-the-sandia-mountains.

Parrish, Julia. "Family Thankful after Two Girls Rescued from Northern Alberta Lake. CTV Edmonton. June 25, 2014. edmonton.ctvnews.ca/family-thankful-after-two-girls-rescued-from-northern-alberta-lake-1.1886846.

Penticton Herald Staff. "Update: Missing Man Found Dead in Manning Park." *Penticton Herald.* Last updated July 26, 2021. pentictonherald.ca/news/article_2a397642-ebec-11eb-a1d2-b37e452ca2fb.html.

Peters, Jessica. "Looking back: Surviving the Snowstorm of '96 in Chilliwack." *Chilliwack Progress.* January 6, 2017. theprogress.com/community/looking-back-surviving-the-snowstorm-of-96-in-chilliwack/.

Phillips, Iris. "Black Lab Survives 40 Foot Fall." *100 Mile House Free Press.* A3. July 11, 2007.

Piller, Thomas. "Missing Senior with Serious Health Issues Located: Shellbrook RCMP." Global News. Last updated April 26, 2018. globalnews.ca/news/4165828/shellbrook-rcmp-missing-man-james-mumm-health-issues.

Pine Tree SAR. pinetreesar.com. 2022.

Potestio, Michael. "Two Years Later, Ryan Shtuka's Disappearance Remains a Mystery." *Kamloops This Week.* February 18, 2020. kamloopsthisweek.com/news/two-years-later-ryan-shtuka-s-disappearance-remains-a-mystery-1.24079034.

Powell River Peak. "Missing Person Possibly Seen; Powell River RCMP Seek Information." August 26, 2021. prpeak.com/local-news/missing-person-possibly-seen-powell-river-rcmp-seek-information-4257020.

Prince George Citizen and Canadian Press. "A timeline of events in the serial-murder case against Cody Legebokoff." Sep 11, 2014. https://www.princegeorgecitizen.com/legebokoff-trial-archive/a-timeline-of-events-in-the-serial-murder-case-against-cody-legebokoff-3713797.

Prince George Free Press. "Extensive Search Proved Fruitless." March 29, 2007. pgfreepress.com/extensive-search-proved-fruitless.

Proctor, Jason. "Rhody Lake's Daughter Wants Death Certificate after Mother's Mysterious Disappearance." CBC. January 20, 2015. cbc.ca/news/canada/british-columbia/rhody-lake-s-daughter-wants-death-certificate-after-mother-s-mysterious-disappearance-1.2918590.

Province of BC. BC Parks. *Cypress Provincial Park Winter Trails.* 2017. bcparks.ca/explore/parkpgs/cypress/winter-trails-and-bac.pdf?v=1654469213667.

Province of BC. *Ground Search and Rescue.* 3rd Edition. 2017. Canada.

Public Safety Canada. Search and Rescue Volunteer Association of Canada. sarvac.ca/about.

RCMP. "Tyner Family Makes Emotional Plea 2-Years after Ben's Unexplained Disappearance." January 26, 2021. bc.rcmp-grc.gc.ca/ViewPage.action?siteNodeId=2087&languageId=1&contentId=68031&fbclid=IwAR2fTC-6wQ19My0vTlxhef0uE9nYf4y-wxMUlB5quk2CLsjNZKNpfQGAMulA.

Redline Guiding. "22 Winter Alpine Travel Tips." December 17, 2016. redlineguiding.com/2016/12/22-winter-alpine-travel-tips.

Reynolds, Dana. "Hikers Missing for Seven Days in the Backcountry Tell Their Story." *Kamloops News.* July 6, 2015. infotel.ca/newsitem/hikers-missing-for-seven-days-in-the-backcountry-tell-their-story/it20988.

Richter, Brent. " North Shore Rescue deploys e-bikes for faster response." *North Shore News.* May 12, 2020.

Ruttle, Derek. "Community Mourns Passing of Young Teen." *The Outlook.* July 26, 2017. theoutlook.ca/news/local/community-mourns-passing-of-young-teen-1.21383548.

Sabo, Don. "Highway of Tears." The Canadian Encyclopedia. June 6, 2016 and May 29, 2019. thecanadianencyclopedia.ca/en/article/highway-of-tears.

The Saint Bernard Club of NSW. "History of the St. Bernard." stbernard.org.au/history-of-saint-bernards.html.

Saltwire Network. "Search for Missing Mountain Biker in Halifax Area Called Off." June 4, 2014. saltwire.com/news/local/search-for-missing-mountain-biker-in-halifax-area-called-off-29713/?location=nova-scotia.

SAR Strategic Plan Working Group. Land and Inland Water Search and Rescue Strategic Plan for British Columbia. November 1996.

Schiman, Elaine. "Commissioner Plays Role in Recognizing Bravery and Public Service." *Yukon News.* July 10, 2008. yukon-news.com/news/commissioner-plays-role-in-recognizing-bravery-and-public-service.

Scouller, Steven. "The Vanishing of Madison Scott." January 8, 2014. youtube.com/watch?v=Xn0ROcjh7ys.

Seeley, James. *The Dangling Dog.* Unpublished story. Written July 2007.

Siren. "Parents sentenced in drowning death of toddler." *Wisconsin News.* November 24, 2014. archive.jsonline.com/news/wisconsin/parents-sentenced-in-drowning-death-of-toddler-b99397166z1-283780451.html.

Stahn, Jennifer. "Sit. Stay. Search." October 18, 2020. youtube.com/
watch?v=MLbP_dgW1Bc.

Steacy, Lisa. "Shaming Those Who Need to Be Rescued in BC Backcountry is Toxic, Dangerous: SAR Volunteer." *Vancouver City News
1130.* January 17, 2021. citynews1130.com/2021/01/17/shaming-
those-who-need-to-be-rescued-in-b-c-backcountry-is-toxic-dan-
gerous-sar-volunteer.

Stenner, Christian. "How Canada's Deepest Cave, Bisaro Anima, Got Its
Name." *Canadian Geographic.* April 8, 2019. canadiangeographic.
ca/article/how-canadas-deepest-cave-bisaro-anima-got-its-name.

—. "New Insights from Canada's Deepest Cave, Bisaro Anima." *Canadian Geographic.* January 24, 2020. canadiangeographic.ca/article/
new-insights-canadas-deepest-cave-bisaro-anima.

Stott, Sandy. "Too Cold: The Death of Kate Matrosova." *Appalachian
Mountain Club,* February 5, 2016. outdoors.org/articles/appala-
chia-journal-blog/too-cold-the-death-of-kate-matrosova.

Stringer, Chris. "A Recreational Passion Leads to a Lifetime of Rescuing
Lives." *The Beacon.* November/December 2020, p. 12. issuu.com/
westvanbeacon/docs/beacon_nov2020_41_web?fr=sZDE2MjY1N-
jcxMw%2520.

Sun Peaks Resort. *Sun Peaks Daily Avalanche Forecast, February 17 2018.*
sunpeaksresort.com/sites/default/files/avalanche-report/180217.
pdf.

—. February 18, *Sun Peaks Daily Avalanche Forecast, February 18 2018.* sun-
peaksresort.com/sites/default/files/avalanche-report/180218.pdf.

Tennessee Department of Corrections, "Felony Offender Information."
John Dylan Adams. June 6, 2022. apps.tn.gov/foil/details.jsp.

—. *Zachary Rye Adams.* June 6, 2022. apps.tn.gov/foil/details.jsp.

Tikkaken, Amy. "Gary Ridgway." *Britannica.* February 20, 2021. britannica.
com/biography/Gary-Ridgway.

Timeanddate. City of Hood River, Oregon, USA – Sunrise, Sunset, and Daylength, January 2021. timeanddate.com/
sun/@7173636?month=1&year=2021.

Transportation Safety Board of Canada. "Aviation Investigation Report
A08P0353." Government of Canada. November 16, 2008. tsb.gc.
ca/eng/rapports-reports/aviation/2008/a08p0353/a08p0353.html.

—. "Swissair Flight 111 Abbreviated Investigation Chronology." Government of Canada. bst-tsb.gc.ca/eng/medias-media/fiches-facts/
A98H0003/chronology_a98h0003.html.

United States Census Bureau. "Camp Fire—2018 California Wildfires."
November 2018. https://www.census.gov/topics/preparedness/
events/wildfires/camp.html#:~:text=It%20covered%20an%20
area%20of,days%20on%20November%2025%2C%202018.

UPI Archives. September 4, 1982. An Army helicopter crashed and exploded into flames Saturday. upi.com/Archives/1982/09/04/An-Army-helicopter-crashed-and-exploded-into-flames-Saturday/9171399960000.

US Air Force. *C-130 Hercules,* June 2018. af.mil/About-Us/Fact-Sheets/Display/Article/1555054/c-130-hercules/.

Van Tilburg, Christopher. Press release. n/d.

—. "Search and Rescue: A Wilderness Doctor's Life-and-Death Tales of Risk and Reward." 2017.

Vander Hayden, Aly. "Missing Army Veteran Found Buried Behind Friend's House Years After He Vanished." *Oxygen.* October 22, 2020. oxygen.com/injustice-with-nancy-grace/crime-news/chase-massner-found-buried-in-friend-brad-clements-backyard.

Vega, Manuela. "21-year-old Toronto woman who loved solo travel dies on Vancouver-area mountain trail." *Toronto Star.* January 16 and 18, 2021. thestar.com/news/gta/2021/01/16/21-year-old-toronto-woman-who-loved-solo-travel-dies-on-vancouver-area-mountain-trail.html.

Wadhwani, Ashley. "Langley Man Dies Near Chehalis Canyon." *Today in BC.* July 5, 2016. bclocalnews.com/news/langley-man-dies-near-chehalis-canyon.

Walton, Lisa. "Hometown Heroes: 40 Years of Saving Lives for Istvan Hipszky." *The Gazette.* March 19, 2014. gazette.com/news/hometown-heroes-40-years-of-saving-lives-for-istvan-hipszky/article_e323392b-b6ab-5b1b-8b48-bf084415d876.html.

Weather Underground. wunderground.com/history/daily/us/nm/kirtland-afb/KABQ/date/2020-9-15, wunderground.com/history/daily/us/nm/kirtland-afb/KABQ/date/2020-9-16, wunderground.com/history/daily/us/nm/kirtland-afb/KABQ/date/2020-9-17, wunderground.com/history/daily/us/nm/kirtland-afb/KABQ/date/2020-9-18, wunderground.com/history/daily/us/nm/kirtland-afb/KABQ/date/2020-9-19, wunderground.com/history/daily/us/nm/kirtland-afb/KABQ/date/2020-9-20.

Weau 13 News. "Body of Missing Prentice Man Found. August 12, 2016. weau.com/content/news/Body-of-missing-Prentice-man-found-389997322.html.

Welsh, Eric. "Good Samaritans help three people survive ATV accident at Foley Lake in Chilliwack." *The Chilliwack Progress.* May 4, 2020. theprogress.com/news/good-samaritans-help-three-people-survive-atv-accident-at-foley-lake-in-chilliwack.

Whistler Arts Centre."Brittania Beach: A Little History." N/d. artswhistler.com/location/britannia-beach-sea-sky-geotour.

Whitfield, Phil. *Fang Cave Rescue 2009*, October 17–18, 2009.

—. Fatal Accident Report. Arctomys Cave. British Columbia Cave Rescue. BC, Canada. 17–21 October 1991.

Williams, Arthur. "Local Climber Recovering from Cave Ordeal." *Prince George Free Press*. October 22, 2009. pgfreepress.com/local-climber-recovering-from-cave-ordeal.

Williams, Tess. "3 men die in avalanche in Bear Mountain area near Chugiak." *Anchorage Daily News*. February 4, 2021.

Wilson, Tom. *Moments of Impact*. April 2015.

WKRN Staff. "Jason Autry Indicted on Federal Charges after Being Convicted for Role in Holly Bobo Case." December 10, 2020. wkrn.com/news/crime-tracker/jason-autry-indicted-on-federal-charges-after-being-convicted-for-role-in-holly-bobo-case.

Woodrooffe, Sophie. "Injured Mountain Biker Airlifted from Langdale Terminal." *Coast Reporter*. Glacier Community Media. May 27, 2020. coastreporter.net/news/local-news/injured-mountain-biker-airlifted-from-langdale-terminal-1.24142086.

Endnotes

1   gov.bc.ca/gov/content/safety/emergency-management/emergen-
cy-management/incident-summaries?keyword=embc&keyword=inci-
dent.

Introduction

2   Government of Western Australia, museum.wa.gov.au/maritime-ar-
chaeology-db/roaring-40s/vergulde-draeck.

3   Jess Blumberg, *Smithsonian* magazine, March 1, 2016.

4   Government of Canada, National Search and Rescue Program, pub-
licsafety.gc.ca/cnt/mrgnc-mngmnt/rspndng-mrgnc-vnts/nss/prgrm-en.
aspx.

5   northshorerescue.com.

6   Emergency Management BC, www2.gov.bc.ca/gov/content/safety/
emergency-management/emergency-management/incident-summaries.

1. New SAR Members

7   Province of BC, *Ground Search & Rescue*, 87.

8   Province of BC, *Ground Search & Rescue*, 32.

9   smist08.wordpress.com.

10   sunshine.vr-sar.org.

11   Robert Koester, *Lost Person Behavior*, 49.

12   Province of BC, *Ground Search and Rescue*, 87.

13   Sophie Woodrooffe, "Injured Mountain Biker Airlifted from Langdale
Terminal," *Coast Reporter*, May 27, 2020.

2. Avalanches

14   Chris Stringer "A Recreational Passion Leads to a Lifetime of Rescuing
Lives," the *Beacon*, 12.

15 Whistler Arts Centre, "Britannia Beach: A Little History."

16 Chris Stringer, 12.

17 cbc.ca/news/canada/british-columbia/lions-bay-search-resumes-hikers-found-and-recovered-1.4062976.

3. Caves

18 An internal manual only available to BC SAR members who are registered to the member's only area of BC SAR website.

19 When SAR members are caving, they use a second rope for backup and are clipped into their rope harnesses for safety.

20 EMBC, *BC SAR Rope Rescue Technician I*, January 29, 2018, 216.

21 Jim Farrell, "Cave Tragedy Recalled," *Edmonton Journal*, October 21, 1991.

22 Phil Whitfield, *Arctomys Cave Fatal Accident Report*, 17-21 October.

23 "Risk and Rescue in a Northern BC Cave," *Northwood Magazine*, August 4, 2010, northworrd.ca/august-210/risk-and-rescue-in-a-northern-bc-cave).

24 Phil Whitfield, *Fang Cave Rescue 2009*, October 17–18, 2009.

25 BBC News, June 19, 2014.

26 Kathleen Graham. "Kathleen on Teamwork," March 2020, youtube.com/watch?v=ahnvbSRqDOw.

4. Deserts

27 Weather Underground. September 15-20, 2020.

28 Associated Press, September 20, 2020.

29 Annalisa Pardo, "Body of Missing Hiker Found in the Sandia Mountains," September 20, 2020.

30 mvsar.org.

5. Dives

31 Department of Corrections Washington State. Security Levels.

32 Corey Cooper, youtube.com/watch?v=UAqCSQykhKQ&t=570s.

6. Ground

33 Coquitlam SAR, November 24, 2017.

34 A.K. Bruinn and Marcel Poitras, 2018.

35 The Associated Press and NBC Bay Area staff, February 22, 2020.

36 Sue Dremman, *Palo Alto Weekly*, December 4, 2020.

37 California Department of Forestry and Fire Protection, May 15, 2019.

38 US Census Bureau, November 2018.

39 pinetreesar.com.

40 https://appalachiantrail.org.

41 https://appalachiantrail.org/explore/hike-the-a-t/thru-hiking/2000-milers.

42 Denis Dauphinee, 2019.

43 Kathryn Miles, August 24, 2016.

44 Veronica Beltran, *CKPGToday*.ca.

45 youtube.com/watch?v=Xn0ROcjh7ys.

46 *Prince George Citizen*, September 11, 2014.

47 Mark Nielsen, September 11, 2014.

48 Salim Jiwa, October 31, 2009.

49 Mark Nielson, September 11, 2014.

50 EMBC, *BC SAR Rope Rescue Technician I*, January 29, 2018, 224.

51 Swiftwater is one of the most dangerous, if not *the* most dangerous type of rescue that SAR becomes involved with, because there is so little that you can control in that environment. Swiftwater requires specialized training, certification and equipment. Ground SAR members not certified in swiftwater are restricted to the shoreline and are not allowed to enter the water, due to the high level of risk. When Ground SAR members are working along the shoreline they must wear PFDs.

52 CBC, November 21, 2021.

53 Three other BC Ground SAR members who died in the line of duty are memorialized on the monument 2013-2021. bcsara.com/service/wall-of-honour.

54 *A Monument To Remember* can be ordered by sending an email to sar-jim@shaw.ca with your name, shipping address and the number of books

requested. Send $29.95/book by e-transfer to the same email address or send a cheque to Jim McAllister, 10252 Rathdown Pl., Sidney, BC V8L 4C7. Allow 3-5 weeks for delivery.

55 EMBC, SAR Safety Program Swiftwater Rescue, January 2022, 93-116.

56 thecanadianencyclopedia.ca/en/article/highway-of-tears.

57 https://bc-cb.rcmp-grc.gc.ca/ViewPage.action?siteNodeId=23&languageId=1&contentId=27048.

58 *Prince George Free Press*, March 29, 2007.

59 Brent Jang, September 4, 2002.

60 Mary Ferguson, January 15, 1982.

61 Jason Proctor, January 20, 2015.

62 Bryceland, 78.

63 Clare Hennig, June 5, 2018.

64 Robert Koester, 179.

65 When a despondent subject takes their own life.

66 CBC News, October 25, 2012.

67 Government of BC, October 2 to 8, 2017.

7. Ice

68 vincentmasseypottery.com/.

69 Corrie, January 17, 2008.

70 Simon Little and John Copsey, January 15, 2021.

71 Pierre Chauvin, December 3, 2015.

72 Elaine Schiman, July 10, 2008.

73 Scott Howard, n/d.

8. K9s

74 youtube.com/watch?v=MLbP_dgW1Bc.

75 CBC, June 24, 2015.

76 Dana Reynolds, July 6, 2015.

77 Government of BC, February 12–18, 2018.

78 Michael Potestio, February 18, 2020.

79 Robert Koester, 116.

80 *Kamloops This Week*, June 17, 2016.

81 bcsara.com/entries/robert-mcgregor.

82 CBC News, January 19, 2014.

83 mltaikins.com.

84 CTV Vancouver, September 4, 2018.

85 Province of BC, *Ground Search & Rescue*, 191.

86 Robert Koester, 163.

87 Nina Golgowski, September 23, 2012.

88 news@inforum.com, September 24, 2012.

89 Siren, November 24, 2014.

90 Erin McClam and Erin Calabrese, May 26, 2015.

9. Mountains

91 Lisa Walton, March 19, 2014.

92 UPI Archives, September 4, 1982.

93 UPI Archives, September 4, 1982.

94 Christopher Van Tilburg, 2017.

95 Channel 21 News, October 29, 2020.

96 Barney Lerten, Jordan Williams, October 29, 2020.

97 Timeanddate. City of Hood River, Oregon, USA – Sunrise, Sunset, and Daylength, January 16, 2021.

98 Aaron Mesh, February 23, 2021.

99 Mesh, February 23, 2021.

100 Red Line Guiding, December 17, 2016.

101 Ty Gagne, 2017.

102 Kevin Landrigan, June 29, 2019.

10. Mounted Search and Rescue

103 Tim Darnell, December 17, 2018.

104 Ben Brasch, December 17, 2018.

105 Aly Vander Hayden, October 22, 2020.

106 Associated Press, September 9, 2014.

107 Tennessee Department of Corrections, "Zachary Rye Adams," June 6, 2022.

108 Tennessee Department of Corrections, "John Dylan Adams," June 6, 2022.

109 Associated Press, September 14, 2020.

110 Federal Bureau of Prisons, "Jason Autry." bop.gov/inmateloc.

111 Local 24 staff, December 3, 2020, and Alberto Luperon, December 4, 2020.

11. Plane Crashes

112 *National Post*, April 27, 2015.

113 Transportation Safety Board of Canada, November 16, 2008.

114 Ian Bailey, September 22, 2010.

115 TSBC, August 11, 2010.

116 US Air Force, June 2018.

117 Molly Brown, June 21, 2000.

118 NTSB, Aviation Accident Final Report, July 17, 2001.

119 Brown, June 21, 2000.

120 NTSB, Aviation Accident Data Summary, July 17, 2001.

121 Tess Williams, February 4.

12. Ropes

122 James Seely, 2007.

123 Iris Phillips, July 11, 2007.

124 James Seely, 2007.

125 Robert Koester, 42–43.

126 Penny Daflos, February 21, 2017.

127 Robert Koester, 242

13. Swiftwater

128 CBC News, December 14, 2020.

129 CTV Vancouver Island, January 30, 2018.

130 Michael Briones, October 8, 2020.

131 CBC, May 4, 2020.

132 Eric Welsh, May 4, 2020.

133 Robert Koester, 47 and 51.

134 Ashley Wadhwani, July 5, 2016.

135 Jennifer Feinberg, March 6, 2017.

136 facebook.com/adam.laurie.37/posts/1864514173790755.

14. Still Missing

137 Sun Peaks Daily Avalanche Forecast, February 17–18, 2018.

138 Government of BC, *Weekly Incident Situation Report*, February 12–18, 2018.

139 Annette Adams, Ph.D., et al. June 1, 2007.

140 Government of BC, *Weekly Incident Situation Report,* April 2–8, 2018.

141 Government of BC, *Weekly Incident Situation Report*, May 7–13, 2018.

142 *Merritt Herald*, January 29, 2020.

Acknowledgements

To all the contributors of this book—you made my job easy. Thanks for sharing your joys and sorrows. I hope that by telling your stories, your burdens were lessened, your healing furthered and your grieving eased. To Jeff Hortobagyi for his careful, thoughtful editing and many creative contributions. And finally, to the brilliant Vici Johnstone at Caitlin Press, who, after a brief phone call, recognized the importance of sharing these stories.

About the Author

Cathalynn Labonté-Smith wrote this book to bring search and rescue volunteers to the forefront. Her husband, Stephen Smith, is a member of BC's Sunshine Coast SAR (SCSAR) team, and this provided her with major inspiration. She also highlights the dangerous beauty of the wilds of North America so that people are more prepared before they head out to enjoy the outdoors, and to hopefully prevent more tragedies from happening.

Cathalynn grew up in southwestern Alberta, and she moved to Vancouver, BC, to complete her BFA in creative writing at the University of British Columbia (UBC). After graduation, she worked as a freelance journalist. She also became a technical writer for wireless communication and other high-tech industries after earning a certificate in technical writing from Simon Fraser University. She later returned to UBC to complete a bachelor's degree in secondary education, after which she taught English, journalism and other subjects at Vancouver high schools.

Cathalynn lives in Gibsons and North Vancouver, BC, where she writes and edits, plays with her chihuahuas and hangs out with her friends and fellow writers. She is the founder of the Sunshine Coast Writers and Editors Society (scwes.ca).